H
/
A4
v. 497

THE ANNALS

ERICA GINSBURG, *Assistant Editor*

Editorial Office: 3937 Chestnut Street, Philadelphia, Pennsylvania 19104.

For information about membership* (individuals only) and subscriptions (institutions), address:

SAGE PUBLICATIONS, INC.

2111 West Hillcrest Drive   275 South Beverly Drive
Newbury Park, CA 91320   Beverly Hills, CA 90212

From India and South Asia,   *From the UK, Europe, the Middle*
write to: *East and Africa, write to:*

SAGE PUBLICATIONS INDIA Pvt. Ltd.   SAGE PUBLICATIONS LTD
P.O. Box 4215   28 Banner Street
New Delhi 110 048   London EC1Y 8QE
INDIA   ENGLAND

SAGE Production Editors: JANET BROWN and ASTRID VIRDING
*Please note that members of The Academy receive THE ANNALS with their membership.

Library of Congress Catalog Card Number 86-042559
International Standard Serial Number ISSN 0002-7162
International Standard Book Number ISBN 0-8039-3101-8 (Vol. 497, 1988 paper)
International Standard Book Number ISBN 0-8039-3100-X (Vol. 497, 1988 cloth)
Manufactured in the United States of America. First printing, May 1988.

The articles appearing in THE ANNALS are indexed in *Book Review Index; Public Affairs Information Service Bulletin; Social Sciences Index; Monthly Periodical Index; Current Contents; Behavioral, Social Management Sciences;* and *Combined Retrospective Index Sets.* They are also abstracted and indexed in *ABC Pol Sci, Historical Abstracts, Human Resources Abstracts, Social Sciences Citation Index, United States Political Science Documents, Social Work Research & Abstracts, Peace Research Reviews, Sage Urban Studies Abstracts, International Political Science Abstracts, America: History and Life,* and/or *Family Resources Database.*

Information about membership rates, institutional subscriptions, and back issue prices may be found on the facing page.

Advertising. Current rates and specifications may be obtained by writing to THE ANNALS Advertising and Promotion Manager at the Newbury Park office (address above).

Claims. Claims for undelivered copies must be made no later than three months following month of publication. The publisher will supply missing copies when losses have been sustained in transit and when the reserve stock will permit.

Change of Address. Six weeks' advance notice must be given when notifying of change of address to insure proper identification. Please specify name of journal. Send change of address to: THE ANNALS, c/o Sage Publications, Inc., 2111 West Hillcrest Drive, Newbury Park, CA 91320.

The American Academy of Political and Social Science

3937 Chestnut Street   Philadelphia, Pennsylvania 19104

Origin and Purpose. The Academy was organized December 14, 1889, to promote the progress of political and social science, especially through publications and meetings. The Academy does not take sides in controverted questions, but seeks to gather and present reliable information to assist the public in forming an intelligent and accurate judgment.

Meetings. The Academy holds an annual meeting in the spring extending over two days.

Publications. THE ANNALS is the bimonthly publication of The Academy. Each issue contains articles on some prominent social or political problem, written at the invitation of the editors. Also, monographs are published from time to time, numbers of which are distributed to pertinent professional organizations. These volumes constitute important reference works on the topics with which they deal, and they are extensively cited by authorities throughout the United States and abroad. The papers presented at the meetings of The Academy are included in THE ANNALS.

Membership. Each member of The Academy receives THE ANNALS and may attend the meetings of The Academy. Membership is open only to individuals. Annual dues: $28.00 for the regular paperbound edition (clothbound, $42.00). Add $9.00 per year for membership outside the U.S.A. Members may also purchase single issues of THE ANNALS for $6.95 each (clothbound, $10.00).

Subscriptions. THE ANNALS (ISSN 0002-7162) is published six times annually—in January, March, May, July, September, and November. Institutions may subscribe to THE ANNALS at the annual rate: $60.00 (clothbound, $78.00). Add $9.00 per year for subscriptions outside the U.S.A. Institutional rates for single issues: $10.00 each (clothbound, $15.00).

Second class postage paid at Philadelphia, Pennsylvania, and at additional mailing offices.

Single issues of THE ANNALS may be obtained by individuals who are not members of The Academy for $7.95 each (clothbound, $15.00). Single issues of THE ANNALS have proven to be excellent supplementary texts for classroom use. Direct inquiries regarding adoptions to THE ANNALS c/o Sage Publications (address below).

All correspondence concerning membership in The Academy, dues renewals, inquiries about membership status, and/or purchase of single issues of THE ANNALS should be sent to THE ANNALS c/o Sage Publications, Inc., 2111 West Hillcrest Drive, Newbury Park, CA 91320. *Please note that orders under $25 must be prepaid.* Sage affiliates in London and India will assist institutional subscribers abroad with regard to orders, claims, and inquiries for both subscriptions and single issues.

THE ANNALS

of The American Academy *of* Political *and* Social Science

RICHARD D. LAMBERT, *Editor*
ALAN W. HESTON, *Associate Editor*

—————————— FORTHCOMING ——————————

THE PRIVATE SECURITY INDUSTRY:
ISSUES AND TRENDS
Special Editor: Ira A. Lipman

Volume 498   July 1988

CONGRESS AND THE PRESIDENCY:
INVITATION TO STRUGGLE
Special Editor: Roger H. Davidson

Volume 499   September 1988

WHITHER THE AMERICAN EMPIRE:
EXPANSION OR CONTRACTION?
Special Editor: Marvin E. Wolfgang

Volume 500   November 1988

See page 3 for information on Academy membership and
purchase of single volumes of **The Annals.**

CONTENTS

BOOK DEPARTMENT CONTENTS

ECONOMICS

PREFACE

Anti-Americanism is a subject much in the headlines these·days in the form of bombings, murders, hijackings, kidnappings, and the entire repertoire of terrorism. No American who travels abroad or meets many foreigners in the United States can remain unaware of a much less visible anti-Americanism that is expressed in ways that do not make the front pages. We feel ourselves to be confronted by a hostile and thankless world and our personal safety is at risk when we travel abroad. Our choices seem to be turning our backs on the rest of the world in neo-isolationism or asserting ourselves against our tormentors to reestablish the respect that used to be ours by right.

Neither of these choices is a real one. To take the most obvious example, we cannot disengage ourselves from the Middle East as long as we need its oil and maintain our support of Israel. In 1983, however, an assertion of American power in Lebanon—where we had been able to impose our will in 1958—ended in disaster. Not everything is as easy as Grenada.

A HISTORICAL VIEW

The nostalgia for the 1950s, like most nostalgia, is of faulty memory. In September 1954, *The Annals* published a symposium rather like the present one, which began with an editor's introduction that could for the most part be just as well reprinted here.[1] It speaks of our need for foreigners' admiration, our belief that American national character is a "desirable and perhaps exportable commodity in the world market," and our conviction that, "if we are rightly understood, the frictions and obstacles in the course of our national policy will disappear." It goes on to observe that the contributions to the volume "will delight no American Narcissus," and that what appears "is a bewildering variety of pictures, which illustrate the idiosyncrasies of individual viewers rather than the character of the America they are looking at." The present reader will find these same ideas expressed in this introduction and in many of the contributions that follow.

Thus even a generation ago, the United States had an image problem and was profoundly worried about that image. For that matter, one could reach back several generations and find dislike and disdain for Americans and their country—as well as find Americans who were disturbed by these attitudes. Foreign observers, beginning at least with Tocqueville, have been struck by Americans' need for appreciation and even adulation from abroad. The passages quoted in the present issue of *The Annals* by Marie-France Toinet are nearly as valid today, a century after they were written, as they were in Tocqueville's time. Scott Thompson also notes our need for admiration as a historical phenomenon and one that persists especially among the political appointees in the government, who often are good barometers of public opinion. Americans have an endearing conviction that their

1. *The Annals* of the American Academy of Political and Social Science, vol. 295, *America through Foreign Eyes,* ed. Richard D. Lambert (Sept. 1954).

innate goodness and the rightness of their ways must be accepted by others—and if they are not, it must be due to ignorance or malice, both of which can and should be countered by effective foreign information programs.

Before World War II, anti-Americanism was largely a matter of stereotypes such as the rude frontiersman of the nineteenth century or the overbearing wealthy tourist of the early twentieth. These were stereotypes based on the barest minimum of direct contact. Few Americans had ventured abroad, and European travelers to the United States, in contrast to immigrants, were even rarer. Certainly until the Spanish American War and really until World War II, the United States as a country and Americans as individuals hardly impinged on Europe, let alone the colonial areas that were still to attain independence. There were some exceptions: British-American ties were always at a level above those with any other country, and the United States played a larger than usual role in the affairs of China, Japan, and Central America. These special relationships were to have lasting impacts, for better or worse, well into our time.

With the demise of empires and the emergence of the United States as the sole global power following World War II, the premises of anti-Americanism changed. Americans of all kinds appeared in the unlikeliest corners of the world and the rapid development of a global communications network spread the American image so that the events of My Lai, for instance, were a topic of real-time concern everywhere in the world.

The change was not only in the breadth but even more in the depth of the American impact. The role of the United States was no longer distant and abstract. American actions, whether political, economic, or military, could and frequently did have a real effect on the lives of the remotest societies. The United States was in a position to frustrate as well as further the goals of nations and individuals everywhere or decisively harm their interests.

Precisely because the United States was everywhere, it saw itself as the custodian of global interests that transcended the parochial concerns of nations with lesser responsibilities. The United States often acted with sovereign disregard for others' interests, and the victims of our attentions responded with a vehemence that reflected the urgency of their concern. The belligerence, even violence, that had been directed against the colonial powers in India or West Africa before World War II now began to be turned against the United States, for we had become the frontline guardians of an international order that was inevitably felt as oppressive by many. We often behaved with an incredible intrusiveness that was irritating even when well meant. We developed an arrogance in dealing with others and what Alvin Rubinstein and Donald Smith call a "hegemonic imperative" that prevented us from understanding and working with, rather than against, developing trends in the Third World and elsewhere.[2] In retrospect, it appears incredible that Americans took over the economic planning functions of such a substantial nation as Pakistan, that Lyndon Johnson micromanaged Indian agricultural policy as the price for badly needed food aid, and that the Alliance for Progress prescribed detailed reform plans for Latin American recipients. While this kind of behavior only sporadically

2. For an eloquent critique of American failure to understand Asian nationalism, see Selig S. Harrison, *The Widening Gulf: Asian Nationalism and American Policy* (New York: Free Press, 1978).

evoked violence and sometimes was helpful and necessary for the recipient, it left a significant residue of resentment.

These unintentional and usually innocent shortcomings were compounded by a series of policy blunders and even straightforward malefactions as the United States went through a period of unrestrained pursuit of our own good and, as we saw it, the greater good of humankind. We inevitably became involved in regional quarrels, thereby alienating one—and frequently both—of the parties involved. This is most clearly the case in South Asia—with India and Pakistan—but also, as Lester Langley shows, in Central America, where our involvement in internal affairs ultimately brought us more grief than comfort. For the most part, we reacted with hurt and incomprehension to the violent reactions and resentment that was expressed through anti-Americanism. We saw ourselves as well motivated and generous—our tormentors must be evil, ignorant, and, often, the tools of our enemies. We still felt that we were being judged unjustly by purveyors of inaccurate stereotypes. And, of course, to some extent, we were, given that all thinking about foreign nations is stereotypical to some degree. We have our own deep-seated images of the English and Japanese, after all, and strange as it may seem, most people in the world have yet to see an American in the flesh.

Even while present-day anti-Americanism is based on substantial firsthand knowledge and experience, it may still be unfair. The United States had its particular interests to pursue, but it was also maintaining a system that was more just and more productive by far than the likely alternative. The American record after World War II is a remarkable one, vastly better than might have been expected given the fact that we assumed vast burdens, with little preparation, in one of the most tumultuous eras of world history. We demonstrated admirable generosity and managed to develop some extremely farseeing and effective policies. It is not likely that any other nation at that point in history could have done much better, and it is not unreasonable to expect appreciation. Many of us believe that the perspective of history will treat the American role even more favorably, but in the shorter term resentments over current indignities overshadow appreciation of the American accomplishment in our heroic age following World War II. We have yielded much of our earlier role to others who—often as the intended result of our policies—have come to strength and prominence. In fact, as a number of the writers in this volume report—Nathaniel Thayer's observations on Japan are particularly impressive—we have received appreciation.

Over the years there have also been corresponding changes in the way that the U.S. foreign policy establishment views our position in the world. The American self-image has changed; naive self-confidence disappeared in the years of Vietnam and Watergate. Consider also the American need to be liked. The most striking thing that the present-day reader sees in the 1954 *Annals* survey is the agonizing desire of Americans to be liked, coupled with the conviction that, as we become better known, we will become better liked. Indeed, much of the anti-Americanism chronicled in that symposium had to do with attitudes toward Americans as individuals and toward American society, rather than toward the U.S. government.[3]

3. To be sure, that slant was inherent in the way the volume was structured; it was, however, typical of its time.

We find little or no attention given in the current symposium to anti-Americanism at a personal level. It is a sign—perhaps a sad one—of American maturity that the urgent need to be liked is no longer paramount.

PRESENT-DAY ANTI-AMERICANISM

The waning of the need to be liked is, however, a true sign of the times. The United States as a nation-state is now a real and pressing issue throughout the world, and the qualities of Americans and their society are simply less important. Correspondingly, Americans are now concerned with attitudes toward their country more than toward themselves as individuals. First of all, an American abroad will worry less that, for example, a Frenchman will find him personally gauche and his society in general uncultured than that a terrorist will blow up his airplane because of political opposition to the United States with no concern for what the qualities of the people on board may be. In addition, Americans now have more reasons to be concerned about attitudes toward the United States than they were a generation ago. In 1954, the American position was unchallenged; today it is vulnerable and under fire from many directions.

Another factor at work is the better awareness that Americans now have of the world at large. Those of us who were something of pioneers in distant parts in the 1950s—I worked with the U.S. Information Agency in India at the time—went out with the shared conviction of American righteousness or perhaps even self-righteousness. It did not take long, however, for most of us to realize that a country such as India had good reason to view the foreign policy globalism of the United States with considerable suspicion and that these countries had values and priorities that were at least as valid for their own societies as those we were offering.

Ironically, virulent anti-Americanism is reaching new heights just at the time when the premise underlying much of it—the global dominance and self-assurance of the United States—is waning. We could—and did—overthrow governments and manipulate regional power balances in the 1950s; today we are rarely able to do so. Much anti-Americanism is simply directed to the wrong target, but old habits die hard. Perhaps, however, this overstates the case. Thompson suggests that the reassertion of American strength under the Reagan administration and an increasingly firm foreign policy will reverse some of the trends of the past years and thereby reduce at least the public, forceful expression of anti-Americanism. The Central American countries, as Langley points out, have not forgotten that the United States, whatever its weaknesses, cannot be ignored. For the present, however, the diminished relative strength of the United States probably remains a temptation to even more outrageous acts of anti-Americanism because our ability to respond is less sure and fearsome.

It seems just as likely that, over the long term, relative American power and influence will continue to decline. The virtual hegemony that we enjoyed after World War II was, after all, a historical aberration. As Riordan Roett shows, the countries of the Southern Cone in Latin America have taken account of the shift in power, and the old style of anti-Americanism is fading away there, yielding to a "gloomy realism." It is only natural to expect that power—and, therefore, responsibility—will in the future be more widely distributed, especially to some of the newer nations. Countries such as India, Nigeria, or Brazil will inevitably have more to say about what goes on in their part of the world than will the United States. They and their neighbors will also begin to learn the costs of size and pervasive influence and attract hostility away from us. This is clearly the case already in South Asia, where anti-Indian sentiment is rapidly outdistancing anti-Americanism.

Still, anti-Americanism is not the preserve of irate Iranians, uprooted Palestinians, or frustrated Central Americans, all of whom have, or think they have, reason for turning against the United States and its hapless citizens but who may in time moderate their concerns as we become less of a pressing issue. There is another aspect of anti-Americanism that is much less likely to moderate because it is based on deep-seated attitudes about who we are rather than concern over what we do.

AMBIVALENCE AND DISCREPANCY

With all of its faults and weaknesses and relatively lesser strength, the United States still represents a phenomenon with which societies everywhere must come to terms. As several of the authors in this issue of *The Annals* point out, the meaning, dynamic, and success of the American experiment have had an immense impact on peoples and nations everywhere. It has presented a qualitatively different model and experience of modernization against which other societies have judged themselves. For elites and, frequently, intellectuals, the American experience has been a disturbing and even frightening thing; for the masses, it has often been a beacon of hope for a better future, either in their own countries or through emigration. While the Soviets—until recently at least—have asserted the universal validity of their politico-economic model, it was in fact the United States that became the model of what a twentieth-century country could be. We remain the most potent proponent of such revolutionary ideas as open government, a free press, and human rights. But, even for those who accept these values, we are often an impetuous, expansionist country with a dangerously confused and confusing political process, a nation that is both uncontrollable and uncontrolled and hence a potential danger even when well intentioned and pursuing desirable goals. Added to the resentments of those with specific grievances, these characteristics form an important foundation for contemporary anti-Americanism.

Herbert Spiro and others point out the persistence of some of the more traditional kinds of anti-Americanism in Europe, where it is now largely the preserve of an elite for whom anti-Semitism or even anti-Catholicism is no longer acceptable.[4] It is important to understand the extent to which anti-Americanism is an elite or intellectual phenomenon in many parts of the world. In case after case presented in this *Annals* issue, even Canada as portrayed by Charles Doran and James Sewell, anti-Americanism appears mainly as the preserve of the upper classes while the mass of the population is more tolerant of American shortcomings or even seeks to make American culture, if not values, its own.

4. Stephan Haseler makes this point with considerable passion in his *Varieties of Anti-Americanism: Reflex and Response* (Washington, DC: Ethics and Public Policy Center, 1985).

The ambivalence that characterizes societies in their view of the United States extends into the hearts of individuals. Emigration to the United States remains the goal of many anti-Americans, for their children if not for themselves. Langley writes of Central Americans rent by the combination of bitterness toward and admiration of their northern neighbor; the poignant complaint of Carlos Fuentes, cited by Roett, can be heard in nations across the globe.

The case of China, described by David Shambaugh, is also striking, albeit somewhat different. The intellectuals of the Communist Party are ambivalent at best about the United States; the mass of Chinese are more likely to be positive because of reports that they have received from their friends and relatives in the outside world. Contrast that to Vladimir Shlapentokh's description of attitudes in the Soviet Union. Here the critical attitudes of the intellectuals appear to have much more impact on opinion in general. This is due, in part at least, to the monopoly of information that the Soviet Communist Party enjoys. It is due also to the fact that the reports that Soviet citizens receive from émigrés returned from the United States are more negative; presumably Soviet émigrés who remain here have more positive things to say, but these are not widely circulated. In addition, anti-Americanism in the Soviet Union seems to be related to an almost xenophobic Russian patriotism in a way that is not the case in China.

There are also societies whose values are simply at variance with ours, and such discrepancy can lead to a widespread dislike of the United States—or some aspect of it—that is much the same as anti-Americanism. Contemporary global culture, especially the mass variety, is American in origin. Many in other parts of the world—especially the intellectuals—see this new culture as shallow and disruptive of the values that they cherish. The values of one or the other culture are not really relevant nor is the fact that the United States makes little active attempt to export this mass culture. Toinet's plaint about English crowding out French in scientific literature is no less painful for the fact that there is nothing that the United States could do to alter the situation even if it wanted to.

Profound differences that set us apart from other cultures include the divergent views on the nature of man and society that Shambaugh sees the United States and China holding. Such differences do not necessarily lead to anti-Americanism—or anti-Chinesism on our part—but they do put limits on how closely two cultures can interact and can provide a basis for creating anti-Americanism.

There are aspects of our culture and politics that are repugnant to many foreigners and to many Americans as well; it is not only Russians who are dismayed by the loosening of moral standards in the United States and in the West in general. Refugees who reach West Berlin sometimes wonder if they have made the correct choice when they see the pornography displays on newsstands and in shops. Freedom does have its costs. The United States is hardly the source of moral changes throughout the West; since our culture is so prominent, however, we often receive the blame.

On the other hand, the size, power, and special nature of the United States evoke a broad range of immensely positive reactions. Anti-Americanism gets the headlines. It is news when an American library is burned in a Third World country, but it is not news when the users of another library petition the U.S. Information

Agency to keep its library open. In fact, it would not be surprising if some of the persons who were in the mob that burned a U.S. library were steady and enthusiastic users of it. They would be reacting to different aspects of the United States and expressing the fundamental ambivalence of attitudes toward it. We should not be surprised; many Americans show the same split personality when they assess their own country.

One cause of this ambivalence is that while the United States is profoundly revolutionary in some regards, in recent times it has also assumed the role of a status quo power on the international stage. Our support has generally gone not to revolutionaries but to the established order; Richard Parker explains how harmful our overidentification with established elites in the Middle East has been. Our adaptation to the challenges posed by the emergence of a host of new nations and an entire new system of international relations has been disappointing to many, Americans as well as foreigners. Japanese anti-Americanism, we learn from Thayer, reflects the disappointment of Japanese that we do not live up to our own ideals—a charge that many Americans would bring themselves.

This brings us to the three issues that are raised by a number of the contributors to this *Annals* issue.

The first of these is the observation that attitudes toward the United States—positive or negative—are often the result of how individuals see their own country. The French intellectual's enthusiasm for Ronald Reagan is his or her way of criticizing excessive statism in France; Japanese ideas of how their own state should be managed condition their criticism of the United States; Canadians, too, judge us by their standards, not ours. The ups and downs of attitudes toward the United States in the Soviet Union, and to a lesser extent in China, reflect changes in the internal policies of these countries more than anything we might have done. In another sense, the United States can become the victim of too close an identification with foreign governments. Clearly many of the complaints against the United States that Pakistanis expressed to Hamid Kizilbash have to do not with the United States but with our association with an unpopular government in Islamabad. This, too, has a reverse side, however; Poles and some other Eastern Europeans almost automatically reject negative information about the United States simply because it comes from a government they do not believe.

The second issue poses a question: is it possible for Americans to be anti-American? If we look at almost any of the charges that others bring against us, we will have no trouble in finding Americans who echo them—or who were the ones who gave them currency in the first place. There are individuals in the United States who are so profoundly alienated from their country and society that they could be branded anti-Americans, but their number is relatively small. Almost all Americans, however, find some aspects of their country that are disappointing and in need of change, and they do not hesitate to voice their criticisms sharply. They are not seeking to undermine their nation but to strengthen it. Few, after all, would argue that everything the United States does is right or, more important, that we do not need to change in some ways if we are to fulfill our promise.

That raises the third issue—is all foreign criticism of the United States to be counted as anti-Americanism, even when it is the same kind of criticism that well-intentioned Americans make themselves? The answer is obviously no, and several authors make the point that informed criticism of specific U.S. policies should not be thought of as anti-Americanism.[5] The hypersensitivity that was understandable a century ago for a nation just finding its way onto the international stage sits poorly on a nation that has now dominated that stage for more than a generation.

At some point, of course, policy-specific criticism can grow into a fundame anti-Americanism. Parker points out that Arabs have historically been w disposed toward Americans. Nevertheless, a substantial number of them ha apparently been so embittered by U.S. policy in the Middle East that they hav made a fundamental judgment that it is not worthwhile to distinguish between Americans and their government. Kizilbash believes that anti-Americanism in Pakistan is not a characteristic at the individual level, but some Pakistanis at least were so disappointed with the United States that they sought to incinerate the officials of the American embassy in Islamabad in 1979. Indeed, the wide range of charges that some Pakistanis appear to believe about the United States would, when put together, seem to be such a total indictment that the next step toward comprehensive anti-Americanism would seem to be a short one.

A PRESCRIPTION FOR
VIEWING ANTI-AMERICANISM

Rubinstein and Smith make the point that anti-Americanism has become much more dangerous and violent in recent years, and it has taken on new forms. Mass anti-American demonstrations in the Third World and elsewhere are nothing new; the willingness to kill substantial numbers of people just for being American is, however, a disturbing novelty.

A related manifestation is anti-American terrorism. For many Americans, the terms "anti-Americanism" and "terrorism" are nearly synonymous. Although the vast majority of terrorist actions in the world are not directed against the United States—indeed it is surprising that there are so few—there are anti-American terrorist actions enough. The high visibility of the United States and its perceived association with injustices make it a particularly attractive target. Although terrorism is carried on by only a small number of individuals, it is the mobilization of widespread anti-American feelings that provides these terrorists with a more or less safe environment in which to operate.

There is a great danger in assuming that anti-Americanism and terrorism are much the same thing. Our reaction to the word "terrorism" is so visceral and negative that extending it to anti-American manifestations in general could poison our attitudes toward much of the world and lead to inappropriate, self-destructive responses. It would be much more useful for us to think through just what anti-Americanism is and how we should respond to it.

---

5. Haseler makes this point well in *The Varieties of Anti-Americanism*. He adds that it is also not anti-Americanism when nations oppose particular American policies or administrations, when they change their attitudes based upon reassessments of the direction in which power is moving, or when they forcefully assert their right to self-determination and independence.

First, anti-Americanism cannot be regarded in isolation. It must be considered on the spectrum of attitudes toward the United States ranging from enthusiastic acceptance to bitter hatred. It is the bombings and hostage takings that grab the headlines, but, in the everyday world around us, these are isolated events, usually not characteristic of another nation's attitudes toward the United States. A country that makes as varied an impact on the rest of the world as does the United States will inevitably evoke a wide range of responses. Depending on the society involved, there will be many positive responses, and in many cases, these will constitute a large majority. Fortunately, this is especially true in the countries that are most important to us.

Second, even this spectrum does not show the full richness of responses given that, as we have seen, competing pro- and anti-American attitudes often coexist within individuals. This means that we have important assets even among our apparent enemies and, of course, that we evoke concern even among our friends. Few glasses are fully full or empty; if we have a positive image of ourselves and behave intelligently, we have a good chance of ensuring that the levels rise.

Third, we have to respond in proportion and according to the intent of the manifestations of anti-Americanism. Much anti-Americanism can and should be ignored, for it has to do with others and their image of themselves rather than with us. When Frenchmen, Canadians, Russians, or Japanese use the United States as a surrogate to fight their own domestic issues, there is little we need do beyond ensuring that the facts are on the record and waiting until the country concerned finds its own intellectual equilibrium and—in all likelihood—puts anti-Americanism aside as no longer helpful. Similarly, much of the anti-American rhetoric we hear is little more than the unfocused worry expressed by others about our size, our cultural pervasiveness, and our economic power and about change in the world in general. As long as we are convinced that our own priorities are in order and that we are bearing our responsibilities as decently as we can, we can largely ignore this kind of criticism.

Fourth, however, when an honest assessment of our own behavior suggests that the critics may be expressing legitimate complaints, we would be foolish not to take it to heart. The international outcry about American treatment of our black citizens in the early 1950s was not pleasant to hear. Many Africans and Asians were radicalized into profound anti-Americanism in the process, and the Soviet Union—itself hardly free of racism—used the theme relentlessly to undermine our international standing. It would have been, and for some was, easy to turn our backs on all of this criticism, claiming that it was nothing but an expression of anti-Americanism that was "hostile," in the useful distinction that Doran and Sewell make. Had we done so, however, we would have been doing a great disservice to our own society. By listening to foreign critics—a Swede, Gunnar Myrdal, did much to prompt our consciences—we at least began to right a historic injustice and heal our own society.

Had we been more attentive to the criticism of the Third World countries when we sought to exclude mainland China from the international community, we could have saved ourselves considerable agony. When, today, international human rights organizations criticize the United States for invoking the death penalty, we would do well to listen and judge the merits of their charges rather than dismissing them out of hand.

We are a nation of imperfections, just as are all others, but because of the immense international shadow we cast, our imperfections are known and criticized the world over. Well-meant criticism is not anti-Americanism; even hostile anti-American criticism, when valid, is something we need heed for our own good.

Fifth, where we find hostile and unjustifiable anti-Americanism, we need to counter it. The Soviet Union and others do devote considerable resources to blackening our image, through both exaggeration and falsehood. True, there is danger that some of our superpatriots will automatically ascribe all criticism to Soviet disinformation and will respond in ways that will, at best, make us look foolish. That does not, however, mean that we should not nail disinformation where it genuinely exists.

Sixth, we have to accept the fact that some anti-Americanism is going to exist and that we will have to live with it. The United States cannot change what it is—large, dynamic, and powerful—and we would not want to change that. These are, however, characteristics that will trigger concern, fear, and resistance. Others encounter this problem on a regional level; we encounter it globally in a way that is only now possible with the globalization of politics. Certainly, enlightened policies can ameliorate the problem, and the passage of time, as the United States comes to occupy a less uniquely pervasive and dominant role in the world, will reduce anti-Americanism. If it is some consolation, our fellow superpower is encountering some of the same problems.[6]

These are only a few observations that one can make about dealing with anti-Americanism. Much more can be and has been said by others. It is not the purpose of this volume to provide quick fixes to the problem; if any one thing emerges from these articles, it is that there are none. Our contribution is more to the crucial first step of understanding the problem.

The direction these articles have taken reflects some general basic approaches. There was no attempt to reach a specific definition of anti-Americanism; several authors have offered definitions and all are useful for their purpose. The contributors have not provided catalogs of anti-American acts; the interested reader can find those, in profusion, in the press.

We have worked within the framework set by the title of this volume. We have sought to present anti-Americanism in a historical context, for history is one of the continua on which anti-Americanism is to be understood. It has specific origins and it changes over time. An understanding of these historical processes can help us deal with the phenomenon more effectively.

We have sought also to put anti-Americanism into the other context, with opinion about the United States ranging from acceptance to hatred. Americans who rightfully worry about their country's image need to realize that the bright and gray spots greatly outnumber the black ones, painful as the latter may be.

As editor, I had to accept the fact that a work of this kind could never be

6. The *Washington Post* carried on 15 Nov. 1987 an interesting article by Graham Fuller in which he summarized and in part translated an article by one Leonid Pochivalov bemoaning the shortcomings of his Soviet countrymen when they travel abroad and the anti-Sovietism they evoke.

comprehensive enough to deal with the full range of events and problems posed by the subject. I set two criteria: the first was to find people who were likely to have something interesting and important to say; the second was to produce a representative survey of the subject. Given these constraints, it was important to avoid duplicating previous efforts along similar lines, especially the volume *Anti-Americanism in the Third World: Implications for U.S. Foreign Policy,* edited by Alvin Rubinstein and Donald Smith.[7] The best way to deal with this was to ask Rubinstein and Smith to contribute to this volume, setting forth some of the main conclusions that they drew from their earlier work. The existence of the Rubinstein-Smith volume reduced the need to cover the Third World comprehensively here; we have, for instance, no contribution on Africa because they covered that subject extensively. It also pointed up some specific niches in the Third World—such as Central America—where more work was needed.

Over the past several decades, the focus of anti-Americanism has shifted markedly to the Third World—scarcely a quarter of the 1954 *Annals* issue was devoted to the Third World—but we still need to look closely at anti-Americanism and related attitudes in the First and Second worlds. Our primary ties remain with our allies in the North Atlantic Treaty Organization and Japan and, in another way, with the powerful Communist nations of China and the Soviet Union, where anti-Americanism is a very different kind of phenomenon. One could, of course, also examine the masochistic anti-Americanism of the American Left that flourished richly a decade or two ago, leaving some lasting impressions and grist for the mills of anti-Americanism abroad. That, however, is a different phenomenon, best left to others. It did, however, seem useful to ask a former government official who was deeply concerned with the U.S. image abroad to provide an overview of anti-Americanism as seen from Washington.

Ultimately, any collective work of this kind can hope at most to provide a few key pieces of this complicated mosaic—perhaps enough in the right places to give the reader a clearer outline of the subject than he or she has had previously. I am grateful to my colleagues in this endeavor for the great usefulness of the pieces that they have crafted.

THOMAS PERRY THORNTON

7. Alvin Rubinstein and Donald Smith, eds., *Anti-Americanism in the Third World: Implications for U.S. Foreign Policy* (New York: Praeger, 1985).

ANNALS, *AAPSS*, **497**, May 1988

Anti-Americanism and the U.S. Government

By W. SCOTT THOMPSON

ABSTRACT: Anti-Americanism is a sometime preoccupation, rather than a specific policy problem, within the U.S. government. There is ample evidence at popular levels, where polls can be taken abroad, that American ideas and policies are understood and respected. With respect to governments abroad, the U.S. government has a more complicated problem. As a world power center, it receives the blame for problems beyond its own making, including some originating as disinformation in the Soviet Union. Anti-Americanism, in balance, has receded worldwide, and American governmental sophistication in dealing with such of it as remains has grown substantially.

W. Scott Thompson was associate director, United States Information Agency, from 1982 to 1984 and is now on the board of the U.S. Institute of Peace. He received a D.Phil. from Oxford in 1967, since then he has served on the faculty of the Fletcher School of Law and Diplomacy. He has been a delegate to the United Nations and is author and editor of eight books on foreign affairs.

NOTE: The author wishes to thank Frederick Knecht, Esq., of Sullivan and Cromwell, New York, and Charles Putnam of the Fletcher School of Law and Diplomacy for their helpful assistance in the preparation of this article.

WHY do we as Americans examine the question of anti-Americanism, in the Third World or elsewhere, if we are proceeding as analysts without policy orientation? Is it only because anti-Americanism is a major political phenomenon in the international system? If so, a preliminary question that may well be asked is, So what? The British in their heyday spent their efforts reinforcing imperial rule rather than in asking the somewhat self-answering question of why there might be anti-British sentiment in Delhi or Aden. The Soviets seem inclined to do likewise today, especially throughout Eastern Europe. The French, with their *mission civilisatrice,* could dismiss anti-French sentiment as uninformed.

It is a peculiarly American subject, for three reasons. First is the oft-noted need of Americans to be liked, an especially apparent aspect of public policy in the 1960s, particularly during the Johnson presidency. It was Johnson who was once quoted as saying that he had never met anyone abroad who would not like to be an American, an assumption whose pathology reveals its own antinomy, for from it comes the notion that anti-Americanism, the essence of being disliked, is salient. One assumes that this particular felt need derives from the peculiar mixture of historic isolationism, the perception of generosity toward the rest of the world, and certain historic—if gratuitous—insecurity about worldliness in the national character. Although Americans are fiercely proud of being American, they are simultaneously a people without a strong, common cultural identity. Perhaps for this reason, as well, Americans look without rather than within to define themselves, seeking their self-image in the reflections offered by non-American opinion. The

degree to which foreigners broadly approve of and emulate Americans, therefore, looms much larger in the American psyche than in the French or British as a measure of self-validation.

As America has learned, however, it is a sad truism that good works do not necessarily bring affection. One thinks of the perhaps apocryphal story of the British viceroy in Egypt who, upon learning that one of his chief counsels was plotting against him, asked his secretary, "But what have I done for him lately?" Americans seem too often to have taken Machiavelli's advice—that of "not being hated by the mass of the people"—without pondering the other side of the coin, namely, the maintenance of respect.[1]

Second, there is the growing importance of public diplomacy—a growth fostered by the United States in its own interest—which by implication makes the acceptability of the proposing power and its people an aspect of the popular acceptance of its policies. Public diplomacy, to be sure, rose in importance with democratization and mass pressure on the processes of foreign policymaking throughout the world, even, to a modest extent, in the Communist world. But nowhere has public diplomacy gained so much currency as in American foreign policy. That public diplomacy should have increased significantly as a strategic factor in U.S. foreign policy is in part a function of external forces, especially the democratization of foreign policymaking, but is also largely due to internal forces unique to the Reagan administration. Historically, the U.S. government has presumed that rational non-Americans would be driven by political

1. Niccolo Machiavelli, *The Prince* (New York: Random House, 1950), p. 67.

and economic self-interest into the arms of democratic capitalism.[2] But Reagan has, domestically and internationally, revived the unapologetic advocacy of values and the forceful promulgation of ideas as an essential element of policy. Thus the administration advocates a theory of public diplomacy that is strategic and not merely tactical, for the purpose of public diplomacy is no longer seen as merely the shoring up of private diplomatic efforts but rather the long-term influence of values and opinion abroad. Conceptually, it is an endorsement of the approach traditionally taken by the public diplomacy practitioners at the U.S. Information Agency (USIA) and the State Department, and the effect on the Reagan administration's view on the subject has been the problematic but generally greater integration of their expertise into the foreign policy-making process.

The third reason has to do with the special way America and Americans have interacted with the world—especially the Third World—as compared with other great powers. The American system—imperial, in a value-neutral sense,[3] political, international, legal, and economic—has operated largely without territoriality as such. To use Arnold Wolfer's celebrated distinction, we have had milieu rather than possession goals. Americans have, therefore, tended to see themselves in a different light from other imperial powers, when in fact the American way has

precisely been to proceed on these other fronts.

The American approach rests on an acceptance of American market and legal premises, which is extended through the popularity of American products, fashions, and trends and through alliances, bases, and military sales. As much as many Third World or European intellectuals may dislike American bourgeois values, their populaces are usually in a race to gain their benefit. The vitriol of the reaction in some places—namely, Islamic fundamentalism—only underlines how powerful a force the American system has been. Moreover, it illustrates the weakness of the traditional U.S. view that the American paradigm of democratic capitalism held up as a model will alone win over the hearts and minds of non-Americans. Rather, it suggests that an active effort to promulgate value-laden ideas must also be present if the American paradigm is to inspire support rather than resentment. Thus anti-Americanism is a serious subject; it is the intersection of the forces molded consciously or unconsciously by those in opposition to the American system. Only in a trivial sense then does "anti-Americanism" denote personal hostility to Americans per se.

A GOVERNMENT PREOCCUPATION

The aspect of this subject for our particular attention is the American government's view of anti-Americanism. Given the topic's vast scope, any such article must inevitably be to a degree idiosyncratic and a function of the writer's own experiences. A comprehensive analysis of this subject would necessarily first look at the view of each of the great departments and agencies, to make the otherwise obvious point that the govern-

2. Carnes Lord, "In Defense of Public Diplomacy," *Commentary*, 77(44) (Apr. 1984), esp. p. 44.

3. For the sense in which the term is used, see George Liska, *Imperial America: The International Politics of Primacy* (Baltimore, MD: Johns Hopkins University Press, 1967).

mental view is many faceted and dependent in large measure on where the viewer sits.

Governments and their ministries are action oriented—certainly the American ones are. If the Pentagon is endeavoring to arm an ally, the result of which might be to enhance anti-Americanism among the national opposition or across the river in the rival's capital, one can be certain that such anti-Americanism will be little considered in the Office of International Security Affairs, where the arms sale is being negotiated. If State Department diplomats have brought to the fore a negotiation with fellow diplomats in an otherwise adversarial country, and this treaty is thought by them to be in the American interest, the more general anti-Americanism it might provoke somewhere will not be a prime consideration. Central Intelligence Agency professionals are trained to develop sources, assets, cutouts, and other nonnational contacts who can counter anti-Americanism on cue, for a variety of payoffs. It is all a rather practical matter.

An initial distinction might thus be self-evident, namely, that professionals working in what may loosely be called the foreign policy field are less concerned with anti-Americanism as such than is the politically appointed executive branch leadership. The professionals in one way or another, in cultivating American interests abroad, can be said to be working to develop respect for their country in the normal course of their work. The political class as a rule is less experienced and perhaps less inclined to disaggregate broad phenomena such as anti-Americanism into their component—and more easily addressed—parts.

This being said, it remains true that anti-Americanism, in a variety of ways and in its differing manifestations, is a preoccupation, as contrasted with a specific policy problem, of the U.S. government. It also seems clear that anti-Americanism is a far greater concern to Washington than are comparable foreign public opinions to other nations. Nations, like people, to paraphrase Freud, wish to be taken at their own valuation. Americans, after all, have created a world system in their own image, and anti-Americanism, from an analytic perspective, is a hole in an intricate international network of dikes. The honest analyst, who might on balance have no trouble upholding the American system as the best possible for the freedom and prosperity of the largest number of people, could surely understand nevertheless that the system, even in its most favorable characterization, has its victims. Even excluding the motives of the Soviet Union, with its far more ideological and imperial foundations, we can see motive sufficient. The Italian Red Guards, the Irish Republican Army, and Angola's ruling Popular Movement for the Liberation of Angola have self-evident incentive for opposing the American system: their ultimate ends—whatever accommodations may be contrived in the short term—are mutually incompatible with America's.

We can recapitulate by saying that while anti-Americanism as such has traditionally not appeared to be a prime concern in the executive branch, it is a subject that, when disaggregated into its many components, often does attract significant attention in Washington. Thus, for example, in the first Reagan term, the way in which "America is being misunderstood," as USIA director Charles Wick often put it, led to the creation of an interagency task force, Project Truth, the function of which was to put the truth out to America's audiences wherever presumptively false versions were found. On my arrival, some six months after the program's inception, as director of the bureau in which Project Truth was lodged, I found only restrained enthusiasm for it among foreign service officers and the interagency panelists who oversaw its progress. The theory was that Project Truth would hit any target with the truth where falsehood—Soviet inspired or otherwise—was found, but to the professionals in the government this was already being done. Project Truth, therefore, was seen as a redundant political overlay, further compromised by its name, which smacked of 1950s-style anticommunism.

Once it became possible to give the program substance, by, for example, opening an office at USIA for disinformation reaction and another for studying propaganda themes in Soviet literature for the guidance of American officials abroad, hostility to the program lessened. Once integrated in a broader program of information development, supervised at the National Security Council by a high-level Special Planning Group with regular cabinet participation, its name was dropped, much to the relief of its staff. This mechanism was used to develop and coordinate programs on an ad hoc basis when Soviet faux pas or bad behavior presented the opportunity. The Soviet shoot-down of Korean Airline flight 007, for example, gave us an opportunity that, not to put too fine a point on it, could be exploited.[4]

4. Seymour M. Hersh, *The Target Is Destroyed* (New York: Random House, 1986), p. 166.

Anti-Americanism exists as a function of three different levels of social organization. We will organize this article in terms of the U.S. government's perception of anti-Americanism at these three levels. The first is at the societal level, where polls readily reveal popular attitudes. The second is political— parties, government, any organized political forces. The third is the political leadership, at the top of the societal pyramid. There is an inverse relationship, as is evident, between the order of these variables and their long-term import: societal trends, which change slowly, are the foundation and base of relations between states, while leaders come and go with relative rapidity.

POPULAR ATTITUDES

U.S. government data on popular attitudes toward American policies— and on America itself—are obtained by the USIA, which has a substantial scholarly staff. Its polls are carried out most often by foreign nationals on a professional and contractual basis and are routinely made available throughout the U.S. government. On issues of great prominence, USIA polls are scrutinized carefully at the White House.

Unfortunately, the countries on which the greatest amount of data exists are precisely those with the deepest American connection, while attitudes in unfriendly states would as a rule be more interesting to plumb. It is precisely the closed nature of such societies, including the entire Soviet-dominated world, that tends to preclude polling. It may well be that the choice of countries on which we are forced to rely stacks the deck to some degree, if we are to try to derive some general lessons from data on anti-Americanism in countries allied with or in close relationships with the United States. For example, we have data of the type routinely used by the U.S. government from commercial and local pollsters in American-allied Thailand and the Philippines, as well as Korea. Latin America is also well documented. The rest of Asia, the Middle East, and Africa is less accessible—or, in any event, less studied in Washington.

On the other hand, it is possible that the intensity of any American connection might, conversely, enhance anti-Americanism. Surely it has been assumed, given U.S. gunboat diplomacy prior to the 1930s, that Latin America has an adequate supply of animosity toward its looming great neighbor. And the extent of the American penetration of the Philippines, especially after the expulsion of Marcos, might be thought to tilt that country against its former colonizer. The data must then have some standing. Consider Table 1, which presents data from a poll taken in 1984. The poll also revealed a highly informed public, the attentive public, which admired America for "guaranteeing political rights" and preferred America to Japan as a source of foreign investment, as one might expect. And despite America's defeat in Vietnam, a large majority of Thai chose the United States as the country that they would prefer to have defend the kingdom in the event of attack.

In Korea in mid-1985, a sizable minority—41 percent—expressed dissatisfaction with the kind of society in which they lived. This might well have led more analysts to foresee the upheavals of 1987. One aspect of that dissatisfaction was a sense that Korea was too closely identified with the United States: 56 percent of the general public and 78 percent of the youth believed that

to be true. On the other hand, 66 to 88 percent agreed with the position that the United States eased world tension, worked toward arms control, provided economic aid, had allies, and possessed capable leadership. The only negative specific opinion was expressed by the 57 percent who felt that the United States unfairly manipulated policies of other countries. But three times as many South Koreans believed that it was the United States that "works hard to ease world tensions" as believed the same of the Soviet Union.

A Philippine poll of 1985, only six months before President Marcos called for the election that led directly to his downfall, showed only 14 percent supporting removal of the American bases; 70 percent wished them expanded or left as they were—even though the utility of the bases was perceived, intelligently, as declining. Of those polled, 88 percent had at least a "good opinion" of America, and—surprisingly—the numbers were highest in Manila. Ironically, these numbers had barely changed from those taken over a dozen years earlier, prior to the imposition of martial law.

In Latin America, which one thinks of as brimming with anti-Americanism, we find data unsupportive of the received wisdom. In 1985, 80 percent of 400 adults in Brazil's two giant cities thought relations with the United States were good or excellent, up from 48 percent in 1981. In 1981 as well, over twice as many Brazilians had a favorable opinion of America as of the Soviet Union.

In Costa Rica in 1985, support for the contras of Nicaragua ran two to one over support for the Sandinistas, and while it was generally believed that the United States interfered in the region, Cuba and the Soviet Union were thought

TABLE 1
COUNTRIES "LIKED THE MOST" IN THAILAND

Country	Urban Public (percentage)	Attentive Public (percentage)
United States	57	62
Japan	44	56
United Kingdom	28	47
Singapore	20	20
France	17	19
Australia	15	23
Malaysia	15	23
Germany	7	13
Philippines	6	9
Indonesia	4	—
Soviet Union	2	1

SOURCE: Author's file; the poll was taken in 1984.

to be worse offenders. Moreover, it was generally believed that the United States interfered "for the good," that is, through desirable economic and military aid.

One recent poll of opinions about the Central American conflict in eight Latin American countries—Bolivia, Brazil, Colombia, Costa Rica, the Dominican Republic, Ecuador, Mexico, and Venezuela—showed pluralities and often majorities in Venezuela, Costa Rica, and Ecuador explicitly approving U.S. policy in El Salvador and Nicaragua. Colombia was evenly divided, while Mexico, Bolivia, and the Dominican Republic often disapproved. A plurality in Mexico asserted that a victory by the revolution would be better for El Salvador, but more favored a government victory when asked which would be better for Mexico!

The variance among these countries was not, it was found, due to differing levels of education or amounts of information but rather to traditional attitudes toward the United States, pressures in social-political circles, and differences in perceptions of long-term goals. Six of these countries polled in 1983—Costa Rica, the Dominican Republic, Bolivia, Colombia, Venezuela, and Mexico—all held "favorable" views of the United States with only the last two simultaneously holding substantially positive views of the Soviet Union—49 percent and 69 percent, respectively. But despite the revolutionary tradition in Mexico, and the positive historical view of the Russian revolution that inspired it, fewer than 20 percent in Mexico were in general agreement with the Soviets in 1983. That figure has been gradually increasing in the 1980s, however.

The U.S. government has consistently found data on European public opinion to be even more supportive of America and American policy. It would be fair to say that, throughout the alliance, polls show support in the 60 to 90 percent range, depending on the issue and its formulation. In a 1981 poll on "favorable opinion and respect toward the US and USSR," the United Kingdom, France, West Germany, Italy, the Netherlands, Norway, and Belgium all showed greater than 50 percent holding a "favorable opinion" toward the United States.

At the same time, less than 20 percent had a favorable opinion of the Soviet Union except in Italy and France, where the figure was slightly greater than 20 percent. The presence of large Communist parties presumably affects that number.

Even on such a controversial issue as the deployment of intermediate-range nuclear forces (INF), against which the opposition was well organized and well financed, the U.S. government found in 1982-83 that, in all non-Communist European countries, a majority supported deployment if we combined the minority in unreserved support of U.S. policy with the substantial minority whose support was contingent on a continued American good-faith effort to reach an INF agreement with the Soviet Union. The latter minority was located by questioning those whose underlying position was favorable toward the United States. The systematic public diplomatic effort the United States made in Europe during those two years, targeted on and resulting from areas identified by such polls, unquestionably had much to do with the success of the deployment, the failure of Soviet policy to prevent that deployment, and the omission by the Soviets of any of the threatened retaliatory acts.[5]

Beyond Western Europe, data are harder and harder to find. The flow of refugees to the United States is one indicator that the American system remains an important symbol. Similarly, mail from around the world to the Voice of America and mail from the Soviet bloc to Radio Free Europe and Radio Liberty are supportive indicia.

5. W. Scott Thompson, "Some Elements of an American Strategy," in *Arms Control*, ed. William Kintner (Washington, DC: Washington Institute Press, 1987), pp. 304-6.

Yet the American government has too often been out of touch with local opinion abroad. Iran is only the most recent and conspicuous example of the havoc wrought by anti-Americanism. How could Iran happen? When I visited Iran in 1977, I found embassy personnel routinely driven in bullet-proof cars, and I encountered widespread hostility on a personal level, almost unique in my experience of 50 countries. I asked embassy personnel what had happened. The response was, Willie Sutton style, that there was substantial terrorism in Iran, and much of it was directed against Americans. A point worth making about the situation there as elsewhere is that U.S. Information Service officials, who are meant to be closer to public opinion and generally are, play little role themselves in policy formulation and are often shunted aside from the political centers of embassies. Charles Wick, director, throughout the Reagan years, of USIA—the parent agency of the U.S. Information Service—tried to make a virtue of necessity and, I believe wrongly, insisted on maintaining a nonpolicy role for USIA. Nonetheless, the Special Planning Group set up at the White House eventually gave the agency a voice at the policy level, if only briefly. This proved highly useful in such matters as the Korean Airline 007 decision and the INF deployments. Especially in the field, experience might well show that USIA officials are far better sensitized to shifts in public attitudes through their regular contacts with the press and intelligentsia.

The example of Iran demonstrates the point that, in cases where public attitudes are generally favorable toward the United States, at those times when they are not favorable, they tend to be volatile and virulent. Trouble at the systemic level throughout a society is very difficult for an American embassy to counter, and the consequences are likely to be far from trivial.

POLICY RESPONSE

If these data surprise, perhaps the distinction drawn earlier between underlying public attitudes and what we might call politics or policy response can help reconcile the data with those vivid images with which we are familiar—chanting mobs and their anti-American placards and slogans as, for example, in Iran and Libya today. The mere fact that the United States is so central to major international economic issues, long-standing regional conflicts such as those of southern Africa and the Middle East, and, of course—with the Soviet Union—superpower issues perceived as affecting the Third World makes the United States and its policies a touchstone for opposition everywhere.

Consider the issue of the debt of less developed countries—nearly a trillion dollars of it by 1987, almost half of which is owed by Latin America, with two-thirds of that in turn held by private American banks. The calamities that made debt so critical an issue in Latin America are not our subject, but the effects of the austerity programs imposed by the International Monetary Fund to deal with it are. As Professor Gilpin writes, "Although debtor governments strongly resisted these austerity programs and they were not always as austere as alleged by the debtors, the programs bred anti-Americanism and threatened to destroy the unsteady progress of Latin America toward political democracy."[6] Members of the Brazilian

labor union LULA, small wonder, demonstrated against the same old *yanqui* imperialism while their government pondered whether to continue defaulting on the debt so eagerly taken up in the 1970s. People can understandably protest when they see their incomes decline as their governments send more revenues to Washington than they take back. But that propensity cannot be confused with the underlying attitude, which is based on comparative judgments. As the late Senator Aquino used to ask his more radical supporters, "What's the alternative [to an alliance with the United States]?"—a position of which American officials were well aware.[7]

The same paradox is visible in Africa. Recently, for example, a group of Ghanaians proposed to an American foundation that they set up—with, of course, American financial support—an institute for developing enthusiasm for the American system. Few Westerners who have lived in Ghana would be surprised by this. Yet in that same country anti-Americanism has flared since independence, *inter alia,* whenever the International Monetary Fund has administered strong medicine. The presence of a tightly organized group of Marxists, including some in the media thought to be controlled by the KGB, affects the process, too, of course.[8]

A statehood movement has long existed in the Philippines, and the very question of where one stands on America is central to one's orientation in that country. The implication is that a large

---

6. Robert Gilpin, *The Political Economy of*

International Relations (Princeton, NJ: Princeton University Press, 1987), p. 325.

7. Author's interviews with Senator Aquino, 1970, 1982, 1983.

8. See Bob Woodward, *Veil: The Secret Wars of the CIA, 1981-1987* (New York: Simon & Schuster, 1987), p. 162.

group—indeed, the majority—is very pro-American. Yet in the months in the early 1970s immediately prior to the imposition of martial law, anti-Americanism was highly visible in Manila. It was widely known to have been fanned by local industrialists hoping to buy off American-owned enterprises in the fire-sale atmosphere created by the demonstrations that engulfed the Philippine capital. Through their newspapers and television, the richest Filipinos fanned the flames to which they would shortly fall victim.

Contrast that with the new Philippine republic. The United States finds itself highly regarded, however lately it came to the support of democracy there. Underneath the surface, not surprisingly, are policy intellectuals deeply radicalized by the Marcos period. It would not surprise this student of the Philippines to see widespread protests of American actions or policies in the years ahead, notwithstanding the polling data cited earlier.

American officials have as a rule found a positive attitude toward them in the international arenas in which they travel. To the political appointee, this is sometimes a surprise. A distinguished scholar appointed to represent the Reagan administration at a human rights forum in Geneva spoke of his expectation that the general antagonism toward the United States in many of the countries' governments would be replicated, *mutatis mutandis,* at the level of the international organization. To his surprise, he found continuous deference to his person and his position—as well he might, representing as he did the country that the rest of the world considers the most powerful. Some American officials with privileged access to the decoded messages sent by foreign embassies in the United States to their

home foreign offices have noted a systematic disparity between the deference paid by the foreign diplomat to the U.S. official in his or her government office and the anti-American hostility present in the coded embassy message. In short, anti-American talk in the diplomatic world is usually not reflected in real business. America commands respect, or so U.S. government officials have reason to believe.

How much is anti-Americanism at the political level a function simply of covert KGB activities and overt Communist-bloc propaganda? Various conspiracy schools see anti-Americanism as a reflection of faults not in ourselves or in the explicable reactions of peoples to a great and fallible power but in disinformation and other active measures organized by the Soviet Union and its allies. Would that it were so simple; the phenomenon is much too complex for so unsophisticated an explanation. Nevertheless, these plots exist and do explain some of it. To ignore them would be putting on, perhaps, Hamlet without the prince.

The fact is that systematic disinformation campaigns, thoroughly documented in and outside of the U.S. government, have attempted to exploit—or create—local grievances that accrue to the benefit of the Soviet Union. In some countries, otherwise friendly to the United States, senior editors under the control of the KGB have managed to stay in power churning out pro-Soviet pap on a daily basis, toning it down when the regime in power watches closely or cultivates ties with the West and turning it up when it averts its gaze. The U.S. government does a competent job of nailing disinformation items, however, and of using its available force in such situations to obtain retractions of material disseminated through Soviet cutouts. That the Reagan administration was willing to use disinformation itself to throw Colonel Qaddafi off guard, while no doubt useful in its immediate object, has clearly undercut the American claim—which I, as an official, was proud to make—that we do not partake of such tactics. The sum of it all is, however, that the Soviet Union has undertaken substantial numbers of active measures against the United States, but it is difficult to believe that these are the predominant reason for anti-Americanism everywhere it exists. Laborers in Latin America whose real wages have fallen throughout this decade do not need Soviet propaganda to find in the American banks a convenient scapegoat for their grievances.

This takes us to the third and highest level of the pyramid: personality or idiosyncrasy.

POLITICAL LEADERSHIP

I would argue that most political phenomena can be better explained by political, economic, and social structure than by the personality of leaders even despite the deep imprint that initial leaders have had on their countries. Nevertheless, the personality factor matters to some extent, especially in the Third World. We need only observe some instances here that self-evidently show the vulnerability of Third World political structures to personality. The early period of nonalignment in the 1960s can arguably be seen as a product of the anti-Americanism of several prominent leaders: Sukarno, Nasser, and Nkrumah, in particular. Sukarno's narcissism, Nasser's identification of Israeli victories as American determined, and Nkrumah's painful experiences as a

black in the United States of the 1930s are all personality factors that, given the hold each leader had on his society for over a decade, took foreign policy in a direction it was otherwise unlikely to have gone or unlikely to have gone so forcefully. Qaddafi and the Ayatollah Khomeini are reminders that, if the generation of supposedly charismatic Third World leaders has largely passed, there are others still to come.

How the U.S. government nurtures leaders toward more supportive attitudes about America is as varied at this level as at other levels. It is worth noting, briefly, that as the result of the programs that USIA has long had in place for bringing prominent personages to this country on leader grants, even in neutral and unfriendly countries, there is likely to be a substantial alumni and alumnae body of those familiar with the United States and, in some measure, happy to travel therein. The program may at times work against the United States, but that would seem to be the exception. And when the political wheels turn in unstable countries, bringing in leaders better disposed to America, a cadre of friends knowledgeable about the United States is at their service. Revelations of Central Intelligence Agency activity abroad in recent years tend on balance to demonstrate the scope and depth of the American networks abroad—however much such revelations tend to vitiate their existence.

American educational programs on a broader scale are also salient. Although the Soviet Union has many times as many official scholarships available for distribution in the Third World as does the United States, the fact is that our educational relations abroad rest mainly on private programs. That this sometimes works against us is absolutely clear; witness Nkrumah. Yet most American officials are familiar with the radical Third World leader who inveighs against the United States while asking for a scholarship for his children at an American university with no sense of contradiction. It is not Patrice Lumumba University to which Third World leaders aspire to send their children.

CHANGE THROUGH TIME

Has the American governmental attitude toward anti-Americanism evolved through time? I believe some immediately apparent distinctions are salient, especially with respect to the Third World, where American concerns on this subject have been centered. We can divide the subject again into three parts, or periods, since Third World consciousness began to have impact on American foreign policymaking in 1960. That was the year in which dozens of new states entered the United Nations and appeared, in the eyes of Christian Herter, the American secretary of state, to be aiding and abetting American adversaries. His comment, following Kwame Nkrumah's General Assembly address, that the Ghanaian leader was "very definitely moving towards the Soviet bloc," aside from mirroring his mentor's neurotic attitude toward nonalignment, strongly irritated Afro-Asian leaders gathered in New York.[9]

The first phase, from 1960 to roughly 1970, was nevertheless a mixed phase and one more favorable than not, the reverse of what we will find in the 1970s. On the positive side, it was a period in which Third World leaders were attracted to President Kennedy's charm, which even Marxist African leaders—

Sékou Touré, in particular—found irresistible.[10] The Peace Corps, the generosity that a rapidly expanding American economy made possible, the idealism of the new states, and the partial distance of the United States from the ex-colonial states conspired to create a positive attitude in general. And the Soviet Union had ill learned at that point how to project power—political or military—in the Third World.

On the other hand, in this period before the most obvious evidence of American racism was cleaned up— especially that assaulting the sensibilities of black diplomats in segregated Washington—America had problems. As the student of one predominantly black country's foreign policy put it:

The cause of America's fading popularity in many of the emerging nations—usually attributed to the Vietnam War—was more a product of its internal racial problems. The United States's image in the developing world was irreparably damaged by racism. It was extremely difficult for predominantly black nations to ally themselves with a country that embodied within itself the racial divisions that black nations believed marked the international system.[11]

It should be added, however, that one powerful motivation for America's leadership in the 1960s to solve this problem was precisely the anti-Americanism that ensued therefrom.[12]

In the 1970s, the United States was absorbed in Vietnam and its aftermath,

9. W. Scott Thompson, *Ghana's Foreign Policy* (Princeton, NJ: Princeton University Press, 1969); *New York Times*, 24 Sept. 1960.

10. Arthur M. Schlesinger, Jr., *A Thousand Days* (Boston: Houghton Mifflin, 1965), p. 560.

11. Brent Hardt, "Jamaica's Foreign Policy" (Ph.D. diss., draft, Fletcher School of Law and Diplomacy, Tufts University, 1987).

12. "The struggle against segregation at home gave substance to our condemnations of apartheid in the U.N. and helped Africans accept our reasoned objections to sanctions." Schlesinger, *Thousand Days*, p. 583.

to which it sought to bring to bear the entirety of its experience in the Third World: insurgency could be cured by large doses of democracy and development. All good things, as Professor Packenham aptly put it, would go together.[13] But it failed, for reasons beyond the scope of this article. Failure hardly begets admiration, however, and there was now currency to Soviet views—reinforced, increasingly, by gun deliveries and even by gunboats—that the American experience was flawed or even irrelevant to developing countries. Moreover, Americans thought ill of themselves. As Trollope has the Duke of Omnium say, nations are like people—one will not think higher of them than they think of themselves.

So the Third World, engaged in its own failures, this time of the so-called development decade, went its own way, and antagonism to the United States built apace.

There is fairly substantial evidence—though too little directly comparable data—that anti-Americanism has receded substantially in the 1980s. Part of this is the reverse of the duke's aphorism. America is back, and it is distributing its favors with increasing selectivity to its friends or tactical allies.

The change can be seen as a function of three factors. First is the failed aggressiveness of the Soviet Union. The U.N. vote censuring the Soviets for their occupation of Afghanistan was a watershed, bringing most Third World states into a common anti-Soviet stance for the first time. The Soviet Union had gunboats, but it did not have the international political and economic leverage

that the United States possessed and in which it had regained confidence. Soviet military power, in short, was not fungible. The countries on whom the USSR had visited its benefits in the 1970s remained major trading partners of the West.

Second is the revived confidence in market economies. Socialism was the slogan of the day for several decades, but it has become increasingly difficult to find any successes for Third World socialism in the 1980s. It has been increasingly difficult to play down market successes. It is not just the Sinitic societies of East Asia. Any country that has freed up its economy has done well: India suddenly became a food exporter. Ghana finally hit bottom in 1983 and took the foulest-tasting medicine the International Monetary Fund has ever given out, and the rest is history. Ghana is slowly, almost miraculously, coming back.

The failure of socialism has been matched by the successes of capitalism. American business ceased to be defensive in the 1970s and by the 1980s was bullish.

Finally, there was the shift of the models. The notion of the *tiers monde* was born on the Seine, and anti-Americanism was intrinsic to it. But what about when the French people were suddenly the most pro-American in Europe or perhaps the world? In a 1987 poll, the French showed confidence in the United States in overwhelming majorities.[14] And then there were the Swedes, who had campaigned for influence on anti-American platforms in influential Third World states. When they found that their strident opposition to all things American—at least those

13. Robert Packenham, *Liberal America and the Third World: Political Development Ideas in Foreign Aid and Social Science* (Princeton, NJ: Princeton University Press, 1973).

14. *Wall Street Journal,* 1 Oct. 1987.

related to their great prosperity—earned them in Moscow only "whiskey on the rocks,"[15] their public opinion turned around dramatically. Witness the poll question of whether the United States or the Soviet Union was unfriendly to them: between 1973 and 1983, the United States went from 47 percent to 15 percent, the Soviet Union from 10 percent to 43 percent.[16]

CONCLUSION

Has there been a learning curve in the U.S. government on the issue of anti-Americanism over the past generation? And does our brief survey of these data suggest further lessons, beyond the notion that more polling would be useful and that U.S. Information Service foreign service officers might be better used in the policy process? As we said at the outset, there is no official view, as such, on anti-Americanism, but there are underlying concerns, and these have evolved. What is immediately apparent is a non-linear maturing curve, as it were, one with its own ups and downs. But the general direction has plainly been toward more self-confidence, less neurosis about being liked, and growing diplomatic selectivity. The United States indeed found itself again and again in the past decade actually forgoing the advantages pressed upon it by favorable trends in certain countries, on the ground that too apparent an embrace of some leaders might not be in the regime's longer-term—and thus America's—interest.

15. As the Whiskey class of Soviet submarine that ran aground in their waters was called.
16. Paul M. Cole, "The Northern Balance: Changing Relations in Defending Northern Europe," *Defense and Foreign Affairs* (Dec. 1986), p. 35.

Still, when the secretary of defense went in late 1987 to the Persian Gulf, where our ships were maintaining the peace in the immediate interest of Kuwait—which state, however, did not invite him to visit—there was resentment in Washington and still more in other parts of the United States. To be sure, no one could fail to understand the sensitivity of Kuwait's position, especially with regard to the great power that undergirds Israel's military position. Moreover, the very debate between the executive branch and Congress on aid to these Arab states is generally caught on the horns of America's Middle Eastern dilemmas.

America has become a more selective great power in its diplomacy. If the debate on ends and means that the Vietnam war occasioned has not been resolved, by the late 1980s it has certainly had the effect—as has experience itself—of underlining national limits. But the other side of that coin is that if we are to be more selectively engaged, then we ipso facto need to make choices by more explicit criteria, such as U.N. votes or other acts of alliance on which great powers have traditionally depended. Anti-Americanism is becoming far too amorphous a concern for the dissipation of national energies.

This maturing has worked in other related ways. Old concerns about, for example, nuclear arms usually took the form of public demands that the genie be put back in the bottle, that arms control be given a priority above all else given America's so-called moral responsibility to the rest of the world and the anxieties about anti-Americanism that would flow from a failure of initiative in this arena. But it turns out that a more realistic approach, of which arms control is but one subset, works far better. It is the hard-liner Ronald Reagan who produced the first great arms-reduction agreement of history—the December 1987 INF agreement—and it did not flow from any high-level desire that America be liked.

The lessons of policy import to be drawn are perhaps prosaic and obvious. Sound policy will help produce the kind of environment congenial to American interests. An area of forthcoming importance is the issue of the less developed countries' debt. America, it might be argued, should be generous to those countries that it encouraged in the 1970s to borrow from its banks, not because anti-Americanism might otherwise ensue—that would be the least important of the possible ramifications—but because only with additional development assistance can the major debtors continue to buy American products and avert actions that could topple the international financial system.

In other words, the concern for anti-Americanism was an unsophisticated adjunct of the desire to be liked, and that desire was never the fundament of policy. Over the generation that America practiced its new role as the world's most involved power, it grew in its understanding of the levers of influence around the world and developed a more intelligent understanding of what maintained a congenial world system. The prince had learned that power and influence came from respect and fear built on a foundation of goodwill and understanding wherever that was possible. Machiavelli counseled the prince, after all, that he should pay attention to all groups—which for America, we read, perhaps, all countries—and "mingle with them from time to time" and while giving them "an example of his humanity and munificence" always uphold "the majesty of his dignity, which must never be allowed to fail in anything whatever."[17]

17. Machiavelli, *Prince*, p. 85.

ANNALS, *AAPSS*, **497**, May 1988

Anti-Americanism in the Third World

By ALVIN Z. RUBINSTEIN and DONALD E. SMITH

ABSTRACT: Anti-Americanism can be defined as any hostile action or expression that becomes part and parcel of an undifferentiated attack on the foreign policy, society, culture, and values of the United States. This analysis distinguishes four types: (1) issue-oriented anti-Americanism, or a pattern of outbursts directed against the policies of the U.S. government with which a Third World country disagrees; (2) ideological anti-Americanism, involving a more or less coherent set of ideas, frequently related to nationalism, Marxism, or Islamic fundamentalism, that see the United States as the central villain in the world today; (3) instrumental anti-Americanism, or the manipulation of hostility by a government for ulterior purposes, such as mobilizing domestic support or identifying a plausible scapegoat for governmental failure; and (4) revolutionary anti-Americanism, which arises in opposition groups seeking to overthrow a pro-U.S. government and develops as an important ideological tenet of the new regime building mass support.

Alvin Z. Rubinstein is professor of political science at the University of Pennsylvania and senior fellow of the Foreign Policy Research Institute. His books include Soviet Foreign Policy since World War II; Red Star on the Nile; *and* Yugoslavia and the Nonaligned World. *He is editor, with D. E. Smith, of* Anti-Americanism in the Third World.

Donald E. Smith is professor of political science at the University of Pennsylvania. His books include India as a Secular State; Religion and Politics in Burma; *and* South Asian Politics and Religion.

L IKE the Third World itself, anti-Americanism is easy to identify in a broad sense but difficult to describe without reference to a particular country or institution and its relationship with the United States. Both terms encompass a wide range of settings, with very different political, economic, social, and ideological barriers and problems. Both defy categorization or facile generalizations. Anti-Americanism can be viewed as any hostile action or expression that becomes part and parcel of an undifferentiated attack on the foreign policy, society, culture, and values of the United States. It is a highly variable concept whose impetus and content are remarkably diverse. It is, however, widespread and intensifying in many parts of Asia, Africa, the Middle East, and Latin America and as such is a major problem for U.S. leaders, whether they be in government, business, education, culture, or religion.

There is no end of examples: the attempt of Communist rebels to use a leaked memo on a meeting between Philippine Defense Minister General Fidel Ramos and Admiral Roland Hays, commander of U.S. Pacific forces, to foment anti-American sentiment, alleging a conspiracy to use U.S. arms to launch a new offensive against the Communist-controlled New People's Army;[1] a mass rally in Rawalpindi by the Movement for the Restoration of Democracy—an alliance of parties in opposition to the government of President Mohammed Zia ul-Haq—denouncing the United States, after martial law was lifted on 30 December 1985 and Miss Benazir Bhutto was permitted to return

to Pakistan;[2] stiff criticism in Mexico—as in much of Latin America—of the U.S. military intervention in Grenada in October 1983;[3] reports of growing hostility to the United States "among younger South African blacks because of their perception that the Reagan Administration has not helped the struggle against apartheid";[4] and amid the internecine carnage of Beirut's religious-political wars of the militias, denunciations of "Death to America! Death to Israel!"[5]

In recent years, Americans have been forced to leave Lebanon, the Sudan, and Colombia—because of attacks by terrorists in the two Arab countries and threats by big-time drug dealers in the latter. These incidents suggest that the Third World is becoming a dangerous place for Americans. And in a sense it is. Yet, anti-Americanism can be likened to an onion; it has many layers and these need to be peeled and examined separately for what they can teach us about the multifaceted phenomenon itself.

Hostility toward the government, society, and culture of the United States is far from new. In Latin America, it is a venerable intellectual tradition. But the depths of Third World resentments and the recourse to violence are new developments. The charges leveled against the United States are numerous: support for repressive regimes and acts of subversion against progressive ones; neglect and

1. *Washington Times,* 13 Jan. 1987; *Newsweek*, 26 Jan. 1987.

2. *New York Times* (hereafter referred to as *NYT*), 24 Mar. 1986; *NYT*, 11 Apr. 1986.
3. For example, José Woldenberg, "Autodeterminación o colonialismo," *Unomasuno,* 29 Oct. 1983: "The invasion of Grenada is not just a game involving the destiny of a small Caribbean island, but one involving the destiny of Central America."
4. *NYT,* 2 Jan. 1986.
5. *NYT,* 10 Mar. 1985.

inequity in the apportionment of foreign aid and exploitation by banks and multinational corporations; arrogance or indifference and the disruptive influence of rock music, blue jeans, and television soap operas. The array of charges and resentments is awesome, segmented, and complex, constituting an ever changing mosaic.

Anti-Americanism is a post-World War II and postcolonial phenomenon that took root among elites whose policies and perceptions of regional and international issues differed from those of Washington.[6] Initial disenchantment with the United States dates from the mid-1950s, when it was political in character. The Eisenhower administration, keen to extend the containment of the Soviet Union, sponsored a series of military pacts that polarized the Middle East and South Asia and pitted U.S. policy against the national interests of key regional actors. The pactomania that brought Iraq and Pakistan into the military orbit of the Western powers in the 1950s triggered a countervailing animosity from Egypt and India, respectively, each of which saw U.S. policy as a threat and consequently moved to develop closer ties to the USSR. This sowed the seeds of hostility to the United States. More recently, one can explain the anti-Americanism of Syria and Libya, at least in part, in terms of their opposition to the U.S.-crafted peace agreement between Egypt and Israel.

Increasingly, many Third World governments objected to being relegated to what they considered to be the status of pawns in the U.S.-Soviet rivalry. They

saw all bilateral relationships as subordinated to calculations of utility in the cold war or peaceful competition with the Soviets and found themselves important to U.S. policymakers primarily because they might go Communist. According to Third World critics, U.S. policy clothed its foreign policy objectives in the mantle of peace, economic development, human rights, and democracy, but underneath it all was the compulsion to counter communism and Soviet expansion.

Third World grievances over the operations of U.S. capitalism vary greatly in intensity from one region to another, ranging from Latin American and the Caribbean, where investments have long been sizable, to South Asia, where they have been relatively small. Of U.S. overseas investment, 70 percent is now in the developed world, but Third World critics see U.S.-based multinationals as continuing to exploit their countries' resources and populations, perpetuating political and economic dependency that benefits only a small segment of the people.

Images rarely keep pace with reality. The extraordinary U.S. dominance over the international economic system began to end in the 1970s, in part because of U.S. involvement in the costly war in Vietnam, but in major part because of the rise of Japan and West Germany to economic prominence. In the 1980s, the United States is still the major actor on the world economic stage, but it is no longer the commanding power it once was.

In Third World circles, however, where hostility is manifested toward the United States for political and military reasons, the economic power and influence of the United States continues to

6. For an elaboration of this point, see Alvin Z. Rubinstein and Donald E. Smith, eds., *Anti-Americanism in the Third World* (New York: Praeger, 1985), pp. 9-18.

receive much attention, albeit often un-deservedly so. On the other hand, many in the Third World are attracted by the dynamism of U.S. society. Driven by a conscious commitment to use tech-nology to produce wealth and a higher standard of living for larger numbers of people than ever before in human his-tory, and willing to accept the searing dislocation and disruptions that are an inevitable part of rapid social, economic, and cultural change, the United States is lunging into the future, impelled by forces that are uncontrolled and non-selective. Governments struggling to con-trol their dissatisfied populations, whose aspirations exceed productive capac-ities, fear the diffusion of the U.S. consumer-oriented culture and the pres-sures that it unleashes from below for change.

TYPES OF ANTI-AMERICANISM

When all is said and done, the United States is still the lightning rod for much of the progress and chaos, hope and fear, prospects and resentments, in-spiration and revulsion that permeates the thinking and policies of Third World elites. From the bewildering array of beliefs, situations, and events that, taken together, have been labeled anti-Americanism, we identify four basic types of the phenomenon, each prompt-ed by different motives and aims.

Issue oriented

First, and perhaps most prevalent, is issue-oriented anti-Americanism, a pat-tern of outbursts directed against the policies and actions of the U.S. govern-ment with which a Third World country disagrees. It springs from the policy disagreements of two governments pur-suing their respective national interests. It is evident in India's opposition to U.S. military aid—particularly high-per-formance aircraft—to Pakistan, in Saudi Arabian and Jordanian anger at U.S. readiness to provide Israel with modern arms but reluctance to do so to them, in Iraqi criticism of U.S. transfers of antitank missiles to Iran, and in Latin America's sense that U.S. hostility to-ward Cuba and Nicaragua is dis-proportionate to the problem they pose. This brand of anger is also fueled by Washington's frequently heavy-handed approach to specific issues and by the alacrity with which it uses pressure rather than conciliation to bring about some mutually acceptable agreement.

Latin America's anti-Americanism is historically rooted in hostility to U.S. interference in the region, especially in Central America. As far back in the early nineteenth century as the pro-mulgation of the Monroe Doctrine, Latin American elites resented the im-plicit arrogation of hemispheric hege-mony. In recent years, their opposition to the United States has emerged on positions such as their insistence on Argentina's right to sovereignty over the Falkland Islands, or Malvinas; criticism of U.S. efforts to topple the Sandinista regime in Nicaragua; and dissatisfaction with U.S. tariff and trade concessions, meager levels of investment, and in-adequate responses to Latin America's $500 billion foreign debt, much of it owed to U.S. banks. Differences over these issues, which are very serious in themselves, are aggravated by the mis-trust and fear that have become indelibly fixed over the decades in the political consciousness of Latin American elites. Complicating the staking out of posi-tions and the readiness to negotiate in good faith is an underlying frustration, which one astute Latin American analyst described as follows:

There is an almost general belief in Latin America today that the United States has siphoned off the wealth that could have led to the Southern Hemisphere's development. *They* are rich because *we* are poor; *we* are poor because *they* are rich. The argument is that, but for North American development, there would have been no Latin American underdevelopment: that but for Latin American underdevelopment, there would have been no North American development.[7]

In much of Africa, the issue that has occasioned a great amount of the anti-Americanism has been that of apartheid. As so often happens in incipient revolutionary situations, decompression brings acceleration of developments and new uncertainties and not any slackening of demands for change. In 1986, South Africa's President P. W. Botha did introduce some promised reforms, including repeal of the pass laws, the granting of permission for blacks to purchase homes, though only in segregated areas set aside for blacks, and restoration of citizenship to blacks considered by the government to reside permanently in the country.[8] But these failed to mollify anti-apartheid protests and strikes in South Africa or to distract efforts abroad to pressure Pretoria to end apartheid. The Reagan administration's policy of constructive engagement, which sought to persuade South Africa to introduce extensive reforms, lost the confidence of the Congress. In October 1986, Congress over-

rode a presidential veto and passed the Anti-Apartheid Act:

The act banned the importation of South African coal, uranium, iron and steel, agricultural produce, textiles and krugerrands; it prohibited new U.S. loans, investment, credits and the sale of computer technology to the South African Government and its agencies. Landing rights for South African airways were terminated.[9]

The effect of this congressional action should be to diminish African outbursts against the United States driven by the apartheid issue. Even longtime critic Prime Minister Robert Mugabe of Zimbabwe lauded the move.[10]

Ideological

A second variant, ideological anti-Americanism, derives from the belief that the United States is the central villain in the world today and that American society epitomizes bourgeois decadence or godless materialism. Pitched at a higher level of generalization, ideological anti-Americanism continues to generate hostility even without serious policy conflicts between the United States and the elite's own government.

Three important streams flow into ideological anti-Americanism in the contemporary Third World: nationalism, Marxism, and Islamic fundamentalism. Nationalism is the most universal and easily merges with the other two. It encompasses efforts to develop a sense of internal cohesion and unity, to build institutions capable of socializing diverse ethnic and religious groups and inculcating basic shared values.

At early stages of nation building,

7. Carlos Rangel, *The Latin Americans: Their Love-Hate Relationship with the United States* (New York: Harcourt Brace Jovanovich, 1976), p. 44.
8. John de St. Jorre, "South Africa Embattled," *Foreign Affairs: America and the World 1986*, 65(3): 543-44 (1987).

9. Ibid., p. 558.
10. *NYT,* 3 Oct. 1986.

there is a hypersensitivity to foreign inroads and influence, real or imagined. This becomes especially politically charged where the United States is concerned. The U.S. writ is global, and this occasions strong reactions to U.S. educational and cultural institutions. One ultranationalist solution is to ban the English language—or any foreign language—from the educational system and insist that all subjects be taught in one's own language. Few countries—Libya is one—have opted for so extreme a course.[11] Qaddafi's policy of Arabization may some day have to be modified, however, if only because English has become an international medium for scientific and commercial discourse and exchange, and no generation educated only in Arabic could hope to keep abreast of advances in the latest fields of medicine, engineering, science, and the like.

Marxism is the most intellectually consistent of the streams of ideological anti-Americanism, but it derives much of its political force from its critique of imperialism, a nationalist theme. What is striking is the similar way in which Fidel Castro and Robert Mugabe and Ayatollah Khomeini view the role of the United States in the world today.

As a social group, intellectuals in the Third World are hostile to capitalism and committed to the alternate ideas and models of societal change. Their anti-Americanism stems from identification of U.S. capitalism with perpetuation of the system they seek to change. It is also reinforced by a propensity toward Marxism, whose appeal to the Communist and non-Communist Left alike inheres in the ideational combination, at one and the same time, of a

critique of capitalism—that the system Karl Marx analyzed no longer exists is irrelevant to partisans of Marxism; an adaptable model for integrating socioeconomic phenomena; a formula, in its Leninist variant, for acquiring power; and a millennarian outlook. Particularly in Latin America, theorists of development and social systems gravitate toward the *dependencia* school established by Raúl Prebisch and others. Also influential in the strong brew of anti-Americanism is the input of militant Roman Catholic priests, whose concern for social justice is interlaced with criticism of American economic and political domination.

Intellectuals of the Left, be they Marxist or non-Marxist, tend to be anti-American in important measure because they can neither forget nor forgive the success and continuing appeal of the American experiment. At a time of spreading disillusionment in the Third World with variants of socialism, the market economy, contemporary capitalism, or whatever one wants to label the American-style alternative has shown a resiliency and adaptability that is attracting greater attention among groups intent on tackling economic development issues.

Anti-Americanism is not the monopoly of the Left. It is to be found as well among elites intent on revitalizing traditional values, institutions, practices, and social relationships. In the Muslim world, Ayatollah Khomeini's Islamic revolution in Iran and virulent attacks on the Satan America epitomize the resurgence of fundamentalism. That it focuses so strongly on the United States is perhaps understandable, this resurgence being a visceral reaction to the iconoclasm inherent in American cultural exports, an instinctive recog-

11. *NYT,* 4 May 1986.

nition that everything American can have socially disruptive and unanticipated consequences, a fear of the peculiarly American notion of change for the sake of change.

In line with this argument, as one would expect, anti-Americanism is to be found among fundamentalist, tradition-minded groups, regardless of their government's official relationship with the United States. In Iran, the official hostility also permeates the entire society. In Lebanon, Shiite terrorists belonging to Hizbollah, or the Party of God, have frequently evinced their hatred of the United States, for example, in public statements that were made at the end of the ordeal of Trans World Airlines flight 847, which was hijacked and kept on the tarmac in Beirut airport in June 1985.[12] Even in Egypt, where the government of Hosni Mubarak enjoys good relations with the United States, among the ultra-religious and the Muslim Brotherhood there is a bitter hostility toward America. They resist American inroads as antithetical to the perpetuation of traditional values and institutions.

Ideological anti-Americanism has different strands, and this makes generalizing a risky undertaking. In the Arab world, it needs to be differentiated along a number of axes: Shiite and Sunni; religious and secular; radical and traditional. One noted Arab specialist captured the complexity of the phenomenon thus:

The Arab radicals are defined solely by their desire and efforts to undermine the Arab status quo order, and by their antipathy toward Israel and their seeming ambivalence to United States policies in the area. Beyond that, it is important to understand (especially in light of present American sentiments) that

there is no ideologically and/or organizationally united radical movement, no tightly controlled radical conspiracy, no coherent or cohesive radical brotherhood.[13]

The phenomenon may not be "amenable to modification, let alone eradication," and it is a serious problem for the United States, but it is so embedded in the consciousness and policies of all Arab groups and leaderships as to preclude piecemeal accommodations and essential stabilization of political relationships.[14]

Instrumental

Third, there is instrumental anti-Americanism, which instigates and manipulates hostility toward the United States in order to mobilize domestic support, provide a plausible scapegoat for governmental failure, or justify a closer alignment with the Soviet Union. It is convenient, easily generated, and relatively cost free. The United States is a convenient target, because of other mutually reinforcing perceptions of it as an omnipotent, ever intriguing, intrusive superpower and because it is not likely to respond in kind.

Such recourse to explain defeats and difficulties is a prominent feature of international politics. Of the more than 100 new countries that have come into existence since the end of World War II, most are authoritarian, hence able to control the flow of information to their constituencies. Especially those who refuse to permit open elections that allow for the possibility of transferring power from one group to another will seek to avoid admitting mistakes by placing the

12. *NYT,* 1 July 1985.

13. Adeed Dawisha, *The Arab Radicals* (New York: Council on Foreign Relations, 1986), p. 131.

14. Ibid., p. 133.

source of the trouble on some outside actor.

In the summer of 1987, General Manuel Antonio Noriega of Panama, struggling to contain growing internal demands for democratization, attempted to portray his position as one of valiant resistance to U.S. pressure. A government-organized attack on the American embassy resulted in damage estimated at $106,000. "Panama has not escaped the classic scheme of destabilization, submission, punishment and surrender practiced by the United States in Latin America," he declared.

Authoritarian governments have special incentives to utilize instrumental anti-Americanism, but it is clear that they have no monopoly on this variant. India, the world's largest democracy, has made use of it on various occasions. Though the presumed American motivation has remained obscure, Indian prime ministers, particularly the late Mrs. Gandhi, have found the "foreign hand"—the Central Intelligence Agency (CIA)—to be a factor in fomenting various ethnic and regional agitations and separatist movements. Largely as a result of exposés published by Americans, the CIA remains, throughout the Third World, a plausible explanation for things gone wrong.

Instrumental anti-Americanism has been a key ideological weapon in the evolution of the Sandinista regime in Nicaragua, particularly since 1981. The consolidation of the regime, its increasing authoritarianism and movement to the left with growing support from the Soviet bloc are all explained and justified to the Nicaraguan people by the existence of an implacable enemy to the north. The basic charges against the *yanquis*, of course, are not simply Sandinista propaganda but fully verified

facts. The U.S. government has given substantial overt and covert support to the contra rebels, the CIA has mined Nicaraguan harbors and has printed assassination manuals, and so forth. Ironically, the Reagan administration has handed the Marxists in Managua a useful tool, and they are making good use of it.

Even when a Third World government retracts an initial position blaming the United States for an act perpetrated against its territory and/or interests, the regime's opponents may persist in an anti-American attitude, if only because of the dynamics of internal politics. For example, in March 1987, 17 months after Israel bombed the Palestine Liberation Organization's offices in Tunisia, the Tunisian foreign minister said that as a result of the revelations that Jonathan Pollard, a former U.S. intelligence analyst, had spied for Israel and provided it with reconnaissance data that made the air raid possible, the government was "convinced that the United States in no way aided the raid" and the bilateral relations were "solid and unaffected"; the leader of the opposition, however, said that "the damage [was] irreparable."[15]

Revolutionary

The final type of anti-Americanism is revolutionary anti-Americanism. It is found among opposition groups seeking to overthrow regimes closely identified with the United States; attacking such regimes thus involves attacking the United States. After the overthrow of the pro-U.S. government, as in Iran and Nicaragua, revolutionary anti-Americanism becomes a mass phenomenon

15. *Washington Post*, 4 Mar. 1987.

and a force justifying the rule of the new leadership. Accordingly, in Iran, for example, long after the fall of the shah, the Great Satan continues to be denounced as the deadliest enemy of the revolution. The new regime finds it useful to manipulate anti-American sentiment, as in the instrumental variant noted earlier, but it is the revolutionary process that has pushed anti-Americanism to the center of both the regime's ideology and the mass consciousness.

Under Ayatollah Khomeini, Iran's leadership has been vituperatively anti-American. When the Reagan administration's covert efforts to establish ties with Iran and ransom Americans held prisoner by Shiite terrorist groups in Lebanon in return for shipments of sophisticated weapons and spare parts were revealed in November 1986, Iranian spokesmen had a field day, "mocking the United States as a country willing to apologize for past sins and desperate to reestablish contacts."[16] From the evidence collected by the Tower Commission and the congressional hearings held in the spring and summer of 1987, the Iranians have more than enough material to use to denigrate the Reagan administration's amateurish and inept diplomacy.[17]

But all revolutionary regimes are not inherently anti-American, even though they may be pro-Soviet and hostile to U.S. policies because of differences over policy issues and not as a result of antithetical cultural, religious, or ideological outlooks. Ethiopia is one example, Vietnam another. From the reports of well-informed observers, we know that the revolution in Ethiopia

headed by Mengistu Haile Mariam has intensified the desire for modernization and change:

But the cultural habits and preferences of both the modernized segment of the society and those aspiring to join them remain pro-Western. Ethiopian ideological publications read like primers at a Soviet Party school; the effort to adapt Marxism-Leninism to Ethiopian circumstances is all verbal and bureaucratic. There is little evidence that the younger generation has been, or is being, converted—least of all those recruited for study and training in the USSR and Eastern Europe, where they experience the shortcomings and contradictions of Soviet-style society at first hand. They also experience racist prejudice, which Ethiopians, generally lighter-coloured than other Africans, and with an ancient tradition of political independence, resent intensely.[18]

Ethiopia, undergoing a sociopolitical and economic transformation every bit as dramatic and pervasive as Iran's, is nonetheless conveying a very different attitude toward the United States, both at home and abroad.

OBSERVATIONS

Our line of analysis suggests a number of generalizations about the nature and future of anti-Americanism in the Third World.

First, given the prominent political, economic, military, and cultural role that the United States plays in the international system, a certain amount of anti-Americanism is inevitable. The United States may be courted for what it can offer, but its unilateralism, erratic policy, cultural dynamism, and persisting parochialism occasion inevitable

16. *NYT,* 27 Nov. 1986.
17. *The Tower Commission Report* (New York: Bantam Books and Times Books, 1987), pp. 284-338.

18. Paul Henze, "Behind the Ethiopian Famine: Anatomy of a Revolution, III," *Encounter,* 67(3): 26 (Sept.-Oct. 1986).

resentment and suspicion. In an era of rapid change, tensions are to be expected along all kinds of axes, be they North-South, East-West, rich-poor, secular-religious, radical-conservative, or ethnic separatist and ethnic unitarist, and as long as an American component is involved at some point, the United States will draw all kinds of powerful contrary forces. There are no immediate palliatives. In dealing with Third World countries, the United States needs to assess the kind or kinds of anti-American manifestations that exist in a particular relationship and adapt as best it can. The complexity of the phenomenon mandates a differentiated policy: Mugabe's anti-Americanism is quite different from Qaddafi's, Mengistu's from Castro's or Assad's.

Second, not all anti-Americanism is inevitable, and the United States should pay attention to the basic complaints from the Third World that have changed little over the decades. Fear of communism has continued to inspire the hegemonic imperative in our Latin American policy. Overwhelmingly the Third World will continue to oppose Washington's assertion of a moral right to overthrow the Sandinista regime in Nicaragua. Despite monumental changes in U.S. policy toward communism in Asia, we are apparently unable to conceive of pluralism in what we think of as our backyard and in the process have done much to cement the tie between Marxism and nationalism. If a future administration will have the courage to repudiate and abandon the hegemonic imperative, anti-Americanism will decrease significantly.

Over time, helping friends, reconciling rivals—along the lines of the Egyptian-Israeli peace treaty—fostering political and economic liberalization, and sharing technological and educational expertise are the ways to transform the political-strategic environment within which the United States operates in the Third World.

Third, a greater empathy is needed for the politically precarious position of implicitly pro-American elites in different parts of the world. American elites, especially Congress and the media, must be sensitized to the reality that exists in other political systems. In the main, there is no advantage in a Third World elite being openly pro-American, because most of their political systems are fragile and to identify themselves thus would enormously increase their vulnerability to opposition groups whose main aim may be power and not stability or development. As one observer of the Islamic world has noted, "Quiet cooperation with a friendly government provokes less opposition than open declarations of support at public meetings. Strong relations need not have a high profile: ideally, they are almost invisible."[19]

Of course, it is also true that Third World elites must be made to understand that cynically fanning anti-American sentiments will inevitably limit their access to support from the U.S. government and ultimately complicate and narrow their ability to further legitimate national goals. One example concerns U.S. relations with Zimbabwe. U.S. economic assistance—about $400 million since 1980—was stopped soon after a Zimbabwean cabinet minister attacked U.S. policy at the American embassy's Independence Day celebration in Harare

19. Daniel Pipes, "Fundamentalist Muslims between America and Russia," *Foreign Affairs*, 64(5): 957 (Summer 1986).

on 4 July 1986.[20] This breach of protocol, which led former President Jimmy Carter and the U.S. ambassador to walk out of the reception, has as yet not brought an official apology and continues to strain relations.

Finally, anti-Americanism is often more apparent than real, or only one side of the coin in a relationship of profound ambivalence. There is a reservoir of goodwill toward the United States and its society—though not necessarily its policies—that affects the way that elites perceive and relate to the United States. Thus while anti-Americanism in Latin America, for example, will continue to be a serious problem for American policymakers, its antithesis is also strong and serves as a bond between two cultures. The quip "*Yanqui* go home" is painted on the walls of Latin American cities and used by critics, but among those for whom the United States retains an attraction as protector, patron, investor, and source of technological, educational, and cultural riches, there is the wry addition "And take me with you!"

20. *Philadelphia Inquirer*, 5 July 1986.

Anti-American Attitudes in the Arab World

By RICHARD B. PARKER

ABSTRACT: Anti-Americanism in the Arab world today is not an inherent and unavoidable phenomenon of race or religion. It is a reaction to American policies and to the penetration of Western culture. It will be with us for some time to come for a number of reasons, including U.S. identification with Israel, U.S. involvement in local issues, and U.S. overidentification with local leaders. We will continue to have relations with Arab states in spite of it. The seizure of American hostages, which is one current gauge of anti-Americanism, is not a new phenomenon. The Algerians once held 150, and we paid a ransom of over $800,000 to obtain the release of 82 survivors because we had no alternative. Early in this century, Theodore Roosevelt blustered in order to obtain the release of American hostages in Morocco, but success was due more to the efforts of the French than to American armed strength. Neither case offers much of a precedent for handling today's hostage problem.

Richard B. Parker, president of the Association for Diplomatic Studies, was editor of the Middle East Journal *from 1981 to 1987. He served as ambassador to Algeria, Lebanon, and Morocco in the Ford and Carter administrations.*

A S I begin to write this, in January 1987, most of Washington is slumbering under a snowfall, but the Department of State is astir over the kidnapping from Beirut University College two days ago of three American professors. The television news last night featured pundits like Henry Kissinger and Michael Ledeen saying calmly that we should resort to physical force against someone. But against whom? And how? And what has brought us to this pass?

To those of us who knew Lebanon when it was an oasis of security and comfort, it is difficult to believe that civility has disappeared from West Beirut and that there is no safety for Americans there today. That they are the special targets of such animosity on the part of some Lebanese should make all of us stop and ponder the causes. We can speak of historical accidents or of forces unleashed by this or that event, but we must ultimately face the reality that we have become unpopular and that the primary cause is the role we have played in world affairs.

EARLY TROUBLE WITH THE BARBARY STATES

The seizure of American hostages is not a new phenomenon in the Arab world. It began when the Algerians seized the brig *Maria* out of Boston off the Algarve coast of Portugal in 1785. Before it was all over 11 years later, the Algerians had captured a total of 12 American ships, and 150 seamen had been sent to slavery in the notorious *bagnios* of Algiers. We eventually paid a ransom of over $800,000, and 82 survivors reached the United States in 1797. We had to borrow part of the ransom from the moneylenders of Leghorn, the credit of our infant republic not then being good enough for the Algerians.

The seizure of these hostages by the Algerians was not the result of a vendetta against Americans, however, but of the Algerian practice of piracy as a source of revenue and as a religiously sanctioned response to the infidel *reconquista* of Spain and Spanish incursions into North Africa. The Americans were not unpopular; they just happened not to have the British—or French—behind them.

In contrast to the Algerians, the Moroccans opted to recognize the American republic at an early date—they were arguably the first to do so—and the sultan ordered on 20 February 1778 that henceforth all vessels sailing under the American flag might freely enter Moroccan ports and that once in port they would be allowed to "take refreshments, and enjoy in them the same privileges and immunities with those of the other nations" with which Morocco was at peace.

The Tripolitanians, on the other hand, attacked American shipping, and we eventually became involved in a war with the Barbary States, principally Tripolitania under the Karamanli dynasty, from 1801 to 1805. Our troubles with Barbary led eventually to an American naval presence in the Mediterranean, a presence that was maintained intermittently in succeeding years but that has been constant since World War II. In spite of its navy, the United States continued to pay tribute to the Barbary States until 1815, and Barbary Coast piracy was not brought fully to a halt until the French occupied Algeria in 1830. It is indicative of our interest in North Africa during this early period that the first Department of State language training program of which we have record was established in 1826 to train officials in Berber, Turkish, and Arabic to facilitate their work in the Barbary States.

GOOD WORKS IN THE LEVANT

A principal reason for the American presence in the western Mediterranean was the substantial participation of American vessels in the west European coastal trade. In the eastern Mediterranean and beyond, however, American involvement was largely eleemosynary.

The first Protestant missionaries went out in 1822 and the first missionary establishment in Beirut was opened in 1824. By 1844, 60 missionaries had been sent out and by the end of the century they were operating in widely scattered sites from Muscat to Istanbul and from the southern Sudan to Iran. Proselytizing was largely confined to Eastern Christian sects—Greek Orthodox, Armenian, and Nestorian—because conversion of Muslims was not permitted and the Maronites, who are of the Latin rite, were too resistant.

More important in the long run than proselytizing, which produced only a modest number of converts, were the good works—the schools, colleges, hospitals, and clinics that the missionaries established and operated and that eventually matured into a series of highly respected institutions, such as the American University of Beirut, Robert College in Istanbul, and the American University in Cairo.[1]

While skepticism about American intentions was inevitable, particularly

1. For a more detailed discussion, see Bayard Dodge, "American Educational and Missionary Efforts in the Nineteenth and Early Twentieth Centuries," *The Annals* of the American Academy of Political and Social Science, 401:15-22 (May 1972).

among the political and religious elite, Americans were known and respected in the Levant for their selfless dedication and for the substantial charitable work they did, particularly in the famines and refugee crises during and after World War I. In the process, they educated a substantial portion of the administrative and technical elite that emerged when the states of the Levant finally became independent in the 1930s and 1940s. Not only did their schools teach science and medicine and Western languages, but they also inculcated something of American mental attitudes, and it is remarkable how much easier it is for an American to communicate with a graduate from one of the American schools than with one produced by the French system, even assuming no problem of language.

THE AMERICAN PRESENCE

The American commercial presence in the eastern Mediterranean was modest. There was limited trade with Turkey and the Ottoman provinces but no serious economic stake until the development of the American role in oil exploration in the 1930s and 1940s. Similarly, while a number of individual Americans were involved in promoting various economic schemes, such as a ship railway from El Arish to Aqaba, and provided assistance and advice to modernizing governments and armies, there was little U.S. government presence in the area.

Even American involvement in the Middle East Supply Center and the Persian Gulf Command in World War II did not make the United States a first-class power on the local scene, which remained largely a British sphere. Substantial U.S. involvement came after 1947, a fateful year in which two developments thrust the United States into the role of a major power in the Middle East: the Truman Doctrine, under which the Americans took over the British role in Greece and Turkey, and the Palestine partition resolution in the U.N. Security Council, which set the stage for the creation of Israel and of the Palestine problem as we know it today.

If America was a distant power before and immediately after World War II, it was even more so in the period before World War I, when Arab nationalism did not yet exist, or rather, had not yet been recognized as such, Jewish nationalism was only beginning to stir, and there was no Palestine problem. The principal foreign powers were the British, the French, and the Russians. All three had been involved in serious military operations in the Levant at one time or another, and all three were entangled politically with local clientele to a greater or lesser extent—the Russians with the Eastern Orthodox Christians of Syria and Palestine, the French with the Maronites of Lebanon, and the British with the Druzes.

The Americans, while concentrating on good works and the protection of their citizens and of their modest commercial interests, also developed clients, particularly in Egypt, Turkey, and Morocco, where they extended consular protection to local nationals who claimed American citizenship or some special relationship. This practice was subject to much abuse and was a source of great resentment by local nationals and officials, who found the American client beyond the reach of the law.

PERDICARIS ALIVE

The most famous case involving such local clients occurred in North Africa.

Ion Perdicaris, a Greek who claimed American nationality, together with his son-in-law was abducted from his home in Tangier in 1904 by a local chieftain, Raisuli. The latter demanded from the sultan a ransom of $70,000, his own appointment as governor of the area around Tangier, the imprisonment of his enemies, and the release of his friends as the price for releasing the captives. President Theodore Roosevelt dispatched a naval force to Tangier, and Washington sent the famous instructions to its diplomatic agent in Tangier that we wanted Perdicaris alive or Raisuli dead. Perdicaris was eventually released but only after the sultan paid the full price, thanks largely to the good offices of the French, who were even then seeking to establish a special position for themselves in Morocco. The great winner was Raisuli, who became a local hero and a powerful figure as a result of his humiliation of the sultan.

Just what Roosevelt could have done had the sultan not paid the ransom is not clear. He could have shelled Tangier, Tétouan, or Rabat, but the sultan was far away and out of reach in Fez. He could have landed troops at Tangier and seized the customs office or something similar, but the European powers, and particularly the French, would have reacted strenuously against that, and it would have caused more trouble than it was worth. Teddy's bluster was a successful bluff by a second-rate power, largely because a first-rate power, France, did not want to give the Americans an excuse to get involved in its hunting preserve.

The dispatch of the naval force to Tangier was the last American military involvement in the region until World War II, when American troops landed in Morocco and Algeria and began the campaign that led eventually to Sicily and Italy. At the other end of the Mediterranean, the first large-scale involvement of U.S. combat forces—as opposed to service troops—came with the 1958 landing in Lebanon, and that was only temporary.

THE EARLY
AMERICAN REPUTATION

Prior to 1947, and even after it, as representatives of a distant power without imperialistic designs on the area and with a residual reputation for supporting self-determination, and as a possible source of succor to a people badly in need of outside help, Americans were generally personae gratae in the region. There were few hostile actions against them. Sharp distinctions were drawn between them and the British and the French, who were usually blamed for whatever went wrong. America was considered the land of opportunity—and still is. Its technological skills and consumer products were much admired, and Americans were looked on as generous victors and disinterested mediators. Even after the Palestine debacle, many Arabs made a point—and some still do—of distinguishing between individual Americans, who were good, and the American government, which was often seen as evil or, at best, misdirected. This distinction seems to be increasingly blurred, at least among Palestinians and Shiite activists.

There were many indications of this essentially friendly attitude over the years. Perhaps the best known of these was the desire expressed by Arabs in the Levant after World War I that America, instead of France and Britain, be given the League of Nations mandate for Syria and Palestine. Less well known is the fact that in 1871 the Moroccan sultan suggested that we declare a protectorate over his country to ward off European incursions. Moroccan nationalists later expressed appreciation for our support for Moroccan independence in World War II, and Rabat had a Place Patton—now Abraham Lincoln—until the late 1970s. Similarly, while the Algerians were not entirely happy with America's somewhat ambiguous role in their own independence struggle, they named a square after John Kennedy, who had made a speech in support of Algerian independence while a senator, and there was a good deal of informal contact between American diplomats and Algerian revolutionary representatives in the period before independence. The Tunisians also toyed with the idea of an American protectorate in the nineteenth century, and there were notable contacts between Tunisian nationalists and American diplomats in the pre-independence period.

During World War II, the Americans were sympathetic to Lebanese and Syrian aspirations for independence from the French and were generally credited with helping the British ease the latter out of the Levant. The Americans also gave the Arabs assurances that "no decision altering the basic situation of Palestine should be taken without full consultation with Arabs and Jews." This formula, first used in May 1943 and perhaps borrowed from the British, became the standard boilerplate for use on all occasions connected with the Palestine problem.[2] It enabled us to enter the postwar era in the Near East with an image of benevolent impartiality on this burning issue and created in Arab minds

2. For further details, see Evan M. Wilson, *Decision on Palestine* (Stanford, CA: Hoover Institution Press, 1979), pp. 24-35.

certain expectations of fair play from Uncle Sam. By and large, these expectations were not met, as the United States increasingly emerged as Israel's principal source of support.

CURRENT ATTITUDES

Some remnant of this Arab expectation is nevertheless still alive today and is revealed in the statements of conservative leaders such as King Hussein of Jordan and King Fahd of Saudi Arabia, who keep underestimating the depth of American commitment to Israel. It is also reflected in personal friendships between Americans and Arabs and by the continued interest conservative Arab governments have in good relations with the United States, which they see as their principal, and most reliable, support against radical trends in the area.

Some of these governments hope for a miraculous change in the American position on Palestine and Israel, but most of them apparently believe that, whether or not there is such a change, their economic and political interests are bound up with those of the United States. We thus have the spectacle of Jordan and Saudi Arabia continually coming back for more, even after they have been rebuffed, not to say insulted, by the administration and Congress.

These attitudes are probably not shared by most of the politically alert opposition in these countries, however,[3]

3. I say "probably" because there is no reliable guide to public opinion in the Arab world except when it finds expression in popular manifestations. Official censorship, fear of reprisals or of exposure, and lack of functioning representative institutions make it difficult, if not impossible, to know what the public really thinks about most questions of the day. The intelligent observer can guess or surmise on the basis of conversations, newspaper

and while governments may be anxious to cooperate, popular attitudes are frequently unfriendly or hostile. That hostility has perhaps reached its ultimate expression among the pro-Iranian Shiite militias of West Beirut, who have just captured another hostage, Charles Glass of American Broadcasting Companies, as I write these words. That matters have reached such a stage in Lebanon is a result of the lack of effective governmental authority, complicated by the Iranian factor, rather than a result of any inherent religious or ethnic antipathy. Lebanese militias not allied with Iran are notably less hostile toward Americans. Some of them can even be classified as friendly, in spite of the Palestine problem, and the actions of the Shiite militias should not be taken as representative of Lebanese attitudes any more than Rabbi Meir Kahane and the Jewish Defense League should be taken as representative of Jewish attitudes toward Arabs.

This illustrates the danger of generalizing about Arab attitudes, which are diverse and depend very much on local considerations. Within a given locality, they also depend very much on the personal situation of the individual in question and on what his or her personal interests are. It is also dangerous to attempt a measurement of hostility, which rises and falls for reasons that are often impossible to predict and which is subject to manipulation by governments and political leaders.

In 1967, for instance, the government of Egypt had so excited local resentment against the Americans by its claim of U.S. participation in the Israeli attack on 5 June of that year that the governor

articles, and current events, but a surmise is still a surmise and is often unreliable.

of Alexandria could no longer guarantee the safety of Americans transiting that city if they happened to be spotted by the mob in the street. Attitudes in Alexandria a year later were remarkably different.

Certain generalizations may be permitted, however. The first is that, while there have been many ups and downs over the years since 1947, popular attitudes toward Americans are demonstrably less favorable than they were 40 years ago. The aura of American beneficence described previously has largely gone, and the Americans are seen as no better than the British or French. The most obvious measures of this deterioration are the increase in the number of terrorist actions against individual Americans and the decline in the American ability to influence events on the ground. Although there were occasional acts of mob violence, as in Baghdad in 1958, when three American businessmen were torn to pieces by a mob, there was no organized terrorism against Americans until after the 1967 Israeli-Arab war. Americans could walk safely through the streets of Arab cities at night unescorted—more safely, indeed, than they could in Washington or New York. Today there are few places in the Arab world where they can relax in the knowledge that they are completely safe from attack.

AMERICAN INFLUENCE

America's word and its potential use of military force were also powerful persuaders in the pre-1967 era. In 1958, the United States could perform successfully as deus ex machina in the Lebanese imbroglio and bring it to a happy resolution without firing a shot. In 1983, it failed miserably to do the same, in part because it had lost its aura of invincibility. The Lebanese discovered that the marines could be killed as easily as anyone else and that they were powerless to do anything effective in response.

We thus come to an important cause of anti-Americanism, or perhaps we should say an important reason that anti-Americanism has become apparent. Anti-Americanism results from, among other things, lack of respect. Defeat is an orphan, and American bumbling and inability to stay the course in Lebanon have reflected severely on American prestige and popularity. That makes it easier to be anti-American and to act out one's hostility. There are still many Lebanese who remember the positive American role of the past and whose interests are closely tied to those of the United States, but they have been pushed into the background and silenced by those who think they have reason to dislike or hate America, and it is this latter current that is dominant in the suburbs of south Beirut today. Uncertainty about the constancy of the Americans makes their friends unwilling to expose themselves and makes their enemies bolder.

THE FRUITS OF POWER

Even when victorious, however, a major power with at least theoretical ability to affect the movement of characters on the local stage inevitably attracts an animosity it did not earn when it was remote and uninvolved. This is one of the fruits of power and responsibility. Twisting the lion's tail long ago gave way to plucking the eagle's feathers. This game becomes easier to play, although perhaps less fun, when the United States loses the will or the capacity either to respond effectively or to solve the problem that lies at the root of local unhappiness.

The dilemma of the outside power sucked into the political maelstrom of the Middle East is brilliantly described by L. Carl Brown.[4] He argues that the only safe course is for outside powers to have a realistic appraisal of their inability to solve the Eastern question, which is at least two centuries old, and to resist the temptation to tinker with it. This is wise and useful advice, but for a variety of reasons, from the strength of the Israel lobby in the Congress to the readiness of the Soviets to fill any vacuum—witness the U.S. dilemma about protecting shipping in the Gulf— the United States will inevitably be involved in the Middle East as long as it claims to be a world power and to be competing with the Soviets.

ARAB GRIEVANCES

It is not just America's role as a world power, however, that gives rise to antagonism. As noted earlier, the very fact of prominence will itself attract animosity. Whoever is great is envied, and whatever he wants some will oppose simply because he wants it. Such resentment is obviously a factor in Arab attitudes from time to time. The Algerians, for instance, in 1974 adopted a self-destructive position on family planning in part because they were tired of American efforts to bulldoze through a consensus in the opposite direction.

The degree of animosity, however, depends a great deal on actions taken or not taken. Policies followed do make a difference. In the case of Arabs, Ameri-

can policies have led to a profound sense of genuine grievance. The nature of that grievance may change from place to place and time to time, but there are some enduring themes. The most prominent of these is the Palestine problem, in which the United States is seen as opposing Arab expectations of self-determination, but there are other issues, some of which are related by the Arabs to Palestine even though they are quite separate in American eyes. One of them has been the fairly consistent American opposition to the more radical forms of Arab nationalism as exemplified by Nasser, Qaddafi, and Hafez al-Assad. This has been widely perceived as a function of U.S. support for Israel. Another has been American support of one side or another in local disputes, such as the Western Sahara issue, the Iran-Iraq war, and the Yemen struggle in the 1960s.

A third, and perhaps the most pervasive source of animosity, has been American overidentification with local rulers, the most egregious example of which occurred with the Shah of Iran, but of which there have been numerous examples in the Arab world—Nuri Said in Iraq, President Chamoun in Lebanon in 1957-58, Hussein in Jordan, Sadat in Egypt, Hassan in Morocco, and Bourguiba in Tunisia. The Americans have an observable tendency to personalize their foreign relations everywhere, to classify local rulers as being either pro-American or anti-American, and to embrace too enthusiastically those in this first category, seeing them as embodying the country they rule and as being personal friends of the U.S. president. The case of Sadat was certainly the worst example of this tendency in the Arab world, and he was eventually brought down by a force we have yet to

4. L. Carl Brown, *International Politics and the Middle East* (Princeton, NJ: Princeton University Press, 1984).

discuss but that in the long run is likely to be the most important single factor in the equation—Islamic revivalism.

ISLAMISM

There is not space to discuss the phenomenon of Islamism at any length, and it is difficult to dissect and classify in any event. Students of the area are still debating what to call it, although they are generally agreed that the term "fundamentalism," so beloved of American and British commentators, is inaccurate, in part because Islamism, or Islamic resurgence or radicalism or reformism or whatever we call it in its various manifestations, is a political as much as a religious movement and its agenda goes far beyond anything the Christian fundamentalists have in mind. Furthermore, in the sense that fundamentalism means a belief in the inerrancy of the holy scriptures, every pious Muslim is a fundamentalist, because it is a basic tenet of Islam that the Quran is the literal word of God, transmitted through Muhammad, who was merely the vessel for communicating it to the world.

Although Khomeini's brand of Islamism has caught the world's attention and is the most active and successful, largely because of the success of the Islamic revolution in Iran, the movement that now affects Muslim communities from Detroit to Mindanao began well before Khomeini ever caught the public eye. In retrospect, the 1967 Arab defeat by Israel stimulated rejection of modern Arab nationalist theories and a return to religious values that had been neglected by political leaders for years. Islam had always been a very important element of Arab culture and society but modern Arab nationalists had largely ignored it as a guide to political action. The urge for modernization and the creation of national states took precedence over piety and tradition as determinants of political behavior.

The return of Islam to the political arena was in part a reaction to the failure of nationalism in the contest with Israel and in part a reaction to the threat of Western cultural penetration. Over many years, the urge to catch up with the West had led to imitation and to the introduction of Western habits and values. The failure in 1967 led to a rethinking of objectives and priorities on the part of many younger political activists and to a return to traditional religiosity as a cure for the weaknesses of Arab society, which were seen as root causes of the defeat and as being due in large part to the rush to westernize. This trend became particularly important among university students of the hard sciences—an apparent paradox that has yet to be explained satisfactorily, at least in Western literature on the subject. There is no agreement today on where this revival is leading, but it has already brought about visible changes in Arab society from the Atlantic to the Gulf, and Islam is no longer politically irrelevant in any of the Arab states.

A principal source of the immorality that has upset Islamic traditionalists has been the United States, where the license of the past 20 years has created a society that pious Muslims find profoundly disturbing. Arab youths exposed to the temptations of normlessness at American universities and colleges have returned home with alarming views and habits. Others have been exposed to similar corrupting influences through radio, television, and videocassette-recorder films without even leaving home. More upsetting, perhaps, are government leaders influenced by modernist ideas who have attempted to change laws and customs that they have seen as a brake on progress—Tunisian President Bourguiba's attempt to convince workers to stop fasting during Ramadan, for instance. The inspiration for such efforts is widely seen as coming from the West, of which the United States is the leading element.

Over the past 10 years, Islamic reform has become a leading language of political dissent. The priority targets of the reformers are local governments, but when those governments are closely identified with the United States, the latter also becomes a target, by association. Khomeini calls America the Great Satan not just because it has been a corrupting influence on Iranian youth but also because it was so closely identified with the shah. Similarly, there was a strong strain of anti-Americanism among Sadat's opponents because the United States was seen as his principal supporter.

There are Islamists and Islamists, of course, and there is a considerable difference between the various groups in different countries as to aims and methods. Some describe themselves as wishing to work within the system to bring about evolutionary change, while others preach violent revolution and bloodshed. Some are quick to maintain that there is no inherent reason why their movement should harm American interests in any way. Others are openly hostile and see a destruction of U.S. influence in the region as a priority goal.

At the present time, there is no Arab country in which an early seizure of power by Islamist elements looks likely, and one is probably safe in assuming that this movement, too, will pass away, but it will change things appreciably before it does. In the meantime, it is a source of tension and discontent that has surfaced in violence in a number of places—Morocco, Algeria, Tunisia, Egypt, Lebanon, Syria, and Saudi Arabia, among others. When it does, Americans and American interests are likely to be among the targets, even if only indirectly. In Tunisia, for instance, Islamism is a potent political factor today, and the United States is closely identified with a regime that is trying to limit its influence. Anti-regime attitudes among the Islamists will inevitably take on an anti-American coloration, if they have not done so already.

SO WHAT?

The reader may well ask at this point where this all leaves us. In brief, as the leading foreign power in the area, the United States is going to be blamed for most of what goes wrong. While much of the blame will be unreasoned and undeserved, the United States has done enough to earn a good deal of animosity from the Arabs, and the miracle is that relations with the people of the area are not worse than they are.

At the same time, the United States is a powerful economic, intellectual, and cultural magnet. There are, for instance, far more Arab students in the United States today—39,430 in 1985-86 according to the Institute of International Education—than there were in 1948—2,088—and they include students from countries with which relations are hardly warm, such as Libya and Syria, as well as from the conservative states that have traditionally been more friendly. American technology and military equipment are preferred to those of the Soviets, and American trade with the region remains significant. Arabs wanting first-class medical treatment may go to Europe, but more would prefer to come to the United States, and the United States is still the preferred goal of most Arab emigrants. As a result, there is a thick network of personal and national interests criss-crossing the distance between us, and while the experience of 1967, when six Arab states broke relations with us, and the oil boycott in 1973 show that these interests cannot overcome major political trauma, they are a healing factor that tends to bring things back to equilibrium after a break.

Thus when the Egyptians broke relations in 1967, they still had to maintain a cultural attaché in Washington to care for the some 1500 Egyptian students who remained in American colleges and universities on Egyptian government scholarships. Similarly, the Libyans are maintaining an official presence in the United States today to supervise an estimated 1000 Libyan students who are here in spite of the Reagan-Qaddafi confrontation.

LESSONS FOR THE FUTURE

Are there, then, any lessons to be drawn from this brief examination? There are some striking parallels between our early problem with the Barbary pirates and our problem with hostages today. We made no bones about negotiating for the hostages' release with the Algerians in the 1790s because we realistically had no alternative and we were following a practice long accepted by the Europeans. By the time Perdicaris came along, however, we had won a succession of wars—with Britain, with Mexico, with ourselves, the Indians, and Spain—and we were feeling our oats. An activist president thought he should show that we could not be trifled

with. There is thus historical precedent for either accommodation or confrontation as a way to get hostages released.

But the parallel should not be carried too far. Roosevelt was dealing with an entirely different mix of characters, and he was very lucky that France pulled his chestnut out of the fire for him. Furthermore, neither the Algerian nor Moroccan hostage problem grew out of the popular antagonism toward Americans of the sort we encounter today in the Middle East; even in Lebanon today, the hostages are pawns in a game of blackmail. They were captured in an effort to obtain the release of Shiite prisoners in Kuwait more than because of particular animosity toward Americans. Animosity undoubtedly made it easier, but the animosity was incidental.

Arab antagonism will not go away soon, and it will rise and fall with the course of events. Some observers argue that Arab nationalism, whose fundamental hypothesis is that there is one Arab nation, which stretches from the Atlantic to the Persian Gulf, is increasingly losing ground to local nationalism.[5] This should mean decreasing interest in the Palestinian issue on the part of those states not directly involved, and a greater possibility of friendly relations with the United States. Even were the Palestinian problem to disappear tomorrow, however, there would be other problems arising out of local issues, such as Islamism and over-identification with conservative rulers, which will bedevil American relations with the Arabs and will keep animosities alive. But the other problems would be more manageable without the Arab-

5. See, for example, Fouad Ajami, "The End of Pan-Arabism," *Foreign Affairs* (Winter 1978-79).

Israeli problem, and the amplitude of the animosity waves would be much reduced were that problem solved.

It does no good, however, to talk in these hypothetical terms. All of the problems mentioned will be with us for some time, and we can look forward to a continuing relationship with the Arab world that will be marked by instability and periods of considerable animosity. It will not mean the end of our republic, but it will keep us busy for the rest of this century, at least.

There are limits to how much damage can be done, because the American civilian—as opposed to military—presence and economic stake in the area have been reduced since the oil boom slackened and because there is an abiding Arab interest in the United States. This includes an interest in friendly relations based on mutual respect. This is true even of the more radical Arabs, none of whom can ignore for long the importance of the United States, even though they may be unwilling to admit it.

The Americans have not been very adept at exploiting this interest and over the years have made a number of serious errors in their dealings with the Arabs. There will be more errors in the years to come, for a variety of reasons, including the pressures of the military-industrial complex, the fact that American Middle East policy is more a reflection of domestic politics than of strategic thinking, and Israel's lack of enthusiasm for having its patron enjoy good relations with the Arabs. This means that we can expect further acts of violence against Americans, but it does not mean they are the result of an inevitable Muslim or Arab animosity. They are a reaction to American policy and to the invasion of American culture, not an inherent and unavoidable phenomenon of race and religion.

ANNALS, *AAPSS*, **497**, May 1988

Anti-Americanism in Pakistan

By HAMID H. KIZILBASH

ABSTRACT: Pakistanis give three kinds of reasons for negative feelings about America. One involves U.S. policies toward Pakistan such as failure to come to Pakistan's aid during the Bangladesh crisis, using Pakistan for its own interests, and opposition to Pakistan's peaceful nuclear program. A second deals with American global policy, including support of Israel, opposition to Iran's present government, and use of force against small Third World nations. The third includes American involvement in Pakistan—for example, support of the military regime, obstructing a settlement of the Afghan issue, and responsibility for the decline in the value of the local currency. Most Pakistanis are uneasy about the relationship with America as opposed to being hostile. American support of Israel, India, and military dictators has undone a lot of the goodwill gained in other ways. Religious, ethnic, and cultural differences are rejected by most people as a basis of anti-American feelings. Speculation about interference in Pakistan's internal affairs and responsibility for former Prime Minister Bhutto's assassination have provided a basis for more ordinary people to develop feelings of anti-Americanism.

Hamid H. Kizilbash is associate professor of political science, Punjab University, and a founding member of the Society for the Advancement of Higher Education, which works to promote relevant and indigenous education in Pakistan. He received his bachelor's degree from Forman Christian College, Lahore, and the Ph.D. from Duke University. He has been associated with research and training institutions in the United States and has held visiting appointments at Fordham University, the University of Illinois at Chicago Circle, and Lake Forest College. His writings have been published in journals in Pakistan and abroad.

ON 10 April 1986, Benazir Bhutto, a leader of the Pakistan Peoples Party and daughter of the executed former Prime Minister Zulfiqar Ali Bhutto returned home after a long absence abroad. Benazir is considered a strong contender for power in a free and fair election, and people had come from all over the country to welcome her back in what has been described as the largest turnout ever in the historic city of Lahore. One of the banners welcoming her back read, "Down with America," and some of the most often repeated slogans heard in the long procession from the airport to the public meeting were against the United States.[1]

This was the most recent demonstration of anti-Americanism on a mass level that I have witnessed. For students and political activists, anti-Americanism is not an uncommon experience. Feelings against America appear regularly in the slogans they shout, the speeches they make, and the pamphlets they write. It is visible in the chalkings on the wall, it crops up in conversations over tea, and it defines the epithets to be hurled at one's opponents. On the other hand, anti-Americanism is not to be found in the fashion that is popular, the technology that is admired, and the education that is sought. It fails to prejudice the sports that are watched and the films that do well. That it is possible to be loved, admired, and hated all at the same time is a difficult status for Americans to accept or understand.

Pakistanis do not view their relations with America just on the basis of factors like culture or ideology. Contradictions exist in their feelings and need to be recognized if their behavior is to be understood. Taking into account the range of feelings that are found in Pakistan, the following pages make an attempt to examine the possible reasons for these feelings.[2]

Different Pakistanis have different feelings about America and at different levels of intensity. For example, the ruling elite's views are based on a self-interest that sometimes takes an anti-American turn only as a means of blackmailing the United States to take more interest or provide more aid. Middle-class fundamentalists are motivated by what they interpret as a threat to their beliefs and traditional way of life. Liberal-progressives or leftists define their feelings in terms of capitalist or imperialist exploitation, neocolonialism, and humanitarianism. Pakistan's four nationalities—the Sindhis, Baluchis, Punjabis, and Pathans—may differ in their feelings about America. The literate and illiterate, the urban and rural, men and women all have their own specific feelings. Pakistanis of the Shiite sect can differ in their attitudes from the Sunni sect, and those who have been abroad have different feelings from those who have never left the country. And yet negative feelings about America can be found in every class, every sect, every province, and every grouping in Pakistan. More significant, it is very difficult to find much public demonstration of pro-American feelings.

1. During her speech at the public meeting, Benazir urged the people not to burn the American flag or shout slogans against America. The Peoples Party workers have been under strict orders to prevent such incidents since April 1986 but without much success.

2. This article is based largely on 40 interviews conducted between February and July 1987 with students, housewives, businessmen, teachers, political workers, trade union leaders, journalists, and domestic servants. A fourth of those interviewed were women and all of those interviewed belonged to the province of Punjab.

Pakistanis give a broad range of reasons for their negative feelings about America. Some are connected with the policies and actions of America relating to Pakistan. Others have something to do with America's global role and its policies toward Third World countries. Still others seem less concerned with American action and more with local issues and domestic politics.

The first section of this article contains some general observations to help establish a context for understanding anti-Americanism in Pakistan. The second looks at the major causes of anti-American feelings in Pakistan, the third at the impact of America's global role on the Pakistani public, and the fourth at how local problems tie up with anti-American feelings. The last section attempts a tentative evaluation of all this information.

GENERAL OBSERVATIONS

For the purposes of this article, anti-Americanism is understood to mean those feelings of disapproval, hostility, or condemnation that are found among the Pakistani people against the American government and its policies. No significant evidence of feelings against the American people, as opposed to their government, was found, and although the distinction is sometimes difficult to make, it is imperative that the American public learn to do so.

Anti-American feelings as just defined can also be found in America, but the same term is not used to describe hostility or open agitation against the policies of the United States in the United States. To demonstrate against the American policy on Nicaragua in Washington is not anti-American while in Delhi or Dacca it is. Pakistani feelings on Vietnam, Grenada, or the Bay of Pigs are not that different from those of the Americans demonstrating in the United States or the Europeans demonstrating in Britain and France.

The Communist role in creating anti-American feeling, particularly that of the USSR, is overrated. At least in Pakistan, Chinese propaganda has done more to create feelings of aversion to the so-called capitalist-imperialist conspiracy than the Soviet Union has ever managed to do. Local leftist parties and groups have a role in creating consciousness about American policies, but there is no agreement among observers on the extent of their impact.[3]

Feelings against America do not operate in a vacuum. They are part of a worldview, a whole set of favorable and unfavorable feelings that exist in every individual. These can start from as basic an impulse as one brother being anti-Soviet so that the other chooses to be anti-American. They can also originate in activities of student days involving flirtation with Marxism or the laissez-faire philosophy. By and large, feelings against India and Israel tend to be stronger than those about the United States.

Desire for travel, a better status, and financial gain can produce considerable interaction between Pakistanis and Americans, but it does not necessarily produce pro-Americanism. In fact, this is a dangerous assumption to make because a

3. Local leftist parties and groups make substantial claims regarding their role in creating public consciousness against America, but, because of their own disunity and limited following, it is difficult to judge how accurate such claims are. The Awami National Party, the Mazdoor Kisan Party, and the Peoples Party, during 1969 and 1970, as well as sections of the trade union movement have doubtless played a role.

Pakistani's search for livelihood does not always control his or her politics. To struggle for a better life, one may, for example, move to any part of the world while retaining the political views already formed.

There is nothing strange about the love-hate reality of anti-Americanism. One may like a person's performance in the courtroom and despise his attitude toward women. The same kind of multidimensional framework is used by Pakistanis as they look at different activities of America. Moreover, anti-Americanism is expressed differently by different people. Some people feel the resentment but confine their feelings to private expression, while others take to the street, demonstrate, or try to damage American property. It is also important to remember that anti-American feelings were low in the 1950s, higher in the 1960s, high in the 1970s, and somewhat reduced in the 1980s.[4] In addition, anti-American feeling was restricted to campuses, intellectuals, and the section of the public with high political consciousness in the 1960s and has slowly come to include larger sections of the ordinary public during the 1970s and 1980s.

The reasons for these feelings are not always rational, logical, or based on facts. In the discussion that follows, it is imperative that the reader remember that all the reasons that Pakistanis give

4. Most Pakistanis agree that the 1965 war against India and the stopping of the supply of spare parts by the United States constituted the beginning of any large-scale anti-American sentiment in Pakistan. This was further fueled by the lack of American help in 1971 when the promised naval assistance never came to the Bay of Bengal. During the rest of the 1970s, America seemed to withdraw from this region and it was only after the Soviet invasion of Afghanistan that interest was revived.

for their anti-Americanism have been included and not just the reasons that make sense to me.

HOW AMERICA
TREATS PAKISTAN

The policies of the United States relating to Pakistan that arouse anti-American feelings range from a belief that the United States has repeatedly failed Pakistan at its time of need, through opposition to specific policies, to vague concern over U.S. involvement in Pakistan's internal problems. Each of these issues, actual or perceived by Pakistanis, is mentioned as a cause of their feelings against America. Not everyone would agree with the complete list, and most people would tend to list three or four reasons as central to their own thinking. It is noteworthy, however, that these factors are the most influential in determining the feelings of most ordinary Pakistanis.[5]

Failure in assisting Pakistan at an hour of need or taking action aimed at weakening Pakistan at such times has played an important role in determining the feeling of Pakistanis. Friendship is rated highly in Pakistan, and the conventional code requires that one drop everything and come to the aid of a friend in distress. Both the ban on supply of spare parts during the 1965 war with India and the failure to assist during the Bangladesh crisis in 1971 are viewed as betrayals of friendship. This is the most frequently mentioned cause for anti-American feeling among Pakistanis. It is also the source of heavy cynicism regarding the future promises

5. In comparison with U.S. global policies and local Pakistani issues, American policies toward Pakistan seem the most important and were always mentioned by those interviewed.

of U.S. commitment to the security of Pakistan.

A lot of Pakistanis are offended by the American support of autocratic and military regimes. They hold America responsible for maintaining Zia ul-Haq or Ayub in power and condemn America for doing so. Another side of the same coin is feeling that no one in Pakistan can hope to come to power without U.S. approval.[6] Charges are frequently traded by Pakistani politicians that one or the other has received the blessings of Washington. That this demeans the ordinary voters and puts their vote or voice to naught is another cause of American unpopularity. Those who are oppressed by autocratic regimes and deprived of their basic rights blame America for being the patron of such oppressors.

At the mass level, the allegation that America was responsible for the hanging of Prime Minister Bhutto, a popular Pakistani politician overthrown in 1977, has had wide circulation and many Pakistanis believe it. Bhutto himself, during the last days of his rule and while under detention, accused the United States of plotting his overthrow. This story has been responsible for creating considerable negative feelings in the Pakistani public. As one student activist put it, "The hanging of Bhutto created a consciousness of the American role in Pakistan which even the most simple citizen could understand."[7]

American opposition to the peaceful nuclear program of Pakistan is in-creasingly gaining importance as a basis of anti-American feeling. Two aspects of it have begun to sink into the consciousness of the public. The first is that there is a conspiracy to prevent Pakistan from acquiring nuclear technology and that America is the most vocal and active member of this group, which also includes India and Israel. The second is that unfair and bogus issues are generated from time to time to hold Pakistan up to ridicule. Pakistanis do not believe the stories of foul play abroad in connection with the nuclear program, and, in any case, they do not see anything wrong in trying to obtain the technology that is needed. The perception is that Pakistan has been singled out for discriminatory treatment in connection with the nuclear issue. Denial of promised aid because of suspicions that Pakistan is going ahead with its nuclear program is seen as an effort at blackmail and creates strong feelings against the United States.[8]

The war in Afghanistan has now lasted eight years. As the incidents of violence and terrorism increase inside Pakistan and as Afghan refugees move into economic competition with local citizens, the pressure for a settlement of the Afghan conflict is increasing. The United States is believed by many to be opposed to the settlement for its own ends. Feelings of resentment are generated because of the suspicion that the United States wants to keep the Afghan conflict alive.

America appears to have been unsuccessful in creating an image of solidarity with the ordinary people of Paki-

6. The latest in this theory seems to be that Benazir Bhutto has received the approval of the Americans. One student expressed the view that Pakistani politicians must not allow America to play such a role.

7. The assumption is that a lot of the complicated arguments against American involvement in Pakistan are not comprehensible to the citizens of a country with a literacy rate of 22 percent.

8. Pakistanis are particularly unhappy that India is not subjected to the same kind of pressure with respect to its nuclear program, which includes the explosion of an atomic device in 1974.

stan. One often hears Pakistanis talk about a senior civil servant's or army general's having properties in America or having the United States pay the bill for children's education abroad. The elite are known to have a pro-American bias, and to the extent that the public dislikes their politics, it also disapproves of American support for this class.

Pakistanis express some disappointment with specific regard to the nature of U.S. aid. A widespread impression exists that aid is, in fact, a mechanism for enslaving Pakistan and that much of it is spent on the salaries and privileges of foreign personnel not needed to do work in Pakistan. Some Pakistanis also point out that American policy regarding the aid to be given has been such as to provide Pakistan with no means for developing its industry on a self-reliant basis. In this connection, multi-national corporations, which are usually identified with America, are also said to be playing a role against the interests of Pakistan. Newspaper columnists and politicians out of power frequently point to the fact that future generations of Pakistanis are already in debt and that much of the aid being received is going into the payment of interest on loans taken.

"CIA" is one of the most commonly used words in the Pakistani language. All kinds of people and incidents lead to public discussion of this organization and it is no honor to be called an agent of the Central Intelligence Agency. One of the most bizarre incidents involved the alleged attempt by an American scientist attached to the Malaria Institute in Lahore to breed a mosquito for use against the local population. The scientist was withdrawn, but the incident lives in the memory of the people as part of the conspiracy being hatched against

Pakistan.[9] The CIA is also regularly credited with engineering the overthrow of governments of Pakistan.

A small number of people also resent the cultural-educational onslaught on Pakistan by the United States. They complain that many of the programs introduced in Pakistani colleges and universities are American inspired and alienate the young from the local culture and social duties. American books and publications are said to be spreading the wrong ideas in Pakistani society.

HOW AMERICA
TREATS THE WORLD

Although not as significant as policies concerned with Pakistan, the global politics of the United States also appear to have an impact on Pakistani feelings. The most commonly mentioned examples of such "American misbehavior" include Vietnam, Libya, Iran, and countries of Central and South America. U.S. support of Israel as well as South Africa is also brought up in this connection. Feelings tend to be strong whenever a small Third World country is presented as being bullied by the United States. They tend to be held by a larger section of the population when a Muslim country is involved.

Vietnam was a debacle that penetrated the consciousness of a lot of people in Pakistan. The United States was seen as forcing a solution on the people of a small country. The heroic struggle of the Vietnamese and the de-

9. The Malaria Institute incident took place in 1983. Similar incidents involving charges against missionary teachers accused of working for the CIA have also taken place. For a short while in the 1970s, the Pakistan government banned the entry of foreign visitors to universities and colleges without prior permission.

struction unleashed by the United States are mentioned as a basis of a new awareness about America. The image of the United States as a compassionate power on the side of the weak was laid to rest and a new image of the successor to colonial and imperial traditions was established. This awareness of America's role abroad has been a source of considerable negative reaction in Pakistan.

The United States-Iran confrontation after the fall of the shah in 1979 had a serious impact on Pakistani feelings. The Shiites of Pakistan have the strongest negative reaction to anything the Americans do to destabilize the Khomeini regime, and their reaction has been very intense to the events that took place in the summer of 1987 in Saudi Arabia and the Gulf. Feelings of friendship for Iran are broad based, however, and make American anti-Iran acts unpopular throughout the country. The fallout of these situations has worked against the United States. The United States is described as the source of all evil, which is bound to suffer the wrath of God and be destroyed. Alleged bloodletting by the Saudis during the 1987 pilgrimage is supposed to have been done at the behest of America and will, unless resisted, lead the ruling family to one day "hand over the care and control of the Holy Kaaba to the Israelis and the Americans."[10]

At a rally attended by over 50,00 of the Tehrik Nifaz-e-Fiqah Jafaria (Movement for the Establishment of the Shiite School of Thought) on 6 July 1987, America came in for a lot of criticism.

10. See *Najdi Safakon kay Hathon Makka Moazamma main Nihatay Hajaj Karam ka Wahshiyana Qatal-e-Aam* (pamphlet) (Lahore: Anjuman Islami-Irani Talaba, Aug. 1987); *Turjaman* (newspaper) (Tehrik Nifaz-e-Fiqah Jafaria, Lahore) (July 1987).

America was described as responsible for the oppression of Muslims, and Khomeini was spoken of as the biggest challenge to America. A resolution passed at the meeting called on the Pakistani people "to oppose Russia at the borders and America inside the borders." It called for an end to all bases and influence of world imperialism in Pakistan.

American threats against the government of Qaddafi of Libya or the Palestinian organizations are also a basis for anti-American feelings among Pakistanis. Both nations are seen as fraternal Muslim states being threatened by imperialist America. American military action is largely viewed as unwarranted aggression. It also ties in with the view that America actively intervenes in the affairs of Third World countries. To a lesser degree, American dealings with the smaller countries of Central and South America, such as the action in Grenada or the involvement in Nicaragua, El Salvador, and Chile, have also been viewed with disapproval in more informed circles.

Feelings are strongest with reference to the support and aid given by America to Israel. As Arab-Israeli relations have gone from bad to worse and as news of Israeli atrocities against Palestinians in occupied territories and Lebanon become public, the feelings against America have registered a sharp rise. It would not be unfair to say that in the 1980s, Israeli actions are deeply resented and the United States is held responsible for the way Israel behaves.

A nonpolitical, rather shy office worker was having trouble responding to questions about anti-Americanism until the name of Israel was mentioned. That was the only vehicle, along with India, by which he was able to express any feelings of resentment against the United States. Israel's violence is considered to be the result of American military and economic support. Because there is no gray area in people's feelings about Israel, it is a constant source of anti-American feelings. After the stories of opposition to Pakistan's nuclear program are circulated, it is usually Israel that is mentioned as the reason for American actions. It was Israel that was supposed to be planning a preemptive strike on a nuclear facility in Pakistan. Anti-Israeli feelings as a source of anti-Americanism are shared by all sections of the Pakistani public, from the religious clergy to the housewife.

Similar feelings of resentment against the United States are occasionally thrown up by reference to the racist government of South Africa. In some Pakistani circles, a link is recognized between the oppression of the blacks and the activities of the multinationals operating in South Africa. Racism, especially its manifestations of violence and oppression, is linked to U.S. support of the South African regime. The United States is purported to be quietly and in an underhanded manner helping the rule of the racist minority.

Incidents of the use of force against small states by the United States and the resentment aroused by U.S. support of Israel make American global activities a fairly important source of anti-Americanism in Pakistan.

AMERICAN RESPONSIBILITY FOR LOCAL PROBLEMS

A Pakistani trade union leader explains at some length how the rise in electricity charges, the lack of free water supply, the plant-more-trees campaign, the election of a technocrat to Parliament, the use of dangerous pesticides, and a host of other local Pakistani realities are closely linked to the United States. A Shiite intellectual explains how the sectarian rioting in a provincial capital is part of a decision to punish Shiites to get them off the anti-American track.

All local issues, of course, do not always lead to a discussion of American involvement, but the reference is frequent. It begins with the dislike of military governments and includes such issues as responsibility for the hanging of Bhutto, holding the United States responsible for supplying funds to the mullahs ("clergy"), and pushing the Afghan situation to where bombs are exploding all over Pakistan. The important thing to note is that many Pakistanis hold America responsible for local problems. On the face of it, this belief seems absurd, but as one listens to Pakistanis explain their feelings, the role of such local issues cannot be ignored in its contribution to anti-Americanism.

Although all governments recognize and deal with the Zia ul-Haq regime, it is the Americans who are credited with keeping Zia in office. To this extent, many of the frustrations created by martial law and the nearsighted policies of the Zia ul-Haq regime are able to find their way into the feelings of Pakistanis against America.

Whether the link actually exists or not, the people see the decline in their buying power and the economic crunch as connected to the policies dictated by the World Bank and Washington. Recently, this problem was illustrated when the 1988 budget was introduced in Parliament and had to be hastily withdrawn because the taxes imposed and the new prices of essential commodities announced were all aimed at the ordinary citizen. It was as if someone not living in Pakistan had drawn up the budget.

In the course of the last seven years, the situation created by the Afghan refugees has taken a turn where the local population feels threatened. Some incidents of confrontation, like those in Quetta and Karachi, have added a sense of urgency to the solution of the Afghan problem. The United States has become a target of attack because it is seen as blocking the process of settlement.

Pakistan governments without exception have a poor record as far as treatment of the opposition is concerned, and the violation of human rights has been noticeably worse during the martial law regime. Victims of arbitrary confinement, harsh punishments, and loss of means of livelihood feel that the movements to overthrow this reign of terror have failed because the United States has supported the autocratic regime.

A new fear gaining ground in Pakistan is that America is behind the increase in heroin addiction in Pakistan as a means of combating the problem in the United States. People say that this is a way to force the issue to surface as a serious crisis in Pakistan, which can then be solved through collaboration with the United States.

The various Muslim sects—Shiite and Sunni, or Deobandi and Barelvi—have differences going back a long way. Recent incidents of sectarianism, however, are considered by some Pakistanis to be part of the American strategy to destabilize the country. Similar feelings are expressed about the growth of provincialism and regional differences. The anti-American sentiment receives support from such speculation because Pakistanis have become deeply attached to the conspiracy theory of politics and are ready to believe the worst about outside involvement in local affairs.

People blame America for the rise of consumerism and materialism in Pakistan. The emphasis on personal acquisitions and individual comfort at the cost of the society is considered to be an export of America. As shopping plazas and motor vehicles multiply and people are judged by the kind of car they drive, many Pakistanis sense a break with the old values and traditions. The country most mentioned as responsible for the change is the United States. A villager from Northern Punjab gave the example of the clergy selling out for money: when people see a prosperous clergyman riding in a car they call out, "There goes the dollar."

AN ASSESSMENT

What one learns from talking to a small sample of Pakistanis is that anti-Americanism is widespread but that the feeling is not very strong. There are some people who question that there is any anti-American feeling at all, but they seem to say this on the basis of the fact that the feelings are not rational or, alternatively, that they should be much stronger than they are.

The feelings of most of the population are best described as uneasiness and fear rather than dislike or hostility. These fears are related to America's alleged betrayal in the past and its support of those forces that Pakistanis view as their enemies—Israel, India, dictators, or the local elite.

No strong and reliable basis of friendship with the United States seems to have emerged in the minds of the ordinary people. Rather, the relationship seems to be a matter of being used for American objectives and in the process trying to use them for whatever advantage is possible. Differences on issues like the nuclear program and American support of Israel have a great potential for changing the existing climate of acceptance to one of hostility. The events in the Persian Gulf also have an impact on Pakistani feelings, and any government that becomes involved with America's adventures there would face serious problems at home.

It is interesting that alliances with America in the past or the present relationship do not create as serious vibrations as some people claim. The complaint is that America does not live up to its promises, not that Pakistan chose to ally itself. At one level, alliances are seen as a means of strengthening Pakistan's defense and not as a sellout to a superpower.

Very few people support the thesis that the religious, ethnic, and cultural differences between the United States and Pakistan are the cause of Pakistani anti-Americanism. Pakistanis seem ready in large numbers to wear blue jeans, eat at fast-food restaurants, and watch American television programs. Individual Americans are well received and treated with respect. If anything, it is the Americans who distance themselves from the ordinary people and continue to live in ghettos of protected buildings.

The strongest attack leveled at America by Pakistani intellectuals is that Washington is not interested in democracy in Pakistan. They point out that it is easy to manage and manipulate one dictator but that it would be difficult to do the same with a government responsible to the people. This impression of the United States as uninterested in democracy does great damage to its image and credibility as a progressive nation.

The extent of American involvement in every sphere of life in Pakistan is also widely deplored. It gives the impression that a small state's sovereignty and self-government are only a hoax. Pakistanis, like citizens of any other nation, like to feel that they are in control, and news that others are managing their lives creates a feeling of unease. This has come up recently with respect to the desire of the American Agency for International Development to deal directly with nongovernmental organizations of Pakistan when distributing funds. Although charges of mismanagement of funds by local government agencies are justified, the alternative of bypassing the local government agencies is not a happy one. In the enthusiasm to get things done, American agencies are risking alienating a substantial section of the population.

Anti-Americanism in Pakistan, to the extent that it is present, is a reflection of the mistakes being made by the American government as well as the failures and weaknesses of the Pakistani authorities. It is perhaps unavoidable where the interests of the two countries diverge, but it is also present where the desire for cooperation exists. As the Afghan situation takes its toll on the people of Pakistan and as India tightens its hold on the region, the prospects for greater anti-Americanism are present. The American public needs to be more aware of the ways in which the American government behaves abroad. Relations with Third World countries like Pakistan could improve greatly if implementation of foreign policy was subjected to the same careful scrutiny to which domestic actions are subject.

ANNALS, *AAPSS*, **497**, May 1988

Anti-Americanism in the Southern Cone of Latin America

By RIORDAN ROETT

ABSTRACT: Anti-Americanism is strongest in the parts of Latin America geographically closest to the United States. Mexico and the countries of Central America and the Caribbean remain highly dependent on their giant neighbor to the north. Their resentment of this fact is often reflected in sharp expressions of anti-American feeling. In contrast, in the Southern Cone of Latin America, criticism of the United States has, over the last twenty years, become less strident and more pragmatic. This change in views follows a shift in the balance of power in favor of the Southern Cone and away from the United States. As these countries have grown more independent, they have grown less resentful of U.S. power. There may, however, be a resurgence of anti-Americanism in the Southern Cone if the debt-trade crisis is not resolved quickly and equitably.

Riordan Roett is the Sarita and Don Johnston Professor and Director of Latin American Studies and the Center of Brazilian Studies of the Johns Hopkins University School of Advanced International Studies. His recent publications include Brazil: Politics in a Patrimonial Society *(1984) and* Latin America, Western Europe and the U.S.: Reevaluating the Atlantic Triangle *(coauthor and coeditor with Wolf Grabendorff; 1985). He is a member of the Council on Foreign Relations.*

NOTE: The author is indebted to Mr. Daniel A. Seligman for his help in the researching and editing required for this article.

L ATIN American literature on the United States is replete with the drumbeat of anti-American themes. There is a well-established pantheon of writers who have shocked and captivated North American readers with their elegant and savage condemnations of the United States. The most influential among them include the Uruguayan essayist José Enrique Rodó and his oft-quoted *Ariel*, which contrasts the Ariel-like spirituality of Latin culture with the Caliban-like materialism of North American culture; the nineteenth-century Cuban journalist José Martí, dispatching his views about the turmoil and inequities of the United States in the gilded age to newspapers throughout Latin America; the reformist Guatemalan politician Juan José Arevalo, whose mordant imagery of the Shark and the Sardines was vividly realized in 1954 when a CIA-backed coup overthrew the Guatemalan Government; and the Mexican intellectuals Octavio Paz and Carlos Fuentes, whose love-hate views of the United States reflect the special, complex relationship between their country and ours.

These writers tend toward a striking uniformity in their view of the United States. We are admired for the creativity of our artists and writers, for the productivity of our economy, for the ingenuity of our science, and for the responsiveness of our democratic institutions. With almost equal uniformity, however, we are derided for our short-sightedness, heavy-handedness, and crass greed when it comes to policy toward our neighbors to the south. Citing what he views as America's hypocritical intervention in Nicaragua, Carlos Fuentes calls the United States "a democracy inside but an empire outside; Dr. Jekyll at home, Mr. Hyde in Latin America." He adds:

We will continue to praise the democratic achievements and the cultural values of the society of the United States. But we will continue to oppose its arrogant and violent policies in Latin America. We will do so painfully, because we love so many things in the United States. We will not confuse the United States and the Soviet Union, or indeed accept their moral equivalence. The problem is far more tragic: the Russians act as an empire inside and outside. They are perfectly coherent. The United States, by acting like the Russians in its sphere of influence, becomes profoundly incoherent and hypocritical.[1]

Fuentes's views are a logical response to the realities of history. For over a hundred years, the balance of power in the Western Hemisphere has decisively favored the United States. With regard to the parts of Latin America closest to us—Mexico and Central America and the Caribbean—the United States has enjoyed undisputed economic and political hegemony. Throughout the rest of Latin America, especially with regard to the Southern Cone of South America, North American power has far exceeded that of any possible rival. It is not surprising to see that we, as a great power, have frequently acted as a great power, pursuing our interests where and to the degree we see fit, even when this means trampling on the interests of our weaker neighbors. The only surprise is that Fuentes can maintain a fresh sense of outrage 100 years after the pattern of U.S. policy toward Latin America was set.

I would, however, argue that the type of anti-Americanism represented by Fuentes—an anti-Americanism, perhaps, still appropriate in the context of U.S. relations with Mexico and with

1. Carlos Fuentes, "Land of Jekyll and Hyde," *Nation*, 22 Mar. 1986, p. 337.

Central America and the Caribbean—is growing less appropriate in the context of U.S. relations with the nations of the Southern Cone. For good or ill, the relative balance of power between Latin America and the United States has, over the last 20 years, been shifting in favor of Latin America. This tendency is most pronounced in the Southern Cone, that part of Latin America where U.S. influence has always been weakest. This shift in the balance of power has, I will argue, been accompanied by a shift in the tone of Latin American thoughts and feelings about the United States. It is a shift away from the outraged tones of the weak whose rights have been violated and who are powerless to do anything about it. It is a shift toward the realistic, pragmatic tones of those who are in an interdependent relationship with another power, who have specific interests to defend, and who have the means with which to defend them.

MEXICO

The proximity of Mexico to the United States has created a particularly high degree of political and economic dependence. This dependence has, in turn, lent a particularly sharp tone to Mexican expressions of anti-Americanism. Americans like to think of their country as benevolent and just. But Mexicans have not forgotten that half their national territory was absorbed by the United States in the nineteenth century or that their country was invaded several times by American armed forces.

Currently, U.S.-Mexican relations are being exacerbated by trade and investment imbalances, by the imponderables of immigration and drugs, and by the inability of the Mexican political system to evolve toward a more open and democratic form. The frustrations of modern Mexico, the humiliation of its dependent relationship on the United States, provide the makings of a Greek tragedy that require constant and sophisticated ministration. No North American administration has understood that reality. In bilateral relations, the United States inevitably has the more powerful position; we then exploit that advantage with minimal respect for the interests or sensibilities of the Mexicans. When we shut our borders to immigration, the Mexicans are left to absorb thousands of extra workers and the loss of foreign exchange. When Mexico and its other partners in the Contadora group framed a workable peace plan for Central America, the United States undermined it with legalistic quibbles and increased aid to the contras. When Mexico needed help to overcome its bankruptcy crisis in 1982, the perceptions of both countries differed sharply. The United States thought it saved Mexico; the Mexicans thought they had been taken advantage of. The Mexican view was captured in a comment by one official, returning from negotiations in the United States. "We flew home," he recalled, "relieved but strangely ungrateful. . . . Washington had saved us from chaos, yet it did so in an uncharitable manner."[2]

Given the basic facts of Mexican dependence, Mexico is not likely to exercise any real bargaining power vis-à-vis the United States in the foreseeable future. Mexico will continue to feel injured and resentful and the country's writers will probably continue to resort to the kind of anti-American feelings expressed by Fuentes. They will continue to appeal to America's conscience

2. Alan Riding, *Distant Neighbors: A Portrait of the Mexicans* (New York: Random House, 1986), p. 487.

for a redress of the imbalance between us because they have limited means with which to bargain and to appeal to our interests.

THE CARIBBEAN AND CENTRAL AMERICA

The Caribbean and Central America constitute a second and distinctive subset. Indeed, some of the most bitter criticism of the United States flows from the pens of writers in these regions, and rightfully so. Nowhere has American power been flaunted with less respect for the rights of people to determine their own destiny. No image—the big stick, big brother, banana republic—that has emerged from the critical literature can capture the enormity of North American malevolence in that region.

Since the turn of the century, American interventions to secure our national interests has resulted, time and again, in the creation of repressive police states. The inability of John Foster Dulles to understand the difference between reform and revolution in Guatemala led to an overthrow sponsored by the Central Intelligence Agency of the democratic government of Jacobo Arbenz Guzmán in 1954. The legacy of the Trujillo family, long protected by American suzerainty, led inexorably to the North American military intervention of 1965. Our backing of regimes like those of Batista in Cuba in the 1950s and of the Somozas in Nicaragua led to the two revolutions that most plague U.S. foreign policy in the twentieth century: Fidel Castro and the Sandinistas.

American military intervention in Central America and the Caribbean has also been accompanied, especially in the early decades of the twentieth century, by a particularly exploitative form of economic intervention. American multinational corporations, often supported by U.S. military and diplomatic power, soon found willing surrogates within the small, dependent bourgeoisie in each of the countries. The resulting combine led to decades of exploitation, manipulated elections, and ultimately greater security problems for the United States as societies imploded under the impact of modernization and inequality. Today, war-torn El Salvador is one fruit of this process; Panama is another.

The current policies of the Reagan administration in Central America and the Caribbean have reverted to the heavy-handed style that seemed to have been dying in the 1960s and 1970s. It matters little to the U.S. government that positive change—toward democracy and social modernization—is under way in the region. If reform movements challenge the status quo, they will be attacked for the threat they pose, not nurtured for the hopes they raise. By our intervention in Nicaragua, our militarization of El Salvador and Honduras, our disdain for the efforts of the Contadora group, which sought to construct an earlier peace plan for Central America, and our current crass indifference to the peace plan of Costa Rican President Arias, we have confirmed the worst suspicions of both our enemies and our friends. The United States is indifferent. The United States is so overwhelmed by its own security interests that it fails to understand that our neighbors, too, have security concerns. The two sets of concerns should not be mutually exclusive, but in the 1980s, they have been so defined.

THE SOUTHERN CONE

U.S. proximity to and hegemony over Mexico and Central America have led to highly critical images of the United States. U.S. relations with the Southern Cone countries of South America—Brazil, Argentina, Chile, Uruguay, and Paraguay—have historically been very different, however. Although South Americans would accept certain features of the basic image of the United States articulated by, for example, Carlos Fuentes, they would not accept that image completely. In fact, their image of North America has changed as U.S.-Southern Cone relations have evolved over the last twenty years.

Historically, the United States has never projected the same degree of power in the Southern Cone as it has in Mexico and Central America. The Southern Cone nations are geographically remote from the United States and, so, have never figured as heavily in questions of national security. In contrast with Mexico and Central America and the Caribbean, North American troops have never invaded or occupied any of the South American countries. Moreover, the countries of the Southern Cone are not small banana republics but relatively sophisticated nation-states with regional and, in some cases, global interests.

Economically, the Southern Cone countries have always had more complex, variegated, and productive economies than our neighbors immediately to the south. In fact, for a period in the early part of this century, the per capita income of Argentina was actually higher than that of the United States. Moreover, while the United States has always been a key financial and trading partner, the Southern Cone countries have also had extensive economic relations with Western Europe.

Culturally, people of the Southern Cone have always identified closely with

Europe, even after U.S. popular culture began its historic conquest of the world. An important contributing factor to the phenomenon is that in countries like Argentina and Chile there has been very little racial mixing between people of European and of Indian blood. While Mexicans, in contrast, take special pride in their mestizo culture, Argentines or Chileans of European extraction often identify closely with their mother countries. Even today, sons and daughters of the middle class may know Paris or London better than the interior of their own country.

If in the past the United States projected limited power relative to the power of the Southern Cone countries, it is projecting relatively less now. Over the last 20 years, American security interests in South America have diminished when faced with the reality of a more complex, multipolar world. In this same period, American economic influence has diminished as the South Americans have diversified their markets and found new sources of capital and as the American economy has begun to labor under its own trade, debt, and productivity problems. Having said that, it must be remembered that the intervention of the United States in Chile took place less than 15 years ago. Diplomatic, commercial, financial—but not military— the United States' efforts to overthrow Salvador Allende illustrate that, in some cases, this country will pursue its security perceptions with devastating results.

If anti-Americanism of the Fuentes school has always had relatively fewer adherents in the Southern Cone than in Mexico or Central America, the shift in the balance of power between the United States and the Southern Cone has made the old style of anti-Americanism increasingly irrelevant. The best work today by South American writers rejects as useless the tone of helpless moral outrage. Instead, and largely because of an increasingly equal balance of power, these writers recognize that their countries are in an interdependent relationship with the United States, that they have specific interests to defend, and that, increasingly, they have the means with which to defend them. Their writing focuses on four major issue areas: U.S. security and power; the erosion of the inter-American system; the common danger to both the Southern Cone countries and the United States of the current debt-trade impasse; and the overriding theme of consolidating democratic, civilian political regimes.

U.S. SECURITY AND POWER

In marked contrast to the years following World War II, when U.S. hegemonic power effectively limited the options available to the region, today the countries of the region continue to diversify their security and foreign policy options. Argentina's close commercial ties with the Soviet Union have become a significant factor in that country's foreign policy. The arms industry in Brazil and the growth of a nuclear capability have given Brazil added status in the Third World as well as an autonomous position regarding its own security.

Even the pro-defense administration of Ronald Reagan seems content to let the process of diversification run its course. Save for the abortive effort of then Secretary of State Alexander Haig to mediate the Malvinas/Falklands conflict in 1982, the United States has shown little interest in South American security concerns. The Reagan administration has not even tried to renew military training and sales programs cut off for human rights reasons by President Jimmy Carter.

Instead, all of the Reagan administration's efforts in Latin America have been devoted to Central America. It is a common view in South America that, after the election of Ronald Reagan, "U.S. Latin American policy became 'Central Americanized,' while at the same time, Washington's foreign policy toward the region was largely transformed into a defense policy."[3] Reflecting the fact that the Southern Cone countries no longer see eye to eye with the United States on security issues, the Reagan administration has chosen not to consult with them regarding its policy in Central America.

The United States is far more distant today than at any time in recent memory. While South American writers may regret or welcome that development, it is a given in their evaluation of both the future role of the United States and the ability—as well as the need—of the Southern Cone nations to develop independent options.

THE INTER-AMERICAN SYSTEM

The growing autonomy in the Southern Cone countries on security questions is confirmed by the decrepitude in the inter-American system. A vital link of the United States' stand against communism in the Western Hemisphere in the postwar years, it is now a marginal and somewhat pathetic player. In the Malvinas conflict, it played only a minor role. In Central America, it has been bypassed by Contadora and then the

3. Heraldo Muñoz, "Introduction," in *Latin American Views of U.S. Foreign Policy*, ed. Robert Wesson and Heraldo Muñoz (New York: Praeger, 1986), p. 7.

Arias peace initiative. On debt questions, the Cartagena Group and bilateral relations have dominated the debate. With the diminution of overall U.S. power in the international system, as well as within the hemisphere, the inter-American system serves little purpose. Moreover, the residual impression that whatever does take place within the Organization of American States—the institutional backbone of the system—is controlled by the United States further dooms the system to obsolescence.

THE DEBT-TRADE CRISIS

The third area of significance to the Southern Cone states is that of the current debt-trade impasse. The countries are burdened with a massive overhang of debt, principally held by private commercial banks. One-third of Latin debt is held by American banks. The American banks dominate the advisory committees that coordinate debt repayment and restructuring efforts. Moreover, the American deficits play an enormous role in determining the degrees of freedom that South American states will have to renew growth and escape the burdensome interest payments that now absorb large portions of their foreign exchange earnings.

Given the gravity of the debt burden, and the imperative to have access to foreign markets for their exports, the South American states had expected the United States to take the initiative in providing alternative policies. Instead, the unanimous impression in South America is that the Reagan administration has chosen to ignore the crisis. The White House refuses to see the debt as a security issue. Nor has the United States been willing to work with its industrial-country allies to seek a collaborative

approach to easing the burden. Protectionism remains extremely high in the European Common Market—and it is growing in the United States. Real interest rates remain far above historical levels. Because much of the Latin debt was borrowed at variable rates of interest when rates were low, the high rates, and potential increases, compound the problem. Commodity prices for Latin American exports remain depressed. In addition, neither private investment nor new commercial bank loans have been available to provide the capital needed to grow.

From the Southern Cone's point of view, the United States, unwilling to confront its own internal problems of the twin deficits, has chosen to allow the Third World countries to bear the costs of adjustment. That cost has been the loss of growth and development. The Southern Cone attitude is well represented by the following quote by a highly respected Argentine economist:

There should be no illusions regarding the present and future U.S. policy stance with regard to the international economy. The aim has been clearly stated: to reassert U.S. international hegemony. Latin America has nothing to benefit from this approach, as the experience of the early 1980s has clearly shown.[4]

The debt crisis, along with the accompanying trade problems, has laid the basis for a type of anti-American reaction that was characteristic of a past era: "The external debt crisis, initially expected by some to increase Latin American leverage in its economic relations with the United States, has back-

4. Roberto Bouzas, "Trade, Investment, and Financial Policies," in *Latin American Views of U.S. Foreign Policy*, ed. Wesson and Muñoz, p. 60.

fired. U.S. influence throughout the region has been strengthened as a result of Latin American inability to exploit the situation."[5] That reality, unless well understood in Washington, could generate an anti-American wave in the future. It is avoidable—but not if the Reagan administration's policies are continued.

REDEMOCRATIZATION

The final theme, that of consolidating democratic regimes in Latin America, is intimately linked to the preceding issues. The reestablished democratic regimes in the Southern Cone—in Argentina, Brazil, and Uruguay—require resources to demonstrate their capacity to respond to legitimate societal needs. The debt and trade crises have severely limited that capacity. The absence of alternatives will inevitably weaken the appeal of democracy for millions of citizens in the Southern Cone. The economic component of democratic stabilization is critical. We now run the risk of a gradual weakening of the democratic process—and the democratic ideal. The United States, through appropriate trade and debt policies, could do much to alleviate the current situation. It has chosen not to do so. The Southern Cone countries have been left to the magic of the international marketplace.

Latin American democrats have, until now, looked to the United States as one of their key allies in the work of redemocratization. If we do not help them now on the debt issue, we are in danger of losing more than their good opinion. The United States may witness the inevitable immobility that characterizes weakened civilian regimes and the inexorable

5. Ibid., p. 59.

return of military governments.

CONCLUSION

What is remarkable, given the realities of today's relations between the United States and the Southern Cone countries, is that there has not been a greater manifestation of old-fashioned anti-Americanism. This is due to the fact that South American analysts are realists. Regardless of their ideological position, they accept the asymmetries of power between the United States and Latin America. They also recognize, however, the gradual, steady erosion of American power in the hemisphere— and in the international system. That, combined with the unwillingness of the United States to address the key development issues confronting the region, has led to a search for alternative modes of analysis, for other options for the region. For the Southern Cone, the United States obviously remains a reality. But it is a defanged tiger, which it is not in Central America and the Caribbean. No gunboats are to be feared. Neither the marines nor the contras will appear in the interior of Brazil or Argentina. A slow process of South America's realignment within the international system is under way. The United States is a key actor but no longer the primary actor in that process.

Anti-Americanism, as a visceral reaction against the hegemonic pretensions of the United States, is alive and well in Mexico and in Central America and the Caribbean. Geography and development have both mitigated that reaction in the Southern Cone. The countries of that region have always tended to deal with the United States as more of an equal in a more adversarial manner. While recognizing the preponderance of the power of the United States, they have sought degrees of autonomy through diversified diplomatic, trade, and commercial ties. Their rapid growth in the last two decades has given them, as a group, a greater weight in the international system. There has also been a greater willingness to look inward for the causes of underdevelopment while not excusing the lack of interest on the part of the United States in helping to accelerate the process of change and development.

Most of the key writers recognize the reality of interdependence. They do not believe the United States is as cognizant of the fact that we must coexist in the hemisphere or be doomed to continued conflict and confrontation. While there is little inclination to be pro-American, the disposition to be blindly anti-American, at least for the Southern Cone, has yielded to gloomy realism. The United States is what it is and does not appear interested in, or capable of, change. The alternative is for the countries of the Southern Cone to diversify their dependence as quickly and as widely as is feasible. That may be less psychologically rewarding than arousing rabid anti-American feelings at home, but in the long run, it will do more for South America's self-esteem and development.

ANNALS, *AAPSS*, **497**, May 1988

Anti-Americanism in
Central America

By LESTER D. LANGLEY

ABSTRACT: Anti-Americanism in Central America, unlike the outbursts of anti-Americanism in the Islamic world, is fueled not by religious fanaticism or anti-Western political or social conviction. America and Americans and the social and political values they symbolize are often extolled and sometimes just as routinely denounced. From the beginning of Central American independence in 1821, isthmian political aspirants, idealists, opportunists, revolutionaries, and social conservatives have found in America's political tradition an example for Central Americans to emulate but ultimately came to regard Americans, along with other outsiders, as an intrusive threat to isthmian culture. Those who ascribe the modern outbursts of anti-Americanism that reverberate not only in Nicaragua—for obvious reasons—but, to our astonishment, in Honduras, El Salvador, and even in the most pro-American country in the region, Costa Rica, to the determination of the Reagan administration to bring down the Sandinista government and the economic and political dislocations wrought by an isthmus at war overlook the deeper causes of this hostility.

Lester D. Langley received a Ph.D. in American diplomatic and Latin American history from the University of Kansas in 1965. He has published eight books, among them Central America: The Real Stakes *(1985) and most recently* MexAmerica: Two Nations, One Future. *Presently he is professor of history at the University of Georgia.*

ANTI-AMERICANISM has been and will remain a feature of Central American life, yet it has always coexisted with a profound admiration and respect for the United States and a partiality for the American life-style. Currently, however, anti-Americanism among Central Americans is on the upswing. The explanation involves more than the pressures of the American government on Nicaragua and our visible military commitment in Honduras and El Salvador. When we retreat from the current hard-line policies, many Americans believe, anti-American feelings will dissipate. Anti-Americanism in Central America may diminish but will not disappear with the decline of American power. The American military presence may retreat but American culture and its myriad features—from the bands of committed evangelical Protestants who have penetrated a still very Catholic domain to the go-getter promoters who dream of expanding the American marketplace—will not go away. Central Americans are too close geographically to the United States, too influenced by the American presence in their history, and, frankly, fearful of closing themselves off from the United States and the benefits the American connection has brought them. Yet at the same time they are acutely sensitive about this reliance and the sometimes shameful legacy it has wrought.

Their expressions of anti-Americanism are not so much rage as guilt or despondence over having lost control of their own destiny. In the fall of 1986, in a course on U.S.-Central American relations I was teaching at the University of Costa Rica, the students often expressed apprehension that American involvement in Central America would only cause them more trouble and coupled their remarks with some disapproving statements about the Sandinistas in Nicaragua. I conceded the first but queried their logic on the second. If they felt the Sandinistas should live up to their initial pledges for a more democratic Nicaragua, should they not be more supportive of American policies or, at least, should they not be willing to create an army to defend Costa Rican democracy, especially if the threat were as great as some Costa Ricans believe? Their response was, in the context of Costa Rican thinking about national identity, eminently logical: Costa Rica is a democracy and is notably different from the rest of Central America because it has no army, although it does have a civil and rural guard. If Costa Rica created an army to defend its admirable democratic way of life, then, their logic ran, the nation would lose its distinctive identity. I asked, "But what if you were invaded?" Their universal conviction was that Americans knew about Costa Rica's democracy and would not tolerate its subversion. The conversation terminated with a futile effort on my part to persuade them with a hypothetical query: would Detroit mothers be willing to send their sons to defend Costa Rican democracy if Costa Ricans themselves would not die for the cause?

The answer, I believe, lies in the priorities Central Americans assign social, economic, and political values. They extol social order and tradition, they fear disturbance to the culture, but they have learned to live with political uncertainty. Governments, good or bad, right or left, led by the indifferent, the ruthless, the well-intentioned but inept civilian, the crass dictator, and too often the *vendepatria* who literally sells out the country to the foreign intruder—each has passed through Central Ameri-

can political history. The political behavior of a leader is governed less by law
than by force of personality, by legitimacy—which is determined less by an
honest election than by the leader's
instinct for knowing the will of the
people and striving to fulfill their un-
articulated wishes rather than following
the strict dictates of the constitution—
and by credibility. Americans, reflecting
on our historical experience, speak of
the primacy of democratic government,
the secret ballot, checks and balances,
an independent judiciary, the inalienable
rights of citizens, leaders who must take
oaths to uphold the Constitution, and
the myriad virtues of our political culture. These qualities of the American
experience Central Americans admire,
yet they do not assign them a central
place in their own lives and resent our
doing so. They inherited no Lockean
social contract to implant in their political philosophy or structure of government. In addition, they have learned
from experience that the military is less
a defender of the sovereign republic and
the constitution than a reminder of the
dominating social order or the intim-
idating power of the state.

THE BURDENS OF HISTORY

Central America's historical experience with the larger world, especially
with Europe and the United States, has
been marked by opportunity and frustration. When the early efforts at union
failed, largely because of isthmian divi-
siveness, Central Americans blamed the
British and later the American government. When ambitious leaders promoted foreign settlement as a means of
modernizing the isthmian economies,
the result was often beneficial only to a
segment of the population. From the

1840s, American interest in securing a
transisthmian passageway to the gold-
fields of California and the determination of the U.S. government to gain
equal stature with the British in isthmian
affairs provided Central Americans with
new opportunities to exploit their strategic location in world commerce. But
after a flurry of diplomatic and commercial activity, the Americans and British decided to settle matters without the
Central Americans at the negotiating
table. In the following decade, American
promoters descended on the isthmus,
joining the British in carving out transit
routes across Nicaragua and Panama.
Again, Central American liberals, usually the advocates of the foreign connection, sensed the opportunity to secure
their political futures with timely alliances. In Nicaragua, they invited American mercenaries and soldiers of fortune
to help them. The most illustrious of the
newcomers was William Walker, the
"grey-eyed man of destiny," who turned
against his Nicaraguan ally, took over
the transit route, and with reinforce-
ments gained control of the country.
For the only time in their tormented
history, Central Americans united to
oust the American intruders, the dream-
ers of tropical empire, who threatened
their culture. The experience lies forever
embedded in the Central American psyche.

In the late nineteenth century, when
the modern Central American economic
and social structure took shape, the
liberals returned to power. Once again,
they looked to the outside world, especially the United States. From the 1890s,
two crops—coffee and bananas—
dominated Central American economic
life and in turn its politics and social
structure. The first lay mostly—though
not exclusively—in Central American

hands; the second, almost completely under powerful American multinationals like Standard, Cuyamel, and especially United Fruit companies. Their domain stretched from Panama along the Caribbean shore to Guatemala. In some countries, notably Honduras, where Standard and Cuyamel—which merged with United in 1929—centered their operations, their economic and political clout was so strong that successive governments depended on their contributions, legally and illegally obtained, for survival. Though they operated largely along the coast, housed their managers and even their workers in separate towns, and professed a cooperative spirit, their influence reached deep into Central American life. When the leftist Jacobo Arbenz government of Guatemala was dethroned in 1954 by an American-sponsored coup, Central Americans largely attributed its downfall to plotting by United Fruit Company, which had fought expropriation of its lands under Arbenz's agrarian reform plans. The Guatemalan affair is another of the signal events in isthmian history that reminds Central Americans of their vulnerability and dependence.

Nor can they forget the landings of American troops, usually along the Caribbean coastline, where foreigners and foreign companies looked to the American government for protection. Given the political insecurity of these places, the protective shield of Washington seemed justified, but to diminutive countries the dispatching of shipboard marines ashore served as another reminder of the limits of sovereignty. Where the intervenors plunged deep into the country, as in Nicaragua in 1912 and again in 1927, the political impact was more lasting. In both instances, undeniably, there were Nicaraguans, usually members of the

elite, who welcomed American support, but the professed policing role of American soldiers and the guarantees of honest elections have never overcome the deeper resentments that the intervention denied Nicaraguans the right to determine their own future. When in 1979 the Sandinistas felled Somoza, whose father had been installed by the Americans 50 years before, they believed they had defeated the last American marine in their country, the culmination of a half-century struggle begun by Augusto C. Sandino in 1927.

ON REVOLUTION

Sandino's war against 5000 American marines unleashed what the Sandinistas believe is the authentic Central American revolution, not the succession of sometimes comical, sometimes gruesome battles for political power that had gone on in the republics. Sandino had no systematic revolutionary agenda, only an unalterable opposition to American interference in Nicaraguan affairs. Laboring in Mexico in the years after the Mexican Revolution, he absorbed the anti-Americanism then rife in Mexico and returned to a Nicaragua in revolt. The United States, as it had done earlier in Nicaraguan history, tried to manage things with forceful diplomacy and promises to the malcontents, reinforced by a powerful military presence. Sandino joined the revolution. When its leaders were bought off or persuaded to give up the fight, he refused. He went over to the east coast, where for years foreign companies had left bitter reminders of Nicaragua's weakness, and put together an army of men, women, and children. His defiance brought him recruits from every Latin American country save Peru. Even a few marines defected to his cause. The 5000 American troops dispatched to catch him failed in their quest, but the U.S. government left in Nicaragua the Somoza familial rule. Somoza lured Sandino into Managua to attend a conciliatory dinner, then had him taken out and shot. But the myth of Sandino and the cause he symbolized lived on.

Sandino, conservative Central Americans would argue, would not approve of the Sandinistas and what they are doing. They intend to reconstruct Nicaragua along Marxist lines and have created Central America's most formidable military force to achieve their goals. Sandino believed in private property and thought Nicaraguans would be better off without a politicized army. These represent the kinds of distinctions important to the debater or policymaker. They are not central to understanding the emotional or even spiritual urgency of a cause inspired by defiance of history's legacy. What matters is not the lack of a realistic goal but the determination to undo history by striking out, even insanely, against whoever or whatever denies self-determination. Compromise and accommodation have no place in this revolutionary mind-set, thus the fearful prospect that, once begun, the revolution may not stop with the bringing down of political authority but may continue in a gruesome destruction of the social order. Among those who fear its collapse, even if the revolution poses no realistic threat, there exists a persuasive belief that the revolution must not only be defeated but extirpated from the social consciousness. In 1932, having turned back a Communist revolt that took perhaps two dozen lives, the victorious Salvadoran military undertook a *matanza*, summary executions of 20,000 or perhaps even 30,000 people.

The word "revolution" or the mission of a "revolutionary" government can take on a more frightening meaning for Central Americans. We cannot easily accommodate such thinking because there has been little in our revolutionary experience that has menaced the social order. We have been able to sanitize the meaning of revolution in our imaginations. In dealing with the Sandinistas, we have seized on the phrase "betrayed revolution," earlier applied to condemn Castro's revolution, so as to identify moral justification with our decision to aid Nicaraguan rebels trying to overthrow a revolutionary government. But even in the semantic gymnastics, we place an American definition on a universally exploited word. When Americans speak of the American Revolution, they have one kind of revolution in mind. When they speak of the Reagan revolution, the sexual revolution, the women's revolution, the generational revolution, and so on, the implications of the word "revolution" can range from something on the order of the political or economic philosophy one brings to government to that perpetually adult dilemma about what to do with rebellious youth. American commentators will sometimes casually talk about how El Salvador deserves a revolution without contemplating too much what kind of revolution El Salvador deserves or, just as important, what burdens its people have to bear in order to get what they deserve.

Most Americans would accept the view that Central America does not deserve the turmoil it has endured but that Central Americans deserve a better life for themselves and especially for their children, deserve basic civil liberties, social justice, and economic opportunity, and deserve governments and political systems that undergird and sustain those justly deserved rewards. If those are the goals of governments in power struggling against guerrilla insurgencies, as we believe is the case in El Salvador, then our sustenance of the legal government is not only politically but morally the correct course. But where the legally constituted government has betrayed the revolutionary goals for which it struggled and which we ultimately accepted, then, it is argued, the political and moral imperative dictates that we support the revolution trying to dethrone it.

The hostility we encounter in Central America—at times even among our friends—is explained not so much by our professed goals for them but our insistence on American guidelines in achieving those goals. The cries for social justice, economic opportunity, and democracy resound from Central Americans and are heard. Ordinary Americans have gone to Central America to labor in the building of the new social order. Even the Kissinger Commission report, which pleased the Reagan administration with its accusatory references to Cuban and Soviet involvement in Central America and its vigorous reassertion of American security interests in the region, recognized the need for a "peaceful revolution." As Kennedy warned a generation ago, "Those who make peaceful revolution impossible make violent revolution inevitable."

The problem lies not so much in the persuasiveness of our argument but in the Central Americans' inability to achieve those goals in an era of strife and, more important, with the fragile democratic institutions they have fashioned. They cannot have economic development, social justice, political liberty, and the kind of revolution they deserve and wage war at the same time. Yet civilian governments in Honduras and El Salvador that depend on our sustenance remain dependent on militaries with measurably little commitment to the democratic future the United States professes to seek in Central America.

For example, we ask Duarte in El Salvador to fight a guerrilla movement and to sustain economic and political reforms. Half a billion dollars annually in American economic and military aid undergird this policy. The Salvadoran military has, unarguably, become more professional. Paramilitary death squads no longer operate so blatantly. The Salvadoran military, which tortured and then exiled Duarte in 1972, must accept him as the leader of the country because his presence keeps the vital economic aid flowing from Washington. If the generals, heeding the shrill voices of the old order or the increasingly complaining businessmen of the capital, stage a coup, the United States will shut off the financial spigot. They do not deny the aid is crucial, obviously, but they resent our reminders that whoever pays the piper calls the tune. More precisely, the Salvadoran military has not been persuaded that it ought to relinquish its centrality in the political order. The generals have their own role in Salvadoran history to ponder, and that role has not followed the hallowed American prescriptions for civilian control of the military. They look to a higher authority than the constitution of the republic for guidance.

Not only in El Salvador but in Guatemala, Honduras, and especially Panama, the American emphasis on its isthmian security concerns has in turn abetted the militarization of the region.

Doubtless, conservative elements in these countries would have reinforced military institutions without our encouragement, but we cannot escape our share of the blame for the process. We should not be surprised when moderate civilian reformists who want neither the Sandinistas nor the generals as determiners of their political future condemn American policy for placing in their path obstacles to ridding their countries of this lamentable military legacy.

Central Americans have to create democracies, we believe and they know, but they cannot do so with our priorities and traditions. Their political inheritance provides no solid foundation or certainty. We treasure political principles that reassure us and a dynamic economy that creates employment and satisfies our material needs. Our political tradition provides such a stabilizing force in our lives that we can afford, even encourage, a revolutionary culture. We are reassured that our political traditions will be sustained, that the military does not threaten civilian authority, and that the losers in an election will grudgingly but peacefully give up their power to the winners. There is a certainty that government not only works but that it can be made better if something goes wrong. No external force unacceptable to the general electorate or lacking its approval can wield power. With such reassurance, it is easy to see why American culture can tolerate such diversity and even revolutionary shifts and trends.

Why can Central America not have this kind of political reassurance? If it could, would the outcome be the same—economic opportunity, social justice, and a culture that lived with the credos of "Be all that you can be" and "You deserve what you want." These are potentially more revolutionary than the Marxian notion that one ought to have what one needs. I was often perplexed at how unfrightened the Costa Ricans seemed to be about the hostile Sandinistas to the north, even without much to defend themselves with, but how uncertain they were at adapting to the invasion of American culture—food, music, clothes, cable television. Only after living among them for several months did I come to realize that political turmoil is such a congenital feature of Central American life that it offers, in the regularity of its appearance, a kind of reassurance. On the other hand, the expectation that one might have more than one's parents—more wealth, more education, more of everything—and even deserve more is at once tantalizing and frightening. It is tantalizing because the American cultural invasion and the symbolic authority of our economic system intrude into the most out-of-the-way Central American hamlets; yet it is frightening because none of the Central American countries could satisfy that expectation, however democratic its political system.

Walter LaFeber, in *Inevitable Revolutions*,[1] perhaps the best known and most widely read of the interpretive studies on U.S. policy toward Central America, argues persuasively that the extension of the American economic system into Central America fomented the discontent now manifestly and violently present. For a generation, Central America's dependency theorists have advanced similar explanations. Central America is a backwater of the First World's economic system, they believe, and its social and political structure is designed to preserve its dependent status

1. Walter LaFeber, *Inevitable Revolutions: The United States in Central America* (New York: Norton, 1983, 1985).

for the benefit of a perpetually ruling elite that employs civilian and military stooges—some of whom may be admitted to the club—to rule over a captive and often abused population. The United States, obsessed with its economic and military stake in this system, ultimately reinforces it. Such a system not only inhibits democracy but makes inevitable the revolution of its victims.

Robert Pastor, President Carter's Latin American expert on the National Security Council and now with the Carter Library, has astutely observed that the irony in this otherwise persuasive analysis is that if so many revolutions were inevitable, why did so few actually occur? And, more paradoxically, why did the United States support revolutions—usually by withdrawing its aid from a pro-American but odious dictatorship—that eventually turned anti-American?[2] For example, the United States withdrew essential support from both Batista and Somoza in the year before their fall. In the latter case, it is true, there was a frantic effort to establish an anti-Sandinista government in Managua—*Somocismo* without Somoza—but the hesitancy with which the Carter administration conducted its affairs with Somoza's Nicaragua in his last year or so provides ample evidence of our willingness to accept something else—even if it meant a government that, we were warned, might shift to the left.

The point is not that our historic economic and military presence in Central America has made revolutions inevitable but, more critically, that our self-assessed ability to manipulate Central American politics, whether right,

2. Robert Pastor, "Explaining U.S. Policy in the Caribbean Basin," *World Politics* (Apr. 1986), pp. 433-515.

middle, or left, has been exaggerated. Critics of American policy are indisputably correct when they cite the dismal historical record of our interference, intervention, and ill-disguised manipulation in Central America. Where they err is underestimating the ability of Central Americans, right, middle, and left on the political spectrum, to manipulate us. Like generations of political figures who underestimated generations of good-old-boy politicians from the South, so, too, have Americans fallen under the spell of Central American political aspirants who needed a well-intentioned but naive benefactor from *el Norte*. In blunter words, if we have oppressed Central Americans politically, militarily, and economically, as is often argued, we had isthmian friends to help us. We have made a pact with them and have sustained them. And, believing something better lay on the horizon and that an alteration of policy would make for a moderating influence on their successors, we have abandoned them. Unfortunately, the outcome of this sensible and well-intentioned course has been recrimination from the old order for our betrayal, and hostility from the new for the effrontery in presuming that our good intentions ought to make a difference in its priorities.

THE MODERN CRISIS

Many Americans believe and several scholars accept the view that anti-Americanism will dissipate once the United States accepts the so-called inevitable revolution under way in Central America. It is plausibly argued that isthmian revolution has been fomented by the political repression of rightist governments and the inevitable resistance they have provoked, which in turn has prompted severe counter-measures by those in power, particularly in Guatemala, Nicaragua, and El Salvador. These conflicts represent the legitimate uprising of oppressed people or the machinations of Marxist guerrillas, inspired by the Sandinista triumph and abetted by the Cubans, the Soviets and their outlaw Marxist allies, and, I might add, several Western European countries.

It is also argued that isthmian revolution symbolizes a violent protest against the persistent economic inequities in Central America, which, despite some of the most impressive economic statistics from the early 1950s until 1979, benefited mostly the ruling classes and its new members. Further, this argument goes, the beneficiaries of isthmian economic growth have failed to offer those on the bottom of the economic scale—in Central America these number probably 20 million of its 24 million people—a chance to move up. A generation denied its revolution of rising expectations by the resistance of the ruling political order has taken to protest and ultimately violence to redress its grievances. U.S. policy in Central America, particularly our war against the Sandinistas, we are told, clearly places us not only on the wrong side in this struggle but, inevitably, on the losing side.

What is even more frustrating for many Americans is the realization that in taking sides in the Central American conflict we have allied ourselves with lukewarm and, to our surprise, resentful friends. Despite Central American irritation about Nicaragua's internal politics and apprehension over the Sandinistas' newfound allies among Soviet-bloc nations, the protective American military and economic shield has not allayed anti-Americanism. In Honduras and El Salvador, the major beneficiaries of American aid, anti-American sentiment has risen sharply in the past few years. Predictably, Americans, who often expect gratitude and admiration from mendicant countries dependent on our largess, attribute this hostility to wrongheaded policies that demand too much and give too little, thus creating resentment among the beneficiaries.

There is truth in the observation, but it is not the truth, which in Central America can often be infuriatingly complex. There is a curious form of sibling rivalry at work in Central America. Honduran and Salvadoran generals are often as concerned about how American military aid will affect the military balance between them as they are about its use against the common leftist enemy. Democratic Costa Rica, which has created the kind of political climate we profess to struggle for elsewhere in Central America, grumbles about our inattention to its economic crisis, which has lowered the standard of living for its people and threatens that country's democratic tradition.

In El Salvador, the American government placed tremendous faith in the ability of Duarte to sustain a government beleaguered by six years of guerrilla war and to carry out economic and political reforms that are necessary, Americans believe, to win the hearts and minds of the people. To this end the United States has maintained Duarte's government, but the war in the countryside has reached a stalemate and the economy, now totally dependent on American aid, has foundered. Salvadorans, certainly from the Right but also from the middle class, have taken out their frustrations not only in verbal assaults against Duarte but against the United States, his benefactor. In that curious but predictable Central American logic, the United States, which has taken credit for Duarte's successes, must now share not only the blame but also the responsibility for his failure.

In Honduras, critics of American policy contend, we have revived latent anti-Americanism by transforming the country into what is humorously called the USS *Honduras*. But even here the explanation for this resurgence of anti-American feeling does not follow a linear route. As in El Salvador, the emphasis on counterinsurgency, reinforced by American technical guidance, has given the military a more visible political role, which has angered reformers who look to civilian control of the affairs of state. *Campesinos* displaced from Honduran land along the Nicaraguan border because the American-backed contras have transformed the area into a war zone ultimately attribute their dislocation to American pressures. Honduran military officers resent the American buildup of the Salvadoran army because they have unpleasant memories of the Salvadoran invasion during the 1969 so-called soccer war. Not to be underestimated is the social pummeling that hundreds of American soldiers with all-American libidinous drives have given Comayagua and Tegucigalpa. They did not introduce the whorehouse into these places, nor are they the first to corrupt 17-year-old Honduran girls, but they have more money to spend for sexual diversion than the Honduran male and thus constitute a threat to him. In such myriad ways anti-Americanism survives.

But we rightly persist in believing that we can take corrective measures to deal with anti-Americanism in the isthmus. In less than a decade, the American public has acquired at least an intro-ductory course in Central America's condition and a rudimentary knowledge of its background. The average American is nowadays better informed about what is styled the sordid American record in Central America, about military interventions, economic intrusion, and in general the occasionally abysmal mark we have imprinted on the isthmus. This has led, in turn, to self-flagellation and reassertion of American interests in the region. But such contrapuntal forces have implanted a collective frustration, expressed in the Kissinger Commission report: "We can't win, we can't lose, we can't quit the game." Our Central American adversaries and friends read such statements as evidence not of resolve but of our befuddlement over what to do next.

This in turn might be understandable if it were not coupled with that annoying American habit—eminently justifiable, it can be argued, where Central America is concerned—of telling others how to run their affairs or solve their problems. The Central Americans do need our help, but they do not care for the advice that usually goes with it. Our benevolence, public and private, is often rendered, many times unintentionally, in a patronizing way. In part this reflects the ethnocentric character of American foreign policy and even of well-intentioned Americans who journey southward to help the Central Americans build a better world or save their souls. It is not enough to speak the language, go out into the boondocks and teach people how to read and write, or live on rice and beans just to show people in the boondocks that one is willing to eat what they eat. What is objectionable is the unstated yet expressed air of superiority of the American who believes that his or her education and technical superiority reflects a superior culture. There is an assumption that because Central Americans admire the United States, wear American-style clothes, watch cable television—even in Managua—devour American music, and are becoming Americanized, they will soon adopt our political style and will deal with their political problems the way we confront ours—by rational trade-offs and compromises.

The Central American reaction to American demurrals over the August 1987 Central American peace plan, set forth by President Oscar Arias of Costa Rica, offered an illustration of the way Central Americans deal with interstate conflict. The plan, which called for an end to American support for the Nicaraguan contras, was filled with ambiguity and imprecision, leaving, said the Reagan administration and the conservative isthmian press, the Sandinistas with an opportunity to maintain their control with only verbal pledges of democracy. Even the pact's most enthusiastic supporters had some inner doubts about resolving the Central American crisis with only lofty rhetoric, yet their irritation with the American government lay not only in our skepticism but in our unwillingness to see the problem as they see it. They recognized that the agreement contained no guarantees of Nicaraguan compliance and required the cessation of American aid to the Nicaraguan contras. But the dream of peace, even without ironclad assurances, offered a respite to eight years of conflict. A brief pause in the political struggle would give each party a better opportunity to direct attention to the disintegrating social order.

In our demurral we did not recognize their priorities. In their scheme of things, the divisive issues in modern Central America cannot really be resolved because politics is not merely a matter of dividing the pie so that everybody gets a slice. What they want is the certainty of a stable social order. In the political realm, historically fraught with uncertainty, the best that can be hoped for is dialogue between parties who believe that honor can never be compromised and political conflict can never be resolved. Its violent manifestations, however, can be mitigated.

AMERICAN PRIORITIES AND CENTRAL AMERICAN REALITIES

Modern soothsayers matter-of-factly observe that what the Sandinistas are doing in Nicaragua and what the Salvadoran guerrillas will do if they get into power is obvious, that what the Soviets and Cubans are up to in Central America is obvious, and that it is obvious that Central Americans do not want another Cuba, so it is obvious that we must do what we can to prevent these things.

If the threat is so obvious, why the uncertainty in the United States and, especially, why the uncertainty in Central America? Why do they so resent our pointing out what to us is the obvious? We have, doubtless, friends in Central America who herald the elimination of the Sandinistas in Nicaragua and the suppression of the Left in the other countries, but the kind of political structure they would impose in the aftermath would be so palpably offensive, even to American conservatives, that it could not satisfy even the most modest American criteria. There are limitations, I believe, on the price we would accept for Central American stability, and I know there are limitations on what price this Central American generation will pay for it.

The answer involves something endemic in Central America, perhaps in

Hispanic culture generally, and it is the lesson we have never learned. Central Americans not only look at the world differently from the way we do; they assign differing values to words like "democracy," "legitimacy," "order," "the church," "elections," and "the ballot," and they see us in a way in which we refuse to see ourselves. What Central America must have, we believe, is order, democracy, and a more prosperous future for a people who will number 40 million by the end of the century. Actually, most Central Americans want those things, but they disagree, sometimes violently, on the best way to obtain them. Their inner doubts and their own experience tell them the price for these is too high, but if they were certain that their future might bring those things, they might be willing to pay that price. Their pride, which is considerable, assures them that even if they are dependent on the First World economy and even if their politics is rife with discord and their leaders are dependent on outsiders, they will prevail. They beckon,

then resent, the intruder and especially the intruder's advice, however sensible.

And they are defiant. The Sandinistas, who are miserable administrators but authoritative governors of what has become a beggar society, understand the debilitating imprint American intervention has had on the collective Central American psyche, especially the Nicaraguan. In their defiance of the American government, in their publicity campaigns to lure American tourists, in their appeals to a candid world, they have challenged the American Goliath and gained for Nicaragua an international prestige none of our isthmian client states has achieved. Even in their despair and moment of uncertainty, caught between the eagle and the bear, torn apart by warring political factions, riven by guerrilla war, they, like those who led the United States into a war in 1812 that few really wanted and few understood, can raise the flag of defiance and reap the consequences. They may not know what they are doing, and we may believe we do, but they know why.

ANNALS, *AAPSS*, **497**, May 1988

Japanese Attitudes Toward the United States

By NATHANIEL B. THAYER

ABSTRACT: The Japanese look within themselves to find the causes of the Pacific War (1937-45). They have discovered an inner-directed nationalism that exalts conformity and ethnicity. Impressed with the high-mindedness of the Americans, who placed reform over rehabilitation in their occupation of Japan, determined not to go to war again, the Japanese have submerged their nationalism within a pro-Americanism. That state of affairs will continue so long as America seeks peace, looks outward, honors diversity, and lives up to its ideals.

Nathaniel B. Thayer is a professor and director of Asian studies at the School for Advanced International Studies, a graduate division of the Johns Hopkins University.

HAVING trashed an American ambassador's car carrying the president's press secretary and having halted in midflight the visit to Japan of the president himself, the Japanese mob—30,000 in number—gathered in the darkness around the Diet building to stop the final passage of the defense treaty with the United States. That same night, only a few miles away, another Japanese mob—40,000 in number—pushed their way into brightly lit Korakuen Stadium to watch the Tokyo Giants take on the Chunichi Dragons in baseball. The treaty passed. The Giants won.

From atop his sound truck parked in the railroad station plaza, the young Japanese rightist denounces the so-called YP system—the conferences at Yalta and Potsdam through which the Americans, with their allies, set forth their principles for the postwar world order. On a nearby wall, a rightist poster supports the Americans in their anticommunism. From his tower built to obstruct the flight path of the departing jets, the young Japanese leftist has found a way to marry the farmers' protest at having their land sequestered to build the Narita airport with American imperialism. Yet the young leftist supports the land reforms the Americans brought to Japan in the first days of the American occupation.

Japanese newspapers write about three Americas. The first America is historical America. The tone is friendly dispassion. The second America is geographical America, a land whose breadth and width still awe the Japanese visitor, though the visitor may travel to it several times a year and read stories of its acquisition by Japanese real estate companies. The third America is Washington, the site of the federal government, which, like the Japanese government,

has yet to do anything right.

A difficulty, then, in describing Japanese attitudes toward America is to decide which America the Japanese are talking about. What is clear is that the Japanese cannot imagine a world without America.

JAPANESE NATIONALISM

Japanese respect nationalism in other cultures. They see it, for example, as essential to nation building. Many Japanese, however, fear nationalism in Japan. They see it, for example, as the principal force that impelled Japan to challenge and then go to war with the United States. The task, then, of the postwar intellectuals has been to supplant Japanese nationalism with something else. The first effort was to engender popular backing for pacifism. The realities of the world broke up that effort. The second effort was to identify with the United Nations. That effort became less urgent as the United Nations drifted away from the main world current, although even today the Japanese government is still willing to contribute without complaint to the U.N. budget. A third effort, under way today, has been to identify Japan with the free world. Integral to this identification is a positive attitude toward the United States.

Has Americanism come to serve as a surrogate for Japanese nationalism? Japanese readily identify with certain Americans and their ideas: General MacArthur, who believed that Japan could be reformed; President Kennedy, who first enunciated the doctrine of interdependence; President Reagan, who will not think evil of either the United States or Japan. The Japanese reject other American ideas, such as containment, big-power chauvinism, and Japan bashing. Most Japanese understand and accept the American concept of transcendency: times and things can become better. And they have seen the United States fall down and pick itself up a number of times. The Japanese have had great faith in a future America.

Meanwhile, what has happened to Japanese nationalism? In 1982, the Public Opinion Research Office of Nihon Hoosoo Kyookai (NHK), the government-owned—but not controlled—television and radio network, published a book that dealt with Japanese nationalism by comparing it to American nationalism.[1] Japanese who answered, "My country," to the question "What do you really feel strongly attached to?" amounted to only 17 percent. Americans who gave the same answer to the same question totaled 51 percent—three times the Japanese percentage. If the American percentage constitutes a bench mark, Japanese nationalism is no longer concerned with the nation.

The effort for the first half of the twentieth century was to make the emperor the focus of Japanese nationalism. Since 1953, the Institute of Statistical Mathematics has asked a national sample at five-year intervals whether "a prime minister, when he takes office, should pay his respects to the imperial shrine at Ise." In 1953, a majority said, "Better he should go." By 1978, a majority said the prime minister could please himself.[2] Nationalism seems no longer directed toward the emperor.

A Japanese majority agree with the statement "Individual rights are too often ignored for the sake of the public good." A majority also agree with the statement "Individual rights must sometimes be somewhat sacrificed to the public interest."[3] Both statements have the individual as their subject. That is a new Japanese interest.

What about the people's freedom? A majority say it will increase. What about people's peace of mind? A majority say it will diminish. The level of science and technology in Japan is thought to be quite high by 85 percent; 71 percent respond that the level of artistic achievement is quite high; 67 percent respond that the level of economic achievement is also quite high.

The Japanese are now concerned with international measurements.

What about the richness of Japanese emotional life? There is no majority view. The Japanese are still dissatisfied. International success does not totally satisfy them.

There is agreement among 27 percent that "if individuals are made happy, then, and only then, will Japan as a nation improve"; 27 percent agree that "if Japan as a nation improves, then, and only then, can individuals be made happy."[4]

Can sense be made of this jumble of conflicting thoughts? Yes. Japan is in the midst of defining a new nationalism. Much has yet to be decided, but much has already been decided. Japan must look outward, not inward. The individual, not the emperor, should be the focus of the state. No longer important is the singularity of the Japanese nation. Japan must become part of the world—

1. NHK seron choosa sho, ed., *Nihon to Amerika jin [Japanese and Americans]* (Tokyo: Nihon hoosoo shuppan kyookai, 1982), pp. 128-45.

2. Tookei suuri kenkyusho, *Dai Yon Nihonjin no Kokuminsei* [The fourth study of Japanese character] (Tokyo: Idemitsu shoten, 1982), pp. 144-52.

3. Ibid.

4. Ibid.

a respected, integral, and contributing part.

This is the background against which we must measure Japanese attitudes toward the United States. We look first at the nations that Japan dislikes. There are several. Our questions are, Does Japan dislike these several countries for the same reason? Or for different reasons? How does the United States fit into this pantheon of disliked countries?

NATIONS DISLIKED BY JAPAN

Japanese dislike several nations. At the top of their list is the USSR. Next are the two Koreas. South Korea is more disliked than North Korea. China was ill thought of until the middle 1970s. Since then, its popularity has staggered upward. The United States, too, has been both liked and disliked. For two years, 1973-74, the Japanese who spoke ill of the United States were almost equal in number to the Japanese who spoke well of the United States. Aside from these two years, more Japanese have liked the United States than have disliked the United States. That has been true throughout the postwar era. The degree of dislike of these several nations varies, and that suggests that the reasons for the dislike vary, too.

We draw these observations from data supplied by the Jiji wire service. Each month since the late fifties, the Central Research Organization, a polling arm of the Jiji, has conducted nationwide surveys of Japan asking of its respondents, "Which country do you like the most?" and "Which country do you dislike the most?" Table 1 contains the answers. Under the "like the most" heading are two columns. The column "highest percentage" contains the highest number, expressed in a percentage,

of the respondents who said they liked the most the country listed on the left and the year in which that country achieved that distinction. The column "lowest percentage" gives the lowest percentage of respondents who said they liked most the country listed on the left and the year that country achieved that distinction. Under the "dislike the most" heading are two columns, one entitled "highest percentage," one entitled "lowest percentage." These two columns contain the same sort of data as the similarly titled columns we have just described.

The verb used in the question "What nation do you dislike the most?" is *kirau*. It is a word that can be lightly used in, say, talking about a movie. A Japanese would not use this word in talking about a nation, least of all to a stranger met for an interview, unless that Japanese bore active animus toward that nation. This circumstance makes even more impressive the clarity with which the Japanese express their dislike for the Koreas, China, and the Soviet Union. What underlies this dislike?

Internal disorder, even though that disorder is outside of Japan, is a primary reason why Japanese dislike a country. In 1967, the Cultural Revolution in China reached a crescendo. In 1960, General Park Chung Hee toppled the elected government of Chang Myon in South Korea. The years 1967 and 1960 were the years that Japanese antipathy toward South Korea and China reached its apogee.

The greater dislike for South Korea than for North Korea may be explained by the fact that the latter, unlike the former, bars permanently stationed foreign correspondents. As a result, negative events are not regularly reported to the outside world. But Japanese reporters do visit North Korea, and they

TABLE 1
COUNTRIES LIKED AND DISLIKED THE MOST

| | "Like the Most" | | "Dislike the Most" | |
	Highest percentage	Lowest percentage	Lowest percentage	Highest percentage
United States	53 (1961)	15 (1974)	4 (1962)	15 (1974)
Soviet Union	6 (1968)	5 (often)	22 (1974)	55 (1960)
Great Britain	40 (1960)	15 (1974)	1 (often)	4 (1964)
France	31 (1967)	19 (1960)	1 (often)	4 (1964)
West Germany	18 (1969)	10 (1960)	1 (1970)	6 (1960)
Switzerland	41 (1968)	25 (1960)	0 (often)	1 (often)
India	18 (1960)	2 (1971)	1 (1960)	8 (1973)
China	17 (1978)	3 (1970)	4 (1973)	45 (1967)
South Korea	7 (1971)	1 (1960)	8 (1973)	47 (1960)
North Korea	2 (1972)	1 (often)	13 (1973)	33 (1970)

SOURCE: Jiji wire service.

invariably write about the xenophobia-driven isolation, the semi-divine status of Kim Il Sung, the docility of the people. North Korea has much social discipline. North Korea smacks of prewar Japan.

In 1970, at the conclusion of a Chou En-lai visit to Pyongyang, the North Korean and the Chinese governments issued a communiqué condemning Japanese imperialism. That condemnation married Chinese and North Korean excesses and criticized Japan to boot. That year, 1970, marked the height of Japanese antipathy toward North Korea.

Thus internal conditions may be the stimulus but not the reason for Japanese antipathy. Disorder—or too much order—may bring to the surface unpleasant historical memories. The Korean peninsula, for example, was occupied by Japan. Its takeover came when the Koreans had put aside Confucian cosmopolitanism and had eagerly grasped and had been driven by Korean nationalism. Koreans opposed Japanese rule—at times through assassination, at other times through uprisings that were bloodily put down. Disorder in China was a

reason the prewar Japanese military officers offered to justify their takeover of China. The attempt at takeover led to war with China and the United States, a war that lasted nine years, 1937-45, and gave Japan no benefit.

Is fear another reason for Japanese dislike of these countries? During the 12 years between 1972 and 1984, the Japanese were asked at regularly spaced intervals, "Which countries threaten Japan's peace and security?" We record the answers in Table 2. The Kyoodoo wire service conducted the 1972 poll; the Yomiuri newspaper conducted the other polls.

The Japanese see neither China nor the two Koreas as threatening Japan's peace and security. Only a few have ever seen the United States as a threat and those few have become fewer in the 1980s. The United States' threat, incidentally, is not that the United States and Japan will go to war against each other but that the United States will involve Japan in a war that is neither of Japan's making nor in its interest. Since the late 1970s, more than half the Japanese have seen the Soviet Union as a

TABLE 2
COUNTRIES PERCEIVED BY JAPANESE TO THREATEN JAPAN'S
PEACE AND SECURITY (Percentage of respondents)

	1972	1978	1981	1984
Soviet Union	34	53	69	54
United States	17	11	6	8
China	9	11	2	2
South Korea	1	5	1	3
North Korea	2	9	3	5

SOURCES: For the poll taken in 1972, the Kyoodoo wire service; for the 1978, 1981, and 1984 polls, the Yomiuri newspaper.

threat, but the scholar Nisihira Sigeki points out that this sense of threat is abstract.[5]

History also enters into Japanese thinking about the USSR. Its diplomats refused to serve as a conduit for Japan's overtures to end the Pacific War in 1945. Instead, despite a nonaggression pact, the USSR declared war against Japan, that declaration made after the A-bomb was dropped, when Japan had no alternative to surrender. Soviet troops swept into Manchuria, capturing Japanese soldiers and forcing them to work for years in labor camps long after the war was over. Japan has its own appreciation of the gulag. At regular intervals, the Institute of Statistical Mathematics has asked Tokyo residents to characterize Japanese relations with the Soviet Union. The number of Japanese describing these relations as bad has grown from 20 percent in 1972 to 67 percent in

5. The definition of the Russian threat is taken in part from Nisihira Sigeki, *Seron Choosa ni yoru Dooji Dai Shi* [A contemporary history based on public opinion research] (Tokyo: Bureen shuppan kai, 1987), pp. 256-59. Other parts of the present article depend on other parts of this book and a series of articles that Professor Nisihira wrote during the late 1970s and early 1980s for *Jiyuu* magazine. Professor Nisihira and I are in the final stages of a manuscript that uses the data in these writings to depict Japan's sense of the world.

1982. During this decade, however, Soviet policy toward Japan did not change.

What accounts for this growth in bad feeling? I would argue Japanese frustration with the unwillingness of Soviets to recognize and accommodate changes in Japan. If this is so, how to answer the question, Is there something common in the Japanese dislike of various countries? I would answer that these nations make the Japanese face a world they no longer want to consider. They encourage the Japanese to assume prewar attitudes and behavior, obstructing Japan in the definition of a new nationalism, and this is resented.

What about the United States? Table 1 shows that at one time as many as 15 percent of the Japanese registered dislike for the United States. Clearly, some Japanese hold an animus against the United States and are willing to express it. But most Japanese register dissatisfaction with the United States in other ways. Let us turn to the other question that Jiji has asked over the years: "What country do you like the most?" The results are plotted in Figures 1 and 2. Figure 1 compares the popularity of the United States with the popularity of other countries. We turn to it first.

Note Switzerland, France, West Ger-

FIGURE 1
YEARLY HIGHS OF MONTHLY SURVEY ON MOST LIKED COUNTRIES, 1960-87

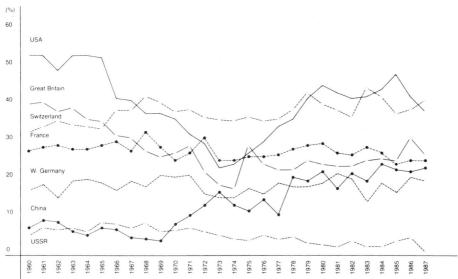

SOURCE: Chuuoo Choosa Services, Jiji Press, Tokyo, Japan.

many, and the Soviet Union. The horizontal lines formed by connecting each year's high point in popularity are essentially parallel to each other and the spread between the highest and the lowest point of popularity is roughly five percentage points. Japanese enthusiasm for Great Britain has dropped over the years because the British, once very active in East Asia, are no longer active. They get as much attention nowadays as France and West Germany. The Japanese have made up their minds about these nations, and that image changes little.

Not so with China. Throughout the 1960s, few Japanese liked China. In the 1970s, though, the Chinese and Japanese governments made known their intent to reestablish formal relations with each other. That kicked off a rise in China's popularity. Why has that line wobbled in its upward rise? Japanese believe each nation should have as its first goal the

building of a prosperous nation. To the extent that the Chinese seem to be succeeding in this goal, Japanese esteem for China rises. To the extent that the Chinese depart from this goal, Japanese esteem drops.

Let us now turn to the United States. Until 1968, it was the most popular of all nations. Then Switzerland took over. Why Switzerland? During the American occupation, General MacArthur said that he was going to turn Japan into the Switzerland of the East. That statement stimulated Japanese interest. The Japanese see Switzerland as small, tidy, well ruled, neutral but identified with the West, respected. These attributes are all goals that many Japanese want for Japan. Switzerland enjoyed being the most liked nation until 1980, when the United States again assumed top position. Note that Switzerland is much the same as the other European countries. Its popularity rises and falls in a narrow

FIGURE 2
JAPANESE ATTITUDES TOWARD THE UNITED STATES, 1960-87 (Yearly highs)

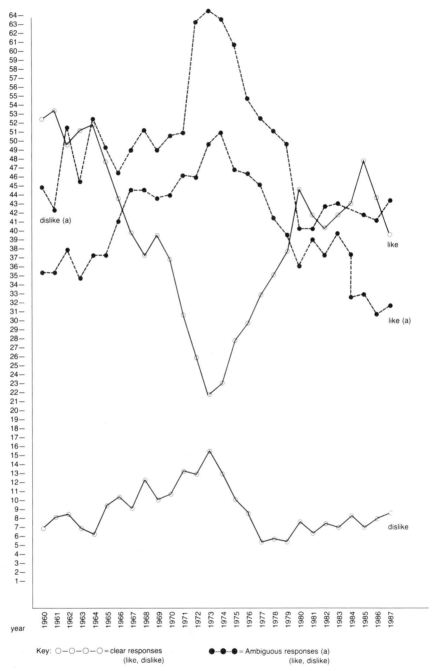

Key: ○—○—○—○ = clear responses   ●--●--● = Ambiguous responses (a)
              (like, dislike)   (like, dislike)

SOURCE: Chuuoo Choosa Services, Jiji Press, Tokyo, Japan, Sept. 1987.

band. It is safe to conclude that Switzerland did not gain in esteem during the decade 1969-79. Rather, it was more popular than the United States because the United States lost esteem. Why is that?

The precipitous drop of 30 percentage points between 1965 and 1973 was brought about by the Vietnam war. Many Japanese saw in that war a strong nation fighting a weak nation and doing great damage to it in the name of an ideology. That the United States could not win the conflict meant that the war was an independence movement, not a Communist takeover. For many years, Japan has had within it nascent pan-Asian sentiment, but that sentiment has been stronger among the intellectuals than among the populace. Nevertheless, that pan-Asian sentiment may account for some of the antipathy toward the United States.

The next downturn came during the first two years of the Reagan administration, when American officials developed the techniques of Japan bashing. This downturn was reversed with Nakasone's accession to the prime minister's office and the close friendship he was able to establish with the American president. The Japanese populace supported their prime minister even though Nakasone greatly expanded the Japanese area of international responsibility. The next downturn started in 1985. Its genesis was trade. Given the volume of goods, their value, and the complexity of interests involved in trade between the United States and Japan, Japanese have accepted the argument that friction is inevitable. Polls show that a third of the Japanese recognize justice in the American position as each issue unfolds. What the Japanese do not comprehend are the threats, the willingness to damage the Japanese economy, that seem to have become part of each negotiation. They particularly resent the thoughtlessness with which Congress passes its anti-Japanese resolutions.

Let us turn to Figure 2. This figure contains four lines—two solid, two dashed. The lower solid line records the yearly percentage high of monthly polls in which Japanese respondents identified the United States as the nation they most disliked (the line is labeled "dislike"). The amplitude of this line is about nine percentage points. The other solid line traces the yearly high response of Japanese who identified the United States as the nation they liked the most (the line labeled "like"). The amplitude of this line is 32 percentage points.

The two dashed lines are formed from the yearly high percentages of respondents who gave ambiguous answers. The uppermost line—labeled "dislike (a)"—is formed from percentages of respondents who gave an ambiguous answer to the question "Which nation do you dislike the most?" The lowermost dashed line—labeled "like (a)"—is formed from percentages of respondents who gave an ambiguous answer to the question "Which nation do you like the most?" As the "like" line dropped, the two dashed lines rose, almost in parallel. This phenomenon suggests these conclusions:

1. Japanese do not like to say they dislike the United States.

2. Nevertheless, Japanese react strongly to questions about the United States.

3. If one allows for ambiguity, as many as 79 percent—64 percent + 15 percent—of the Japanese have spoken out against the United States.

4. Stasis, though, is a pro-American, not an anti-American, attitude.

The yearly percentage highs for respondents who said they liked America often appeared in December or in January. Japanese see the change of years as a time for paying old debts, setting new goals. Japanese hope in America would seem perennial.

Some researchers have described anti-Americanism—and any other anti-nation sentiment—as stemming from a clash of national interests. In the case of Vietnam, Japanese and American national interests did not clash, though their understanding of what the fighting was about certainly did. Most visible in the antiwar movement in Japan during the Vietnam war years was the Vietnam Peace Alliance (Beiheiren), led by young writers and other intellectuals, many of whom had been educated in the United States. "America was wrong," they argued. "America was no longer true to its ideals." This argument received broad popular support. Is this anti-Americanism?

RIVALRY WITH THE UNITED STATES?

If the Vietnam war and the Japan bashing have weakened American support in Japan, memories of the American occupation have strengthened it.

In a bitter war—1941-45—the United States defeated Japan and occupied its islands. Expecting retribution, the Japanese received reform. Specifically, the occupation officials wrote a new constitution, restructured the government and national legislature, and restored elections with contending candidates. The U.S. officials helped rebuild the Japanese economy; today, the United States is Japan's largest market. Finally, with the conclusion of the occupation, the United States accepted a treaty obligation to help defend Japan and

today has military bases in Japan both to do that and to maintain peace and security in the Far East.

In 1975, NHK set out to see how the Japanese perceived American influence in these three areas—politics, the economy, peace and security. They posed three clusters of two assertions each, and asked respondents to agree or disagree. (See Table 3.)

More Japanese than not agreed that in the economic and political spheres American actions have benefited Japan, though these actions have created a dependency within Japan. Japanese views on defense matters were a little more complex. Finally, the NHK researchers asked for an overall assessment of the relations between Japan and the United States. A majority of Japanese—65 percent—said they have been a plus; 5 percent felt they were a minus; 24 percent felt relations were equally positive and negative; and 6 percent gave no answer. Recall that this poll was taken in 1975, two years after Japanese willingness to identify with the United States had reached its postwar low (see Figures 1 and 2). Although less than 25 percent of the Japanese were willing to say they liked the United States, 65 percent of the Japanese found benefit in the relationship.

Not only have a majority of the Japanese found benefit in the past relationship with the Americans, but they also share with them a vision of the future and what should be done to realize it.

In 1980, the Yomiuri newspaper underwrote a poll taken simultaneously in both the United States and Japan that explores this common vision. The question was "What should we be doing to fulfill our role in international society?" (See Table 4.)

TABLE 3
JAPANESE PERCEPTIONS OF AMERICAN INFLUENCE IN POLITICS,
THE ECONOMY, AND PEACE AND SECURITY

	Percentage of Respondents	
	Agreeing	Disagreeing
1. Americans assisted in making Japan a democracy.	40	11
Politics easily swayed by America continues.	47	12
2. Americans were helpful in restoring the immediate postwar and subsequent economy.	53	5
We [Japanese] now have an economy incapable of standing without leaning on the American economy.	40	15
3. The presence of American military bases protects Japan's peace.	23	36
American bases invite unease [the fear of involvement in war].	28	27

SOURCE: Nihon Hoosoo Kyookai, 1975.

TABLE 4
JAPANESE AND AMERICAN VISIONS OF THEIR INTERNATIONAL
ROLES (Percentage of respondents)

Question: "What should we be doing to fulfill our role in
international society? Choose two statements."

	Percentage of Respondents	
Statement	Japanese	American
Relax East-West tension	11	9
Strengthen the Western camp	3	46
Work for peace	68	63
Give economic aid to developing countries	23	5
Help in resolving regional conflict	2	5
Establish international economic order	17	14
Develop alternative sources of energy	33	37
Create a culture based on science and technology	13	12
No answer	10	3

SOURCE: Yomiuri newspaper, 1980.

TABLE 5
JAPANESE RESPONSE TO THE NAME "UNITED STATES," 1987

Question: "When you hear the word 'United States,'
what immediately comes to mind?"

Response	Percentage of Respondents
Freedom; free country	9.8
Strong country; big country	9.5
Trade friction; economic friction	6.5
Vast territory	5.6
World War II; war	5.3
Acquired immune deficiency syndrome	5.1
President Reagan	4.3
A military superpower	3.5
An economic superpower	2.5
Strengthening of the yen; cheapening of the dollar	2.0

SOURCE: Yomiuri newspaper, 18 June 1987.

Seeing themselves as leading the Western camp, the Americans place a higher priority on its unity than do the Japanese. Precluded from a world military role and discouraged from a world political role, the Japanese put a higher premium on economic aid than do the Americans. Both Americans and Japanese place their highest priority on working for peace. They share most other international goals.

What do Japanese think when they hear the name "United States"? Pollsters in Japan have asked that question on two occasions ten years apart. We present first the most recent poll, taken in March 1987. Table 5 shows the ten most frequent replies. Pleasant and unpleasant thoughts both appear among these replies. But pleasant thoughts predominate—even though the Japanese were in a period when fewer Japanese each month were willing to recognize that they liked the United States.

We next present the results of the poll taken ten years ago, in September 1978. (See Table 6.) This poll contains some responses that did not show up on the later poll: race problems, the A-bomb, and democracy. Furthermore, responses that were most frequently mentioned in the 1978 poll were mentioned less in the 1987 poll. This suggests a stately progression of ideas about the United States across the Japanese psyche. Note, though, that freedom, which was fifth in frequency in the 1978 poll, moved to first in the 1987 poll. That construct marches to its own drummer. The 1987 poll is a far more sunny poll than the earlier, 1978 poll.

A question that has received extensive attention in the Japanese media is, "Is the United States in decline?" Most journals have concluded that it is; they differ only in the degree of commiseration they summon to reach this conclusion. Have their readers found their

TABLE 6
JAPANESE RESPONSE TO THE NAME "UNITED STATES," 1978

Question: "When you hear the word 'United States,'
what immediately comes to mind?"

Response	Percentage of Respondents
World War II; war	14.2
Vast territory	6.2
Strong country; big country	5.7
Economic power	4.1
Freedom; equality	4.1
Strong yen; weak dollar	2.3
Military big power	2.3
Race problems	2.0
A-bomb	2.0
Democracy	1.9

SOURCE: Yomiuri newspaper, 18 June 1987.

TABLE 7
JAPANESE AND AMERICAN PERCEPTIONS OF DECLINE OF U.S. STRENGTH

Question: "There are various views regarding the
national strength of the superpower, the United
States. Do you think that the United States has
started to go into eclipse?"

Response	Percentage of Respondents	
	Japanese	American
Think so	44	54
Think not	44	36
No answer	13	10

SOURCE: Yomiuri newspaper, Mar. 1987.

arguments convincing? That was a question that the Yomiuri put to a national sample in March 1987. Interested also in how the Americans saw themselves, they asked the same question of an American national sample. The American and the Japanese polls were taken at the same time. We present in Table 7 the Japanese and American responses. The Japanese split evenly in their responses. Even so, they are more sanguine than the Americans about the American future. How imminent is this eclipse? That speculation the Yomiuri elicited in another question, as shown in Table 8.

A large majority of the Japanese think that present circumstances will continue. In answering this question, they reveal themselves to be less sanguine than the Americans, of whom a third think that America will become stronger in the next century.

Trying to pin down further what the Japanese and American publics think

TABLE 8
PERCEPTIONS OF AMERICA IN THE TWENTY-FIRST CENTURY

Question: "The twentieth century has been called the
'American Century.' What will happen in the next
century? Select one of the answers."

Response	Percentage of Respondents	
	Japanese	American
America will become stronger in the twenty-first century.	10	32
Present conditions will continue.	64	48
By the end of the twentieth century, strong America will be over.	18	12
No answer	8	8

SOURCE: Yomiuri newspaper, 18 June 1987.

TABLE 9
VIEW ON WORLD LEADERSHIP IN THE TWENTY-FIRST CENTURY

Question: "Do you believe that another country
or another region will overtake the United States
and lead the world in the twenty-first century?"

Response	Percentage of Respondents	
	Japanese	American
Think so	21	28
Think not	68	64
No answer	12	8

SOURCE: Yomiuri newspaper, 18 June 1987.

about the future, the Yomiuri asked about world leadership (see Table 9). Japanese and American views are not far apart. Only one in three see the United States' world leadership being supplanted. When asked specifically whether Japan would supplant the United States, citizens in the two countries responded as shown in Table 10.

Varying only in emphasis, 91 percent of the Japanese see no possibility of Japan's assuming world leadership. They are even clearer in their views than the Americans.

The preceding questions suggest that Japanese have no sense of rivalry with the United States—at least in the international arena.

CONCLUSION

What can we conclude? A few Japanese say they dislike the United States. Events do not seem to change this judgment much. More Japanese say they like the United States. Some events affect this judgment. The two events that have caused the Japanese to lessen

TABLE 10
VIEW ON THE POSSIBILITY OF JAPAN'S WORLD LEADERSHIP

Question: "Do you think that there is a possibility that
Japan will supplant the United States and assume world
leadership in the twenty-first century?"

Response	Percentage of Respondents	
	Japanese	American
Good possibility	4	7
Little possibility	19	23
Almost no possibility	41	35
Absolutely no possibility	31	30
No answer	5	5

SOURCE: Yomiuri newspaper, 18 June 1987.

their identification with the United States have been the Vietnam war and Japan bashing, and what both have in common is the belief among Japanese that the behavior exhibited in them is atypical of the United States.

World War II is over, but the American occupation of Japan still reverberates. That the United States chose to rebuild Japan rather than destroy it is the decision that still forms the basis of Japanese attitudes toward the United States. Japanese disparage the United States but are not troubled enough to change their dependency on that country. They identify with the United States' world goals. They find the United States itself to be built on principles they increasingly are coming to believe in themselves.

The Japanese are more optimistic about America's future than are most Americans. The American concern over whether the United States is going into eclipse has awakened a similar concern in Japan. Of those Japanese who voice an opinion, half say that eclipse has started; half say not. But few Japanese see that eclipse as happening fast. Japanese see no possibility of Japan's as-

suming world leadership. Certainly, the Japanese have no wish to challenge the United States for world leadership. Their newly emerging nationalism precludes national rivalry.

Let us return to the question posed at the beginning of this article: has Americanism come to serve as a surrogate for Japanese nationalism? One can argue that nationalism adapts to, encompasses, and finally absorbs and reflects what the people of the nation see as in their best interests. The United States provides a peaceful international environment. The United States created and leads the global economy in which Japan prospers. The United States was instrumental in the restoration of democracy to Japan. These circumstances dispose Japan to view the United States with favor.

But these same conditions could engender a sense of dependence, and that, in turn, can breed resentment. Why is there no resentment among the Japanese? The Japanese recognize the United States to be a pluralistic society: it respects other cultures; it works to tolerate all races; it finds strength in diversity. In short, the American political vision is broad enough to provide within it room for Japanese thought and ideas. It even recognizes, writes the scholar Kosaka Masataka, that "the secret of Japan's success may lie in being different from America."[6] So long as the United States continues to be tolerant, Japan can find within that tolerance room to express its own national wishes yet identify with America's larger concerns.

6. Koosaka Masataka, *Bunmei Ga Suiboo Suru Toki* [The decay of civilization] (Tokyo: Shincho sensho, 1981), pp. 200-201.

ANNALS, *AAPSS*, **497**, May 1988

Anti-Americanism in Canada?

By CHARLES F. DORAN and JAMES PATRICK SEWELL

ABSTRACT: Anti-Americanism is a form of hostile caricature of American values and behavior. In Canada, hostile caricature of things American is sometimes used by politicians for a functional purpose. A government may appeal to a nationalist streak in some Canadians so as to attempt to stay in office or to unify the country against a purported hostile external influence. Anti-Americanism is undermined by cultural, regional, partisan, and individual differences in viewpoint. Governments that too ardently exploit anti-Americanism are thrown out of office. No latent anti-Americanism exists in Canada.

Charles F. Doran, professor of international relations and director of the Center of Canadian Studies, Johns Hopkins School of Advanced International Studies, Washington, D.C., was Claude Bissell Professor at the University of Toronto (1985-86). He is a member of the Canadian-American Committee and president of the Association for Canadian Studies in the United States (1987-89).

James Patrick Sewell, professor of politics at Brock University, St. Catharines, Ontario, has also taught at the University of Toronto, Princeton, Columbia, and Yale and in 1987 was visiting scholar at the Johns Hopkins School of Advanced International Studies. His current interests include the comparison of Canadian and American approaches to effective international action.

D OES anti-Americanism exist in Canada, one of the most open and friendly countries Americans can visit? To answer this question requires precise definition of "anti-Americanism" and other types of derision. The short answer is "yes and no" or "yes, but with a difference." Perhaps more than for any other polity, Canadian derision of things American is mixed with affection. This article argues that, insofar as the phenomenon of anti-Americanism, so defined, is present in Canada, (1) it must be understood in terms of historical and continuing utility rather than as a core element of Canadian political culture, and (2) it is undercut by regional, communal, and individual differences and by the changing fortunes of political parties as government or opposition— variations that together virtually negate its generalized presence and impact. The former theme receives explicit attention in this article; the latter theme runs throughout it.

Anti-Americanism is an attitude and perception that reflects the perceiving nation as much as the object of perception. Because perception influences or even becomes reality, understanding the bases for the perception and their accuracy is essential for both polities. This is especially so for the United States and Canada; both have a great deal at stake.

DEFINITIONS AND LIMITATIONS

For the purposes of this article, "anti-Americanism" will be defined in a twofold way. First, anti-Americanism involves perceptual distortion such that a caricature of some aspect of behavior or attitude is raised to the level of general belief. In addition, based on that perception, it involves hostility directed toward the government, society, or individuals of that society.

Caricature alone is funny and may even prove salutary. Indeed, one mark of a mature culture is that its votaries can laugh at its actual or alleged shortcomings, including those comically overdrawn by outsiders. Hostility may arise as the result of policy difference or a disparity of interests that goes unassuaged and thus becomes a source of continuing irritation. Hostility alone may become the vehicle for policy alteration and thus for progress, given a modicum of attentiveness by policymakers. Criticism, when specific and objective, is not anti-Americanism. But when perceptual distortion is mixed with hostility, the target is unable through action to correct the negative distortion. Anti-Americanism results from this explosive combination of elements.

An unflattering, though accurate, image of the United States by a foreigner is not anti-Americanism, but hostile caricature is anti-Americanism.[1] Cari-

1. For purposes of this discussion, the attitudes held by the noted philosopher Jean-Paul Sartre regarding East-West relations illustrate to the fullest degree the concept of hostile anti-Americanism (1) because of groundless negative statements about Americans, (2) because of the intentional denial of negative statements about opponents of U.S. policy, and (3) because of Sartre's alleged intellectual commitment to objectivity. On the one hand, Sartre refused to admit that the Soviet Union employed concentration camps even though he possessed evidence of such camps, and on the other he accused General Ridgway, in the absence of any supporting evidence, of using germ warfare in Korea. Such complete distortion of truth seldom, if ever, occurs in the Canadian-U.S. setting because most Canadians are less arrogant about their analytical prowess than Sartre and more subject to the useful self-corrective of cross-border dialogue.

cature achieved through the use of half-truths or insufficient information—that is, by information consciously held back; remember the Ems Dispatch—can likewise constitute anti-Americanism.

Anti-Americanism lends itself to ideological propagation in the way that other isms are cultivated. Information that may or may not be accurate is spread to the uninformed, and hostility is intensified by offering this information as explanation to those bearing grievances. Anti-Americanism presumably germinates where there is a lack of accurate information or where there is purposeful distortion.

Both sets of circumstances are largely absent in Canada. Canadians tend to view information about America and Americans as an unending series of truth tests and hence are not easily persuaded by anti-American explanations. Nor have most Canadians shown themselves to be inordinately susceptible to grievance-mongering, even though opinion leaders with contesting views of what is wrong are not lacking. Thus a quest for anti-Americanism in Canada is apt to unearth fragments of bias held fleetingly by segments of a diverse populace rather than a deep-seated, broad-based hostility. Yet such fragments of anti-Americanism nonetheless often have great significance for the conduct of foreign relations between the two countries. And the uniqueness of Canadian anti-Americanism makes it all the more imperative for both nations to understand.

In one fundamental sense, Canada's very essence is anti-American. Soon after what some Canadians think of as the second North American civil war—the first being the Revolutionary War, which founded the United States—the

Canadian federation was launched. It was a deliberate effort to create a political society distinct from the United States while accommodating both European founding nations. The saga of extending the Dominion from sea to sea similarly bespoke an aim of protecting the Canadian project from its neighbor and its neighbor's way of life. Thus Frank Underhill could later remark that Canadians hold the world's record as the oldest continuing anti-Americans.[2]

If anti-Americanism is a chronic fever, however, it is surely a low-grade one. Today adverse sentiments are apt to be cast in terms of complaints about neglect or insensitivity more often than fears about U.S. takeover. Margaret Atwood redefines the forty-ninth parallel boundary as the world's longest one-way mirror. Nowadays what Americans do to threaten the well-being and say to offend the self-regard of their northern neighbors they are usually thought to do only semiconsciously. Canadian experience is that "Americans have a galling habit of regarding [Canada] as a regional aspect of a national problem."[3]

Canada has long striven to be accepted as a foreign country, preferably as an independent foreign country,[4] and this modest ambition seems often to go unrecognized in the acts and words of those who appear to believe they can have only Canada's and others' best interests at heart. Canada often feels that it is treated as "a kind of aurora

2. Thomas S. Axworthy, ed., *Our American Cousins* (Toronto: James Lorimer, 1987), p. x.
3. John W. Holmes, *Life with Uncle* (Toronto: University of Toronto Press, 1981), p. 45.
4. John W. Holmes, "Canada's Stake in the New Internationalism: Introductory Comments" (Address delivered at Trinity College, University of Toronto, Toronto, Ontario, Canada, 22 May 1986).

borealis on the northern horizon, all reflecting lights without substance"[5]— unless the reflection talks back. How do Americans interpret this talking back? A Michigan congressman has called Canadian criticism of a U.S. policy "downright un-American"; a Rhode Island senator, following a meeting with Prime Minister Brian Mulroney, concluded, "We're lucky to have Muldoon as Prime Minister . . . because he got into office not by American bashing but by saying kind words about us."[6] This article argues that much anti-Americanism in Canada is, in the final analysis, as much a talking back to break the self-image of Canada as a mere reflection of the United States.

The most common form of anti-American statement heard in Canada is the half-truth, or truth absent important contextual information. For instance, public statements by Canadian observers that the United States was "destroying world agricultural markets" with its high price supports were of this type. Lacking was the additional information (1) that the recent flood of American subsidies came as a response to huge European subsidies whose purpose was to offset higher European marginal costs of production and whose

impact was to drive American wheat off Third World markets, and (2) that Canada itself had responded with price supports of a value at least equivalent to U.S. subsidies. How much contextual information is necessary is a matter of judgment.

A particular difficulty in addressing anti-Americanism in the Canadian-U.S. setting is that half-truths about or hostile caricatures of U.S. government policy held by Canadians are almost always likewise held by some sector of U.S. opinion. Can Americans themselves be anti-American? To this non sequitur one can perhaps respond that Americans can sometimes be lamentably misinformed about themselves to the point of hostile caricature and that Canadians should not entirely be blamed if some of this misinformation rubs off on them. It must also be noted that the diversity of viewpoint that Americans recognize and expect in their own country is present in their northern neighbor as well.

By focusing on two important areas, the economic and the defense areas, this article will show how certain aspects of Canadian society and government distinguish the Canadian perception of America from that of other nations and how this perception influences Canadian policies. In brief, the Canadian viewpoint on economic and defense issues is driven by differences in attribute and role, and hence the anti-Americanism in those views is essentially functional in nature. Furthermore, the diversity of viewpoint—individual, communal, and regional—within Canada, on the one hand, and the values and interests Canadians share with Americans, on the other, modulate any tendency to let anti-Americanism become anything more than functional.

5. Quoted by Richard Gwyn, *The 49th Paradox* (Toronto: McClelland and Stewart, 1985), p. 263. John Sloan Dickey maintains that an independent-minded Canada benefits the United States by exposing Americans to "knowledgeable scrutiny from the outside which is free of both the hostility of an adversary and the acquiescence of a sycophant." *Canada and the American Presence* (New York: New York University Press, 1975), p. 139.

6. Quoted in Margaret Royal, "Reviving the Special Relationship: The Mulroney Government and Canada-U.S. Relations" (Paper delivered at the meeting of the Canadian Political Science Association, Hamilton, June 1987). Originally quoted by K. MacQueen et al., "A Ringing Slap at Success," *Macleans*, 31 Mar. 1986, p. 23.

INSTRUMENTALISM OF
HOSTILE CARICATURE

Knowledgeable Americans soon learn that their greatest sin as a nation, from the Canadian perspective, is their geographic location next door to Canada. Their second greatest sin is that they cast a political and economic shadow that is ten times as long as Canada's. A third sin is that they do not seem to realize how Canadians regard this elephantine shadow, cast so often across them. In fact, Americans seem to Canadians always to be facing in another direction, ignoring Canada. Together these sins are difficult to forgive. The emotional result is troublesome for both Canada and the United States. It also is not subject to easy correction.

A Canadian cartoon of 1901 illustrates this Canadian perspective, which has been a difficulty throughout the history of Canadian-American relations. The cartoon pictures Uncle Sam in a sequence of poses reflecting how he and, at the end, the rest of the world will view the rise to world leadership that was visibly within his reach at the beginning of the century. First he is observed in the "American media drug house" indulging freely in a substance labeled "supremacy." In vignettes that follow he "sees himself as the greatest nation on the face of the earth"; "dreams that he controls the world's money and other markets"; "dreams that he has licked all creation, and throws bouquets at himself"; ponders expansively his armed forces as the most powerful and finest, "his daughters the most beautiful, his colleges the best, his statesmen, writers, artists, actors, athletes and possessions the greatest, his merchants the wealthiest and his constitution the grandest in the world." Uncle Sam "gathers the world into his grip and is reaching for the other planets" when he awakens from his reveries to find himself "the cause of much amusement" for onlookers.[7]

Notwithstanding the wisdom underlying the cynicism of the final vignette, the cartoon does not do justice to the shrewd and expedient way in which Canadian leaders have used such a caricature to manage internal problems and to define an international political role. Of course, Canadian leaders are not unique in their instrumental use of hostile caricature to rally others behind them, but here certain features deserve special attention.

One reason for the success of the instrumental caricature for political purposes is that it works within natural limits. A natural brake operates within Canadian politics, restraining any anti-American impulse even as that impulse is being used to the fullest. If Canadian opinion shifts too far in the direction of anti-American attitudes, the country begins to institute policies that make it miss opportunities for gain in bilateral economic and political areas. Canadian public and press opinion is quick to measure these costs, and in response to the new climate of opinion, the dynamics of Canadian political competition yield a new cabinet or a new government to redress the losses. Thus anti-American caricature operates in Canada only when it is a focused and limited form of hostility.

The peculiar nature of Canadian instrumental anti-Americanism arises out of the differences between the two cultures. Despite historical ties, similar cultural traditions, and many mutual or coin-

7. Cartoon signed "Chic/Moon," reprinted in Peter Desbarats and Terry Mosher, *The Hecklers* (Toronto: McClelland and Stewart, 1979), pp. 56-57.

cidental interests, Canada and the United States are very different countries. Differences in political values and institutions within a democratic ethos and differences in international role are among the attributes that most distinguish the two polities. Differences of outlook are bound to arise in this closest of international relationships, and these differences are normally managed with acumen. Anti-Americanism as hostile caricature does not arise naturally at the level of the mass public because the mutual respect and familiarity of the two peoples is too well established. But when policies collide, hostile caricature in some quarters—like as not focused by a political party in opposition—can emerge to impinge upon the Canadian-U.S. relationship.

Hostile caricature on the part of Canadians toward Americans contains more caricature—much of it playful—and less hostility than most brands of anti-Americanism. But caricature of things American in Canada, albeit less hostile, has deeper roots than in other countries. Canada is relatively underpopulated, and the Canadian population borders the United States along a band that stretches for more than 3000 miles. In addition, this population is strikingly segmented in regional and ethnolinguistic terms. The south-north pull continually threatens to overwhelm the east-west axis. Caricature of Americans and American policy, therefore, proves especially useful in Canada because it helps provide the cement to which Canadian politicians from time to time resort in order to keep the polity together. Hostile caricature of Americans and American policy becomes a problem in Canada only when Canadians begin to believe it and let it misdirect them into policy choices that are not beneficial to

the relationship or that are even harmful to their own interests. We will now examine how this instrumentalism works in the two areas of trade and defense.

ECONOMIC ATTITUDES AND
COMMERCIAL BEHAVIOR

Frustration associated with the U.S. political and economic shadow in Canada is sometimes evident in discussions of trade reform when the admixture of cultural identity carries overtones of anti-American feeling. Canadian cultural identity is regarded as in peril because of the American presence. Anything that opens trade between the two polities or increases bilateral trade is, therefore, suspect in certain circles. Hostile caricature emerges when the United States is thought to be purposefully attempting to undermine the Canadian identity. The image is sometimes carried further in that the United States is held not only to be trying to Americanize Canada but to fragment the polity or perhaps even to annex portions of Canada. These views are expressed most strongly on the political Left and in Ontario, where the heart of the industrial base is located and where a large proportion of the population—predominantly English speaking—lives. Significantly, however, these fears of cultural takeover are clung to most strongly by members of the intellectual elite rather than by the mass public. According to one viewpoint, the masses manifest greater confidence in the vitality and autonomy of Canadian values and institutions; from another viewpoint, they manifest merely an overriding appetite for the consumption of American media offerings. Elite opinion regards the less educated masses as indifferent to their cultural fate and as easy targets for Americanization.

Fear of cultural takeover containing anti-American overtones has historical roots. It was, after all, an errant statement from the U.S. Senate floor asserting that the next step was annexation of Canada that allegedly destroyed the chances for a free-trade agreement with Canada in 1911 and that eventually helped to bring down the Laurier government. Americans, however, were scarcely serious about such loose talk, whereas Canadian fears, like all fears, were looking for something upon which to feed. Anti-Americanism has a paranoid side that sometimes can undo self-interest.

Analytically, the problem with the mythology of Americanization and the alleged desire to fragment or annex is that in seeking to counter falsehood, the tendency may be to go too far in the opposite direction. It is easy to show, for example, that the true U.S. interest in Canadian-U.S. relations is a strong and united Canada. What does not follow is that Canada has no difficulty in maintaining unity or that the Canadian identity is robust. Nor can one deny the obvious overflow of values and behavior across a border that is so long and porous. Perhaps the surprising thing is that this overflow leaves regional differences in Canada virtually untouched. Vancouver is more interested in the Pacific Rim than is central Canada, and Halifax follows in its local newspapers the daily activities of London, England, in a way found nowhere else in either Canada or the United States. But overflow does occur, as evidenced by architectural styles in Windsor, Ontario, even if handguns are banned and the crime rate is remarkably low, certainly judged by the standards across the bridge in Detroit, Michigan.

Anti-American nuance is found in the occasional implication that the United States would prefer a fragmented to a united Canada or that Washington, D.C., is prepared to gobble up portions of Canada at the smallest opportunity. Similarly distorted is the view held by a number of Canadians that trade itself is responsible for the erosion of patriotism or nation-state affinity. Indeed there is perversity here. Historically, high tariffs, more recently reduced in the Tokyo Round, created alienation within Canada, denying the West and the Maritimes the opportunity to trade to the fullest extent in north-south terms, where commodity and raw material sales brought the most revenue and imported manufactured products were cheapest; instead, trade was diverted toward central Canada. Likewise, the present balkanization of Canada through buy-province preferences and provincial nontariff barriers, as the distinguished MacDonald Commission observed, is not contributing to political unity but to its opposite. Thus trade has become a cultural whipping boy in Canada when it is at best neutral and could possibly be made to support political unity within Canada through the freer flow of goods and services.

Yet the mysterious linkage between trade and culture has a more immediate focus in the contemporary trade talks, namely, the so-called cultural industries. Here misconception parts with caricature. Because Canadians allow virtually 100 percent of their feature films to be distributed by foreign-owned companies, import the larger fraction of their textbooks, listen to more foreign-recorded popular music than Canadian, read more American magazines than Canadian, and watch more U.S. television programming than that produced at home, they believe that their own cultural industries must receive continued subsidy and protection. From the American perspective, this desire for protection, like any other, is economically motivated. Distribution of U.S.-made films, for example, is a large earner of foreign exchange worldwide. But from the Canadian perspective, the continued participation of Canadian owners, managers, producers, writers, and performers in work that has Canadian content can readily appear as a matter of cultural survival. Economics is secondary.

Hostile caricature is not present in this aspect of the trade-cum-culture discussion, but American misconception quite possibly is. When Canadians say to Americans, "Put yourself in our cultural shoes," this intellectual exercise is quite revealing of the Canadian quandary. If put in Canadian shoes, Americans would express feelings on this aspect of the economic-cultural dimension not dissimilar to the present Canadian outcry.

A final area of gross misconception verging upon caricature occurs in the realm of U.S. foreign investment. Despite recent efforts by the Mulroney government to encourage foreign investment, to remove constraints on U.S. investment in the energy industry, and to tether the foreign investment screening agency, refurbished as Investment Canada, a lingering suspicion in the U.S. business community holds that curbs on U.S. foreign investment in one industry or another at some time in the future are likely to return. Part of the reasoning is that the level of U.S. foreign investment remains very high, perhaps 80 percent of the total foreign investment in manufacturing, for example, with that total itself amounting to almost 40

percent of all manufacturing investment in Canada. But another part of the reasoning is that U.S. ownership is often the subject of caricature in Canada.

There is a sense, for example, that American firms in Canada are not good corporate citizens. They do not do much research and development, they tend to produce high-cost facsimiles of American products only for the domestic Canadian market, they prefer to import factor inputs rather than to rely on Canadian sources, and they tend to avoid competition with lines of production emanating from their U.S. plants. American firms do not so much dispute these accusations as criticize the explanations offered for the behavior. In other words, hostile caricature emerges, according to them, because of half-truths regarding commercial practice.

Foreign-owned plants of the type that are common in Canada arise because investment seeks to get inside tariff walls. It is protected investment like that of domestic Canadian firms and is not competitive by world standards. Therefore, exports outside the protected Canadian market are unlikely. Neither Canadian-owned firms nor foreign-owned firms do much research and development. But in any case, whatever research and development is done occurs at the great university-industrial research centers near the home offices. Research tends to thrive on concentration.

The instrumentalism of anti-Americanism in Canada is also exemplified at the corporate and individual levels. This instrumentalism is interesting because of the remediability of the policy problems revealed. It is also interesting because it further illustrates the sociopsychological dynamic that underlies the peculiar type of anti-Americanism found in Canada.

American corporations with operations in Canada are observing a strange attitudinal problem on the part of their Canadian nationals employed in Canada. These Canadian nationals "want to do business with virtually anyone else but the home office in the United States."[8] What is the origin of this alienation? The Canadian employee is bitter, and this bitterness is directed at American counterparts and superiors within the same corporate hierarchy. The problem is so severe that middle management must spend an inordinant amount of time mediating disputes between the home office in the United States and the branch in Canada.

Probing more deeply, one finds the source of the alienation, a source that in part is rooted in the public policies of the two federal governments.[9] Canadian employees in Canadian branch enterprises describe their situation as that of a ghetto. Their prospects for mobility within the corporate hierarchy at the home office are virtually nil. The reason for this ghettoization is that immigration rules between the two countries foreclose mobility. Obtaining a green card to work in the United States is difficult, slow, and expensive. Likewise, obtaining the right to work in Canada for an American is nearly impossible. Hence the branch operation in Canada employs almost no Americans, and Canadian managers have no future in the top administrative ranks of the firm in the United States. Bit by bit the Canadian employee becomes more and more disenchanted, blaming the American firm for his or her frustration and lack of job mobility.

Opening up the border to greater labor mobility would ease this instrumental anti-Americanism. Resentment that is manifested as anti-Americanism would disappear. A better balance of Canadians and Americans throughout each level of the corporate hierarchy would probably erase much of the bitterness and focused irritation. Canada may fear a talent drain from easier cross-border mobility, yet government-imposed restrictions are scarcely the answer. Creating the right job atmosphere and opportunities at home is the only plausible longer-term response. Neither government may want to open up the border to easier immigration in a period of potentially high unemployment, yet such a public policy step is the key to healthier corporate and individual attitudes in Canada toward the United States and perhaps vice versa.

8. Confidential interview with a manager of a *Fortune* 500 firm, 8 Sep. 1987. Expressed in terms of organization theory, this response is a breakdown of the "crucial determinant," the "organization's response to the environment." W. G. Bennis, "A Funny Thing Happened on the Way to the Future," *American Psychologist*, 25(7): 595-608 (1970).

9. The problem of the social mobility of the individual and the need for a sense of personal control vis-à-vis the corporation is a principal theme of the twentieth century. Pareto emphasized individual mobility in his "circulation of elites." T. B. Bottomore, *Elites and Society* (New York: Norton, 1974), p. 105. Democracy within firms is part of the recent answer. Robert A. Dahl, *A Preface to Economic Democracy* (Berkeley: University of California Press, 1985), pp. 111-35. In the Canadian-U.S. context, intercountry restrictions on immigration hinder mobility within the firm and lead to anti-Americanism on the part of the frustrated Canadian employee.

CONCEPTION AND MISPERCEPTION OF U.S. DEFENSE POLICY

Canada is a loyal member of the North Atlantic Treaty Organization and a partner with the United States in the North American Aerospace Defense Command. While its defense spending in the past as a percentage of gross national product has been near the bottom of the North Atlantic alliance countries despite its wealth, a new Canadian defense policy under Prime Minister Mulroney promises changes that are aimed at bolstering Canadian territorial sovereignty at the same time that it attempts to reconcentrate its defense effort on the Central Front in Europe. Each of these changes is deeply affected by how Canadians from all three political parties—the federally ruling Progressive Conservative Party; the principal opposition party, the Liberals; and the socialist social democratic party, the New Democrats—see the United States. Although most Canadian opinion is stable and generally supportive of alliance goals, attitudes in some circles tend to characterize defense policy narrowly as a mere confrontation between the United States and the Soviet Union, Canada's other superpower neighbor. According to these attitudes, "Canada has no enemies."

The characterization of the U.S. defense role vis-à-vis Canada is a caricature in a number of respects. The notion that defense is not collective but only reflects a disagreement between the United States and the Soviet Union is a troubling distortion. It suggests that Canada has no role in collective defense, cannot affect alliance decision making, and has little responsibility for the security of others. If Canada has no enemies, either present or potential, it has no need of security beyond standing on guard in defense of its own sovereignty and no responsibility for helping to defend others in its own self-interest. Moreover, if the East-West confrontation can be oversimplified to a dispute between the Unit-

ed States and the Soviet Union alone, the dispute can more readily be attributed to the way the United States conducts its foreign policy. The next step is an easy one to the conclusion that the only reason the United States, in contrast to Canada, has enemies is that the United States has a belligerent foreign policy that leans on opponents and friends alike. A logical extension of the idea that defense is not collective is that there is no need for collective defense.

This notion that America's allies have nothing at stake in the East-West confrontation was reinforced by policies of the Reagan administration that appeared unilateral, especially in implementation, despite efforts at earlier consultation. U.S. leadership endeavors, regarding, for example, a response to the Afghanistan invasion and debate over the Siberian pipeline, tended to isolate U.S. foreign policy and gave support to the caricature of a one-on-one U.S.-Soviet quarrel. For those seeking reinforcement for the unilateralist thesis, the invasion of Grenada, the bombing of Libya, and even the arranged exodus of the dictators Duvalier and Marcos all looked like confirmation. A caricature of American foreign policy emerged that some sectors of opinion in Canada equated with the image of the cowboy.

One of the dangers of the cowboy caricature lies in the strategic nuclear field. For those who relish a cowboy image of American foreign policy, nuclear war is more likely to occur because of an intemperate American policy than because of any threat, direct or indirect, stemming from the Soviet Union. While many members of the Canadian peace movement see U.S. alliance leadership realistically, others find the cowboy image of U.S. foreign policy extremely appealing as a source of caricature and at the same time extremely frightening because they begin actually to believe the caricature.

Perhaps the principal area in which U.S. foreign policy has been subject to caricature and where this caricature has in turn impinged negatively on U.S. interests concerns the Canadian sovereignty debate. To a degree, American misunderstanding of Canadian politics brought about the hostile caricature of the U.S. position. On two recent occasions, the United States has attempted to cross the Northwest Passage, first with the oil tanker *Manhattan*, more recently with the icebreaker *Polar Sea*. Each time Canadian opinion was extremely negative and the Canadian government responded with legislation that in effect expanded Canadian claims to the territorial sea and adjacent waters.

Caricature emerges in that the United States is seen as wanting to divide up Canadian territory and to trade Canadian sovereignty over its own territory for some ephemeral idea of collective defense. The United States is cast in the role of an expansionist power seeking to subjugate and divide an enfeebled and overly compliant Canadian polity.

It is not hyperbolic to observe that the most recent Canadian defense white paper would not have been written in the way that it was but for the existence of the caricature of U.S. interests in the Arctic. The commitment to build 10 to 12 nuclear submarines, which is at the core of the white paper, is designed to appease Canadian opinion concerned with a proper assertion of sovereignty over Canadian territory. To the extent that the opportunity costs are very high for this defense policy extending well into the 1990s, the United States has the caricature of its own foreign policy

initiatives and its own prior foreign policy insensitivities to thank. The commitment to a defense of territorial sovereignty may well come at the expense of a commitment to European defense, not out of indifference or pique regarding European defense but out of lack of sufficient expenditures to cover all of Canada's defense priorities.

Thus hostile caricature of U.S. defense intentions and behavior is not absent from some discussion of overall defense objectives in Canada. A lack of interest in defense questions, some observers may protest, is a greater danger than misperception and distortion. Yet when caricature mixes with disinterest, any government in Ottawa finds the formulation of a plausible and effective defense policy that has the interests of alliance stability at its heart an extremely tough enterprise.

DOES LATENT ANTI-AMERICANISM EXIST IN CANADA?

An older strand of thinking in some Canadian quarters held that American ways were culturally inferior to English ways. Given that Canada was an English offshoot, as viewers in these quarters saw it, Canadians were bequeathed a relatively lofty position in the social firmament. That the bases of such sentiments were eroding in the play of economic and political forces was suggested fictionally as early as 1904 by Sara Jeannette Duncan's *Imperialist*, set in a controversy over Canada's trade and identification with Britain as compared to the United States.[10] But the assumption of English cultural superiority

10. Republished with an introduction by Claude Bissell (Toronto: McClelland and Stewart, 1971).

remained strong during the 1940s and 1950s. If today this premise is much less evident, no doubt it is due to a variety of factors, among them the predominance of U.S. mass media—really their global predominance—and the decreasingly English composition and orientation of the peoples of Canada. In addition, the English, among others, apparently have Americanized themselves, providing Anglo Canadians with a weaker reference point for discrimination than before. Canadians so inclined have, therefore, had to develop other expressions of their status consciousness.

Robert Fulford calls the earlier attitude the old anti-Americanism, and against it he contrasts a more recent brand of outspoken hostility: "The new anti-Americanism begins with the proposition that the United States is a colossal empire and a corrupt one, and that its imperial designs are forcing its corrupt nature on us."[11] George Grant might arguably be called a spiritual forefather of the newer anti-Americanism.[12] Lesser and more hysterical figures followed during the 1960s. Many of the roots of the newer anti-Americanism are indigenous to North America. Its major impulse arose from the U.S. military engagement in Southeast Asia and gained strength with a tide of draftable, often vocal young Americans seeking haven in Canada.

Fulford's new anti-Americanism, which he had feared might prove as

crippling to the Canadian spirit as had the old anti-Americanism, weakened during the 1970s, but it lives on in a quiescent phase. The corrupt-colossus thesis draws most of its sustenance today from issues in which Canadian interests are directly engaged with the United States.[13] Some of these have been considered in the preceding pages. At the same time, a knowing, we-have-seen-this-before air pervades certain Canadian circles when the U.S. militarization of yet another part of the world is observed. The Canadian conscience—what Dean Acheson, at a proper distance from his Toronto heritage, once derided as the "stern daughter of the voice of God"—asks today whether the spirit of can-do does not deserve checking and balancing by the question of should-do.

Canadians also increasingly criticize American political institutions. Over the years, thoughtful Canadians have taken quiet satisfaction in their own system; of late, they have disparaged more publicly that of their neighbors. This forthrightness may arise partly from a new Canadian self-respect born of major, if uncompleted, constitutional successes at home. No doubt it is emboldened by the U.S. executive absurdities exhibited during the 1987 Irangate and watched like a morality play north of the border. Today the colossus is not deemed corrupt so much as "tired and a bit senile" by a wise and moderate observer who is "still betting on the good guys" but recalls for their reflection Edmund Burke's 22 March 1775 praise of magnanimity in politics and his admonition to the British, in the face of rebellion overseas, that "a great empire

11. "The New Anti-Americanism," *Saturday Night* (Mar. 1970). Fulford was editor of this magazine at the time. Reprinted in Hugh Innis, ed., *Americanization* (Toronto: McGraw-Hill, Ryerson, 1972), pp. 18-20.

12. Grant would deserve this recognition especially because of his seminal *Lament for a Nation* (Toronto: McClelland and Stewart, 1965), republished by Macmillan of Canada in 1978 and thereafter.

13. Cf. Stephen Clarkson, *Canada and the Reagan Challenge* (Toronto: James Lorimer, 1982).

and little minds go ill together."[14] Nor, despite Canada's own debt problems, does U.S. standing as a super-debtor counsel silence in the politically charged atmosphere of Canadian-U.S. trade talks.[15] Certainly much of the new and uncharacteristic outspokenness stems from Canadian frustration in dealing with a government that will not, perhaps cannot, bind its several institutional parts, even in commitments with a friendly neighbor—even though the relations between Ottawa and the provinces seem parallel from a southerly vantage point. Whatever the constellation of causes, however, this criticism bears pondering, if only because it highlights important differences between the two systems.

Canadians likewise take seriously their credo of peace, order, and good government. Reflective Canadians are apt to contrast it with the more individualist—if not hedonist—American ode to life, liberty, and the pursuit of happiness. Surely freedom is important to Canadians, who by and large sense no shortage of it, but authority looms much larger in their system than it does in the United States. One Royal Canadian Air Farce skit depicts an attempted bank heist thwarted by the teller, who insists that the robbers not jump the waiting line. Most Canadians feel that freedom and authority have always stood in balance within their system; some feel that the two have never been accommodated within that of their neighbors. Canadians find it difficult to understand how Americans perpetuate their license

to bear arms and foul their own—and others'—nests. Of course, Canada has its own proponents of the unencumbered right to tote guns and its practitioners of pollution. The writ of the peaceable kingdom, moreover, has never run to hockey rinks and box lacrosse arenas. But Canadians are conditioned to hear and read about those who run amok and of other displays of violence and self-indulgence in the republic next door, and in their habitual perspective they are given ample opportunity to stay in training.

Good government means strong government, tough government, ever-present government, as Pierre Berton emphasizes.[16] More invidious, to reflective Canadians it means effective government and also responsible government as only a parliamentary form such as their own can yield. A Canadian sees the U.S. Constitution as "antiquated," providing a "government with no one in charge."[17] Never does doubt arise in Canada about who is accountable for budgets and for other functions of governance.

Canadians also tend to draw tacit distinctions when they use the phrase "good society" and similar words. Upon occasion, Canada's nationally read newspaper has made quite explicit the contrasts of public policy between Canada and its southern neighbor, as, for instance, in an editorial response to Pres-

14. John W. Holmes, "The Future of the American Empire" (Speech delivered at the Couchiching Institute on Public Affairs, Geneva Park, Lake Couchiching, Ontario, Canada, 6 Aug. 1987).

15. Henry Hess, "Free Trade with 'Dying Star' Is Poorly Timed, Experts Warn," *Globe and Mail*, 8 Aug. 1987.

16. *Why We Act Like Canadians* (Toronto: McClelland and Stewart, 1982), esp. chap. 1. Good government also means expensive government, as James A. Gibson explains in contrasting the two systems. "Principles of Partnership," in *The Role of Canada in North America*, Public Lectures of the New York Central District High School Board (New York: New York City Government, 1966).

17. Holmes, "Future of the American Empire."

ident Reagan's 1986 State of the Union address. The *Globe and Mail* quotes Reagan's claim that the United States is "the model to which the world once again turns," then offers a series of uncomplimentary comments on American social programs:

We do not turn to the United States as a model of social justice or even intelligent self-interest when it comes to domestic policy. Far from it. . . . America is not the ideal . . . in many of the civilized aspects of life, though the dynamism of the U.S. economy is impressive and attractive. America pays too little attention to the community.[18]

The editorial suggests alternative national models, including Canada.

These criticisms of American political institutions and values hardly approach anti-Americanism as defined previously in these pages. For one thing, Canadians are too diverse to see anything one way. Some Canadians covet the Great Republic's political system. Even among those who are critical, silent dismay, private smugness, and quiet pity are more common reactions than the newfound public candor. Many see no past American pattern and believe that a better day will come with the passing of the current presidency. Others, less hopeful about human succession, pin the blame for ineffectuality on Congress. If some Canadian views seem distorted, it may be recalled that the distortion is often shared by various individuals and groups in the American polity itself.

Nor for the most part are these Ca-

nadian criticisms of the American political system really hostile. Thus the second necessary element of anti-Americanism also remains unfulfilled here. Hostility does overcome humor, however, when the United States, whether viewed as a system or as particular individuals making official decisions, seems arbitrary in economic actions toward Canada or unreliable in reaching firm bilateral economic and political— including environmental—agreements and keeping them. It seems that anti-Americanism occurs in Canada only when it is politically functional.

Perhaps the most useful way to interpret current views of America is in Canadian terms. Just as it is wrong to label recent outbursts anti-Americanism, it would be somewhat misleading to call them the expression of a new Canadian nationalism. Nationalism, at least in a singular form, has always been resisted by the multiple cultures with discrepant historical memories settled mosaiclike across this second-broadest land mass. The choice of Ottawa as a political meeting ground of Francophones and Anglophones, more recently with newer comers, continues to say more about Canada than does the sign designating this city the "nation's capital." Much, too, is revealed of Canada by the fact, let alone the substance, of the periodic summits of 11 first ministers—the prime minister and 10 provincial premiers. At this writing, Canadians are arguing among themselves about whether or not too much of the remaining power of the federal government is being surrendered to all the provinces in order to bring Quebec on board the new constitution. It has, then, been sufficient challenge for Canadians to hold together their state without trying to build a nation. The recent rise

---

18. "That American Model," 7 Feb. 1986. "When we look at Americans," says Allan Gotlieb, Canadian ambassador to the United States, "we often do so to seek reassurance about our image of ourselves." "Some Canadian Myths about the United States" (Address delivered at the Empire Club, Toronto, Canada, 9 Apr. 1987).

in standing of the New Democratic Party, a political party less given to pro-U.S. posturing than so-called Turneroney has been during the post-Trudeau 1980s, shows that instrumentalism played on the distinctiveness of Canada still helps.

Yet today a gentle pride also suffuses many segments of the Canadian populace. Canada's leaders express this pride; others partake of their vision. Canada has long been in the making and now Canadians sense that it has come of age. The willingness to undertake serious trade talks with the United States is but one sign of a new spirit of self-confidence. Nobody has articulated the vision better over the years than has Mr. Canada, John W. Holmes:

Canada's destiny, I believe, is to be the most international of all countries. . . . We are a modern state designed to protect and further the interests of diverse peoples, not to weld them into some mystical unity. It is a model far more appropriate to the needs of other new states than those which have generated wars over language and totems.[19]

The twenty-first is to be Canada's century, and it approaches.

One seeks hard to find, let alone isolate, traces of anti-Americanism in Canada. Evidence once identified tends

19. "Canada's Role in International Organizations," in Role of Canada in North America; Holmes, Life with Uncle, p. 116.

to dissolve when brought directly into contact with the individual American. Whatever their view of Uncle Sam as an abstraction, Canadians for the most part show themselves to be genuinely fond of their American cousins in the flesh. Even regarding the states as a system, Canadian admiration far exceeds Canadian criticism. Above all, Canadians envy Americans their postal service.

CONCLUSION

Unless Americans understand the instrumental uses of hostile caricature in the Canadian context, they may become alarmed at the anti-Americanism that periodically is detected. But just as Americans sometimes exaggerate the significance of the noise that characterizes federal-provincial relations in Canada, fearing that it means the fabric of unity is being torn asunder, so Americans sometimes overreact to hostile statement or misguided attribution stemming from north of the border. A useful tip to remember is this. Anything Canadians say in criticism about Americans pales when compared to what they say about each other. As far as Canadian cohesion is concerned, if the United States did not exist, Ottawa would have to invent it. A little sensitivity in Washington to these political realities will serve both countries best.

Anti-Americanism in Western Europe

By HERBERT J. SPIRO

ABSTRACT: Anti-Americanism consists not of opposition to particular policies but of "persistent patterns of gross criticism of the main values of the U.S. Constitution." It is a historic attitude of the ruling classes in continental Europe, to whom every American success meant a failure of their own, of either prediction or achievement or both. Ordinary Europeans have generally admired the United States, to the point of migrating there. Americans have not reciprocated with anti-Europism, perhaps because of Europe's nonexistence as an entity and the waning weight of its components. Today, anti-Americanists damn the United States if it does and if it does not, for U.S. security, economic, and cultural policies. They resent the American conversion of the primacy of foreign policy into the primacy of domestic politics. Anti-Americanism will diminish, however, as the procedures of American domestic politics spread over the world.

Herbert J. Spiro has been the professor of politics at the John F. Kennedy Institute for North American Studies of the Free University of Berlin since 1980. He served as a member of the Policy Planning Staff, Department of State, from 1970 to 1975, and as U.S. ambassador to Cameroon from 1975 to 1977. His books include A New Foreign Policy Consensus?; Politics as the Master Science; World Politics; The Global System; *and* Government by Constitution.

UNDER the headline "Statue of Truman in Athens, Bombed in 1986, Is Restored,"the *New York Times* reported, "The Greek left condemns the Truman Doctrine and Marshall Plan aid as representative of American domination over Greek political affairs. The pro-Moscow Greek Communist Party today charged that the restoration of the statue 'conflicts with the anti-American sentiments of the Greek people.'"[1] The story suggests that there are at least four different kinds of attitudes that are referred to as anti-Americanism:

—the popular kind, or people's anti-Americanism, which the Communist Party here invoked, but without much credibility, as the statue had in fact just been restored to its previous pedestal without visible or audible popular opposition;

—cold war, or anti-anti-Communist, anti-Americanism, which the Greek Communist Party was trying, unsuccessfully, to perpetuate or revive in this case;

—policy-specific anti-Americanism, which was tested in this instance, as approval for the restoration had to be obtained from Prime Minister Andreas Papandreou, who received his Ph.D. in economics from Harvard University and served as a professor at the University of California in Berkeley for many years; and

—elite, or ruling-class, anti-Americanism, which will be the main focus of this article.

We can most easily eliminate policy-specific attitudes and actions from our

purview. It is a mistake to describe as anti-Americanism temporary opposition to the temporary policies of this or that administration in Washington. This is illustrated by support for, and participation in, European antinuclear demonstrations by such quintessentially American models as Coretta Scott King, Daniel Ellsberg, and Harry Belafonte. On the contrary, instead of evincing anti-Americanism, most if not all circumstantial European opposition to specific policies of successive administrations in Washington is largely a derivative product of domestic opposition to the same policies previously articulated within the United States.

For example, in the case of the Green Party in the Federal Republic of Germany, Petra Kelly, one of its principal founders and leaders, graduated from an American high school and the American University in Washington, D.C., and worked for the presidential campaign of Robert Kennedy. She obviously learned a general substantive political stance and the possibly transplantable procedures of the politics of protest from a long experience in the United States during her impressionable youth. That is not the stuff of which genuine anti-Americanism is made.

Nevertheless, Petra Kelly during antinuclear demonstrations and Prime Minister Papandreou during tough negotiations with the United States over naval base renewals within the North Atlantic Treaty Organization—which also includes Turkey, Greece's archenemy—have some things in common. Both returned from deep immersion, and engagement, in American democratic—and Democratic—popular politics to their comparatively hierarchic, elitist, closed, conservative-to-reactionary home countries. They con-

1. "Statue of Truman in Athens, Bombed in 1986, Is Restored," *New York Times*, 7 Aug. 1987.

tributed considerably to introducing to
West Germany and Greece, respectively,
greater use of the procedures of American domestic politics. In the course of
doing so, they came into conflict with
some foreign policies of the Carter and
Reagan administrations. They shared
their grounds for this opposition with
some Americans, who opposed specific
policies of these administrations within
the domestic politics of the United
States.

In consequence, these two, and similar, European elected leaders were
bound to develop, at the least, a certain
ambivalence toward the United States.
Here they had been trying, in a sense, to
bring the American democratic outlook
and American methods of politics, as
they understood these, to their compatriots, only to run smack into the
naked use of power by the U.S. government, more or less openly aligned with
conservative forces in both Germany
and Greece. But no matter how strong
the ambivalences generated by such experiences, they do not amount to the
kind of permanent or endemic anti-
Americanism, which is the subject matter of this issue of *The Annals.*

THE CORE OF
ANTI-AMERICANISM

What, then, is the core of anti-Americanism? To paraphrase the act of Congress requiring annual reports on human
rights violations around the world, I
find anti-Americanism wherever there is
a persistent pattern of gross criticism of
the main values enshrined in the U.S.
Constitution. These values are largely
procedural ones, formulated negatively
as prohibitions on what government
may do to citizens. For example, "Congress shall make no law . . . abridging the

freedom of speech, or of the press"; "no
religious test shall ever be required as a
qualification to any office"; "the right of
the people to keep and bear arms, shall
not be infringed." Government may
literally do nothing, either internally or
externally, without the consent of officers regularly elected by the voters. This
means, very concretely, that specific
government actions and policies are
made acceptable not by the expertise,
the heritage, the education, the con-
nections, even the length of service to
the government of the United States, or
the aura of mystery—or, for that matter,
of publicity—of the persons putting
them into effect, but by the consent of
the governed, given directly and indirectly through elections, confir-
mations, appropriations, public criticism, debate, and discussion in the
widest meaning of the term.

Whatever the actual manifestations
of anti-Americanism may be at any one
time, in any particular country of Western Europe, its source can be traced
back to either the incomprehension or
the rejection of the procedural constitu-
tionalism and substantive democracy of
the United States of America. A random
sampling:

—Lord Keynes's statement to a U.S.
  delegation: "But you don't *have* a
  government in the ordinary sense
  of the word," because "the Administration, not being in control of
  Congress, is not in a position to
  enter into commitments on anything";[2]
—West German Chancellor Helmut
  Schmidt's condescension toward
  President Jimmy Carter's alleged

2. Quoted by Raymond Vernon, "International Trade Policy in the 1980s," *International
Studies Quarterly,* 26:485 (1982).

lack of economic expertise and general intelligence;

—widespread fears among continental Europeans after President Reagan's first election about his, and his team's, alleged lack of expertise about foreign policy in general and Europe in particular, which some Americans—though not I—might see as a case of having been prematurely right for the wrong reasons;

—President DeGaulle's refusal to tie France's military power in with NATO; and

—Continental reactions to both the Watergate and the Iran-contra affairs of a cynical "So what?" and the question, "Why drag it all out into the open?"

THE ROOTS OF ANTI-AMERICANISM

The historical roots of continental European anti-Americanism are easy to identify. But first, the rather different British attitude should be explained. The British were the first to become reconciled to the loss of their colonies. They learned from that experience to grant their other dependent territories independence after the colonists, and/or the natives, had made anti-British efforts more or less analogous to those of the fathers of American independence. Even the British governing class—whose members rightfully claim continuity with that of 1776—can console themselves over the American succession to world primacy the way parents do over the greater success of their offspring. Moreover, just as this class maintained its sway at home by means of the practice of co-optation from below, so it succeeded, into the 1950s, in maintaining Britain's global influence in part by means of co-opting the United States from the outside.

But to the Continental elites, every American success has always appeared like a failure of their own, for a variety of combinations of reasons. The United States simply could not succeed, certainly not to the extent it actually did, outstripping each of the European powers separately and all of them combined, either in terms of military, economic, diplomatic, and cultural power or as the largest and oldest continuously functioning constitutional democracy. The United States could not succeed, in the views of the Continental ruling classes, because:

—its rationalist constitutional founding cut the United States off from the only true sources of legitimacy and cohesion recognized in Europe: tradition, descent, religion, geography, tribalism as it evolved into nationalism, and the omnipotent and ubiquitous state's monopoly of the organized means of violence;

—it had no standing army, needing none against Canada and Mexico, and without a standing army, and with its prevailing atomistic individualism, it was unlikely to achieve the kind of unity without which a great national state cannot be built, according to Hegel;[3]

—its population, though never "melted" in any "pot," was too multiracial, and no single pure race predominated, depriving it of the

3. Robert M. Hutchins and Mortimer J. Adler, eds., *Great Books of the Western World*, vol. 46, *Philosophie der Geschichte*, by G.W.F. Hegel (Chicago: Encyclopaedia Britannica Educational Corporation, 1952), pp. 192-93.

driving biological energy required for great cultural achievement; and —it lacked a ruling class, or an aristocracy, or had a more or less phony substitute for one—for example, according to Tocqueville, the lawyers.[4]

Mention of Tocqueville calls for an admission. Neither were all members of Continental ruling classes anti-American, nor was each one, whose anti-American sentiments or actions are on the record, consistent in his or her attitudes. Like their contemporary successors, many were ambivalent, like Tocqueville himself, Friedrich Engels, and Goethe. In most cases, the pro-American side of their ambivalence was rather condescending, providing a foundation for current European critiques of the American "experiment" as simply having gone wrong.

All these defects or deficiencies should have permanently kept the transatlantic republic from becoming a power like the old great powers of Europe, with which the Founders in the Declaration of Independence had both sought, and declared, their full equality. As the United States did nevertheless achieve and then transcend the original European arch-model, its Continental critics and foes would be forced to question their own fundamental assumptions about the existence of their states, the *raison d'être* of their *raisons d'état*. Either they were right about themselves, in which case the United States should never have amounted to much; or the United States would move from strength to strength,

to become the primary model for all the world, and their European states would lose—as they have lost—both actual power and intellectual self-esteem. Hence their basic animosity, or at least ambivalence, toward the United States today.

ANTI-AMERICANISM AS A CLASS PHENOMENON

Let me propose three very simple theses, though, in any other context I would call them hunches, based as they are on a lifetime's immersion in the living subject matter:

1. Anti-Americanism has been endemic among the ruling classes in continental Europe since 1776 at the latest.

2. Ordinary continental Europeans have generally shown themselves to be pro-American, sometimes existentially and enthusiastically so.

3. The British governing class has shown an attitude that could easily be mistaken for anti-Americanism but has in fact always come closer to the detached critical posture English parents take toward their sons in order to further the latter's independence and, thereby, their progressively improving tenure in whatever bequest the parents leave them.

To say that there is no anti-Americanism in Great Britain, compared with Continental countries, amounts to only a slight understatement. At the popular level, attitudes can perhaps best be illustrated by the well-meant jocular finding, made at the high point of the American military presence in Britain during World War II: "The trouble with the GIs is that they're overpaid, oversexed, and over here." There has been virtually no cold war anti-Americanism and less of the policy-specific kind than in major Continental countries, regardless of wheth-

4. Alexis de Tocqueville, *Democracy in America* (New York: Random House, Vintage, 1944), 1:288. Cf. Herbert J. Spiro, *Government by Constitution: The Political Systems of Democracy* (New York: Random House, 1959), pp. 282-83.

er Conservative or Labour governments have been in office. An additional reason for this absence of anti-Americanism may be the lack of a separate intelligentsia in Britain. There are, of course, people whose objective functions in society are very similar to those of intellectuals on the Continent. Because of the governing class's practice of co-optation, however, these intellectuals have only rarely had occasion to let lack of tangible responsibilities tempt them to construct the kind of ideologies that easily generate endemic anti-Americanism on the Continent.

The ruling classes of continental European countries, including their intelligentsia—whether "utopian" or "ideological" in Karl Mannheim's sense[5]—evinced anti-Americanism in its various forms long before the United States reached its current position, poorly described as a "superpower." That term suggests that the United States has achieved an enhanced measure of the status, marked mainly by military and economic power, that Britain, France, and Spain possessed at one time or another and that the United States shares in today's so-called bipolar world with the Soviet Union, that is, a quantitative enlargement of a historical model altogether familiar to Europe's ruling classes. If that were all they saw in the United States of America, their own historical perspective and patience, inbred by their deep knowledge and awareness of the scientifically established past, as propagated by their intelligentsia, would reconcile them to the passing of the mantle to another imperial power, ruled by another ruling class, in which they recognize an updated mirror image

of themselves in their own most powerful period. It is precisely the fact that they cannot recognize anyone much like themselves, in what they consider to be more or less analogous to a ruling class in the United States, that turns a merely critical attitude into the mind-set of anti-Americanism. This mind-set of contemporary ruling classes in continental European countries continues the attitudes of their nineteenth-century forerunners—like Hegel and perhaps Mrs. Trollope[6]—who were put off or puzzled by what they saw as the absence of a ruling class in the United States. Tocqueville's view of American journalists stands in the same line of descent:

The hallmark of the American journalist is a direct and coarse attack, without any subtleties, on the passion of his readers; he disregards principles to seize on people, following them into their private lives and laying bare their weaknesses and their vices. That is a deplorable abuse of the powers of thought.[7]

Ordinary Europeans, on the other hand, have shown their pro-Americanism by voting with their feet or moving to the United States on bottoms, that is, ships, whose ruling-class owners profited from mass passages in steerage. A minority of ordinary Europeans migrated to the United States, and the majority who stayed in Europe generally showed much more positive attitudes toward things and people American than their intellectual, social, and economic betters. In fact, one useful criterion for distinguishing between mem-

5. Karl Mannheim, *Ideology and Utopia: An Introduction to the Sociology of Knowledge* (New York: Harcourt, Brace, 1947).

6. Frances Trollope, *Domestic Manners of the Americans*, ed. Donald Smalley (New York: Knopf, 1949).

7. Alexis de Tocqueville, *Democracy in America* (Garden City, NY: Doubleday, Anchor Books, 1969), pp. 185-86, cited in Martin Mayer, *Making News* (Garden City, NY: Doubleday, 1987), p. 168.

bers and lackeys of the ruling class, on the one hand, and, on the other, the ruled classes of a Continental country is their location on the spectrum that runs from anti-Americanism to pro-Americanism. The more anti-American one is, the more likely to be self-identified with the rulers, partly because of the discomfort engendered by the perceived absence of the European rulers' counterparts in the United States, partly because of sheer envy. The more pro-American, to the extreme of wanting to emigrate to the United States, the more likely one's opposition to and alienation from not only one's own ruling class but also the idea of rulership in general and the more likely the assumption—possibly illusory—that rulership has been overcome in the United States by way of Abraham Lincoln's ideal of government of the people, by the people, for the people.

Members of the Western European ruling classes can take one or both of two contradictory positions. Either they can admit that they and their intellectual forerunners were simply wrong, that the United States has been the wave of the future from 1776 onward; or they can insist, in the face of all the evidence to the contrary, that the deterministic predictions of the impossibility of American success were correct; or they can try to take both of these contradictory positions simultaneously, with the usual ambivalent results. The few who admit the historic wrongness of the original forecast of failure for the United States do not generally share the prevailing anti-Americanism of the ruling classes. Indeed, they sometimes turn into grotesque pro-Americans, in a pattern frequently found among converts, who try to make up for their, and their intellectual or natural ancestors', supposed

guilt. They become more assertively pro-American than the most vociferous America firsters. This then feeds the anti-Americanism of both the consistent true believers and the ambivalents.

Those who insist that predictions of America's failure were correct sometimes seem to suggest that the United States somehow cheated history, just as its merchants, according to Hegel, had "the evil reputation of cheating while protected by the law."[8] Trying to cheat history in this way will, of course, eventually have catastrophic consequences not only for the United States but also for Europe and the rest of the world.

THE LACK OF ANTI-EUROPISM

"Anti-Europism," or "anti-Europeanism," is never used to describe anti-European attitudes held by Americans. That this is so not only because Western Europe has not yet become an entity is suggested by the nonuse of the nouns that would go with anti-British, anti-French, anti-German, anti-Italian, anti-Austrian, and similar attitudes. The Europeans complain about American economic policy and the U.S. economy. Americans do the same in reverse and often describe the policies of the European Economic Community as anti-American, whereas the Europeans are more likely to describe the parallel U.S. policies as protectionist or irresponsible. NATO has been in apparent disarray over U.S.—and Soviet—arms-reduction proposals and negotiations. From the United States, European reactions are again more often described as anti-American than the American proposals

8. G.W.F. Hegel, *Sämtliche Werke,* in *Amerika im Spiegel des deutschen politischen Denkens,* ed. Ernst Fränkel (Cologne: Westdeutscher Verlag, 1960), p. 112.

as anti-European by the Europeans.

American culture, both high and low, in the broadest sense of the term, has been engulfing Europe and the world. This, and the reactions it engenders, are not novel phenomena. In 1922, a German scholar of the history of religions, Heinrich Frick, published a work on missions that featured an extended critique of *Amerikanismus*.

With their naive Bible societies, their rough itinerating methods, their superficial approaches to unity, and their failure to distinguish between unchurched heathen and Christians who simply belonged to the wrong church, the Americans had shown that their aims were fundamentally not religious at all. What they really wanted to do was to convert everyone, Hindus and Germans alike, to an American style of religion and civilization.[9]

To that kind of perception of Americanism, anti-Americanism is the obvious continental European response. British missionaries had been included in the accusation against the "Anglo-American" societies.

While European protests against the flood of American culture are often proclaimed and received as anti-American, the reverse has not been true. The contrast can be explained in part as resulting simply from differences of scale. The United States appears to the Europeans like a colossal monolith, whereas the various European countries appear to Americans as effete if persistent nuisances, whose obsolescent eccentricities we can more or less afford to tolerate. This dismissive kind of attitude may have found its nutshell expression in the concept of "Eurowimps."[10] If their

criticism, noncooperation, or resistance becomes too counterproductive, the United States simply squelches European opposition and criticism.

This suggests a lack of parallelism, or of proportionality, between anti-Americanism and what one might conceive of as its U.S. counterpart or riposte. British Francophobia has its counterpart in French Anglophobia. Germans and French used to consider each other archenemies, and recent expressions of fear about developments in the Federal Republic, expressed by French political figures like former Foreign Minister Michel Jobert, elicit corresponding anti-French utterances in West Germany. Is Western European anti-Americanism then mainly a response to the overwhelming power and presence that the United States has acquired and deployed despite the predictions and preferences of Europe's ruling classes?

I think not. The difference is not mainly a quantitative but a qualitative one. When members of different European nations are critical of one another, their discourse takes place within one and the same universe. This is true especially of anti-Communist Western Europeans and the Soviet targets of their hostility, who in turn describe their critics as anti-Soviet. After all, the Russian and German founding fathers and grandfathers of Soviet communism were very European in both their antecedents and their state-focused goals.

Soviet Russian policies toward Western European states have generally been susceptible of being understood, by the Western Europeans, as having a great deal of continuity with earlier Czarist Russian policies. The United States of

9. William R. Hutchison, "Innocence Abroad: The 'American Religion' in Europe," *Church History*, 52:81-82 (Mar. 1952).

10. "Some may go so far as to call us Eurowimps." Richard von Weizsäcker, "The Un-

finished Business of the Marshall Plan," *Harvard Magazine*, 80:21 (July-Aug. 1987).

America, by contrast, deliberately cut itself off from Europe and its traditions of rulership, hierarchy, and secrecy, to found the new order of the ages, characterized by government based on consent and on openness. The very proclamation of these principles, out of the Founders' "decent respect to the opinions of mankind," challenged the European rulers' legitimacy, as it had been intellectually rationalized by statist intelligentsias. Their anti-Americanism has, therefore, been profoundly ideological from the outset, and it continues to be so today.

Perhaps the more ideological and virulent strains of American anti-communism—called anti-Sovietism by the Soviets—are the functional equivalent of the missing anti-Europism. This is suggested, among other things, by the even more virulent anti-Americanism propagated by Continental pro-Moscow Communist parties at the height of the cold war, as illustrated by Communist denunciations by the French Communist Party of Coca Cola as a case of "coca-colonization." The Soviet journalist Ilya Ehrenburg claimed that Coca Cola advertised in Chicago with a poster showing Jesus Christ on the cross, with the caption "He died deeply satisfied."[11] This early postwar link between the major Communist parties of Europe, especially in France and Italy, also points to the strength of pro-Americanism at the popular level, because the masses of lower-class people, who then voted for those parties, were converted to Communist anti-Americanism for only a brief period or not at all.

In any case, the European elites may

11. See Spiro, *Government by Constitution*, pp. 122-24.

not be acting in awareness of the paradox of the challenge to the legitimacy of their rule that the success of the U.S. model presents. It poses a greater threat to the fundamental underlying assumptions of the Continental states than does Soviet communism, which evinces much greater continuity with its German originators, Marx and Engels, than does American openness with its English antecedents. This is one aspect that lends anti-Americanism in Western Europe its troubling persistence.

ANTI-AMERICANISM IN THE CURRENT SITUATION

The reader is familiar with the current state of U.S.-European relations. What role does Western European anti-Americanism play in those relations?

The United States is the leader of the free world, first of all, in the military sense. It is the most powerful and principal founding member of NATO. The European members, for decades, have acted so that the United States is damned if it does and damned if it does not. The Europeans criticize the United States either for imposing its will—without adequate consultations—upon the continental Europeans or for not providing enough leadership. Even during those rare and brief periods when they voice neither criticism, the Europeans are likely to attribute the temporary correctness of U.S. policies to a selfish or even brutal pursuit of American national interest, which simply happens to coincide or overlap temporarily with the European allies' national interests. In any case, over any time span of more than four years—a presidential term of office—the continental Europeans always condemn U.S. military policies as erratic, unpredictable, insufficiently in-formed by a constant strategy, and too much at the mercy of the passing fads of domestic politics inside the United States.

U.S. international economic and finan-cial policies are treated in the same basically anti-American way by the non-sycophant wings of the Western Euro-pean elites. They tend to approve of these policies only when they persuade themselves that the Americans listened to German—as from Chancellor Schmidt—or French—as from President Mitter-rand—or European Economic Commu-nity expert advice, which steered them away from committing another grave or crude error. Otherwise, the United States is, for example, damned because the dollar is too strong, or because the dollar is too weak. It was damned by many, if not by all, during the last decade or two of the effectiveness of Bretton Woods, and it has been damned ever since the Nixon Shock, which put an end to the effectiveness of that agreement. Whereas the Europeans tend to explain European—and Jap-anese?—protectionism, in its various overt and covert manifestations, in eco-nomic terms such manifestations in the United States are described and ex-plained as flowing from causes at least as singularistically American as any set of causes concoctable by the most singu-larist American economic historians. Anti-Americanism easily lets Europeans attribute a particular U.S. policy that displeases them to the Americans' crude desire to exercise economic power, with-out scientific economic expertise and the sense of responsibility or even of noblesse oblige that enables a European ruling class to extend its true vision of national interest to the broader inter-

national interests of the free world or the global economy. Non-Marxist, or anti-Marxist, Europeans think along the same lines as Hegel did: "Here the basic [American] character is indicated, which consists in the endeavor of the private individual after acquisition and profit, with the predominance of particular interests, which devotes itself to the general interest only for the sake of its own advantage."[12] Western European Marxists, on the other hand, recognize as true fascism the direct action in the world economy of private multinational corporations that do not even bother to avail themselves of the American state as an instrument of their predatory international behavior.

What the Europeans misperceive as the cultural policy (*Kulturpolitik*, in German) of the United States, to an even greater extent than U.S. economic policy, is actually the effects upon Eu-rope of a multiplicity of American indi-vidual and organizational activities. The actions of the United States Information Agency (USIA) constitute a minute com-ponent of this total, but the European ruling classes, which identify themselves, positively or negatively, with their re-spective states, wrongly assume that the USIA is the weightiest mediator for American culture abroad. This seems to be true especially in West Germany, where an *Amerika Haus* was established in every major city soon after the end of the war to aid the process of democ-ratization. These USIA centers, more than forty years after World War II, still bring a steady flow of American aca-demics, artists, and officials to the Fed-eral Republic, alongside a flow of private

12. Hermann Glockner, *Sämtliche Werke*, vol. 11, *Philosophie der Geschichte*, by G.W.F. Hegel (Stuttgart: Frommann-Holzboog, 1929), p. 129.

sector *Kultur*-Americans, who are often of better quality than the officially sponsored ones. Because German intellectuals have a positive attitude toward their own state institutions, however—regardless of their current policies—they assume that U.S.-government-sponsored culture must be the most authentic one available.

Most members of Western European intellectual elites prefer to assume that American culture in Europe is U.S.-government controlled and directed, even though they may have their doubts about the reality of this, because it would simplify the problem of the diversity and confusion of American culture and its impact upon their peoples. The identification of American culture with the U.S. government also enables them to maintain their condescension toward American culture by identifying it with what they regard as the relatively low level of the official USIA product. This then leads to, or is connected with, anomalies like the refusal to recognize the equivalency of, for example, bachelor of arts and doctoral degrees from American colleges and universities like Haverford, Harvard, or Johns Hopkins, though these have requirements generally at least one degree higher than their German counterparts—an honors B.A. is worth at least a German M.A. or *Diploma*, an American Ph.D. a German *Habilitation*. With respect to culture, as to economics and military and diplomatic power, the assumptions underlying the arrogance of the continental European elites have been long overtaken by events. They try to live off intellectual capital that, if they ever possessed it, has been long mortgaged or spent. Though they are in fact *nouveaux* broke and because they are, they look down upon American culture as the pretensions of the *nouveaux riches*.

DERIVATIVE CHARACTER OF ANTI-AMERICANISM

Anti-American Europeans are most likely to approve of particular American policies—political, military, economic, or even cultural—when they perceive these as being conducted by Americans whom they can consider to be actual—or honorary—Europeans, for example, for a variety of reasons, Dean Acheson, Henry Kissinger, Zbigniew Brzezinski, or even someone like Paul Volcker, in the eyes of some. Because such men do not appear, to the Europeans, to come out of American domestic politics, and because of their real and/or perceived affinity to Europe's elites, they jar European sensitivities less than the genuinely homegrown, not obviously university-related policymakers. The following passage, from Peter Wright's *Spy Catcher*, conveys one dimension of this attitude:

There was, in the end, a fundamental difference in approach. Both F. J. [Furneval Jones, Director-General of M.I.5] and Dick [Goldsmith White] saw themselves as servants of the Crown, and their services as part of the orderly, timeless configuration of Whitehall. They were insiders, whereas [Richard] Helms, [James Jesus] Angleton, and [J. Edgar] Hoover were all [sic] outsiders. There was a streak of ruthlessness and lawlessness about the American intelligence community which disturbed many in the senior echelons of British Intelligence.[13]

Americans like Acheson and Kissinger may have conveyed the impression of conducting the foreign policy—

13. Peter Wright, *Spy Catcher: The Candid Autobiography of a Senior Intelligence Officer* (New York: Viking, 1987), p. 303.

in the singular—of the United States in keeping with the Prussian historian Leopold von Ranke's dictum about the "primacy of foreign policy." This has never been applicable to the United States, however, and for two reasons that mutually reinforce the Europeans' misunderstanding. First, the Constitution subjects foreign relations to extensive controls by the elected Congress—including the senators' advice and consent on appointments, and on treaties by a two-thirds' vote, and appropriations. Second, the Continental languages have only one word or concept—and, I would add, practice—for the two English terms "policy" and "politics." Their word *Politik, politique, politica*, and so forth, means "policy" much more than it means "politics." If the Europeans' perspective were less distorted, they would perceive that von Ranke has not only been stood on his head but twirled into irrelevance. The foreign relations of the United States are driven by domestic, internal—rather than foreign, external—considerations and are embedded in the matrix of variable, volatile, unpredictable but highly accountable, because open and popularly responsive, localized politics. They are not focused on state policy. The United States differs in this respect from every European country. Indeed, it is unique.

Europe's ruling classes resent this, because they can do nothing to reverse the trend that is imposing the American pattern upon world politics, replacing the centuries-old practices of the aristocratic, secretive, administered diplomacy of international relations. They resent it the more because the whole framework of post-World War II international relations was created—as they think, sometimes on European suggestions and initiatives—by Eurocentric Americans like Dean Acheson, who asserts that he was "present at the creation."[14] But there is nothing they can do to reverse or retard this trend.

THE PROSPECTS

The prospects for anti-Americanism in Western Europe are these: First, the anti-Americanism of the ruling classes will continue, but with diminishing effects, as their members are gradually being deprived of their ruling functions from below, through the replication of the model of American domestic politics; and as they gradually adopt American methods from the outside. This adoption will occur through their increasing direct exposure to American politics in the United Nations, NATO, and similar international organizations, but also, and more important, to the contagious influence of the grass-roots politics of American business and science, American culture and crime, and all American life.

Second, pro-Americanism at the popular level will grow as the distinctions between rulers and ruled become blurred, under the irradiating influence of the model of the United States, and as individuals and groups oppose specific U.S. policies for derivative reasons, with help from, and using the replicated methods of, the original domestic opponents in the United States.

Eventually—and I expect this will take less time than Lord Keynes's long run—only policy-specific anti-Americanism will survive. With the waning in Western Europe of elite, popular, and

14. Dean Acheson, *Present at the Creation: My Years in the State Department* (New York: Norton, 1969).

cold war anti-Americanism, specific American policies will find support, indifference, or opposition on their perceived apparent merits or demerits, just as specific policy proposals do within the domestic politics of the United States. When that happens—and it may happen long before either Americans or Europeans become aware of it—the original promise will have been fulfilled.

In the seventeenth century, John Locke wrote, "Thus in the beginning all the World was *America*, and more so than it is now."[15] For the twenty-first century, I will venture to prophesy: in the future all the world will be America, and more so than it is now.[16]

15. Quoted in Spiro, *Politics as the Master Science: From Plato to Mao* (New York: Harper & Row, 1970), p. 178.

16. See also Spiro, "Foreign Policy and Political Style," *The Annals* of the American Academy of Political and Social Science, 366:139-48 (July 1966).

ANNALS, *AAPSS*, **497**, May 1988

French Pique and *Piques Françaises*

By MARIE-FRANCE TOINET

ABSTRACT: If there is something that can be called anti-Americanism, the French variety goes back a long way, to the end of the eighteenth century, when France hoped that its contribution to American independence would translate into a special relationship. It was never able to achieve this and has never understood its failure. Since then, a very peculiar love-hate relationship has characterized French attitudes toward and dealings with the United States, based on both misunderstandings and conflicting interests. It has varied in different periods and among the various groups of French society. Recently it has been paradoxical to note that Gaullism, whatever its supposed anti-American content, has meant a more serene and mature French attitude toward the United States. A basic source of conflict remains, however, in the cultural area. The French thirst for the universality of its values has resulted in a profound divide between fascination with and rejection of the competitive democratic values that the United States is seeking to project.

Marie-France Toinet is directeur de recherche *at the Fondation nationale des sciences politiques in Paris, France. She specializes in American politics. She has been a Harkness fellow (1968-70), a congressional fellow (1969), and an Eisenhower fellow (1987). She has taught at the University of California at Irvine, the University of Iowa, Yale, and the University of Michigan. She has recently coedited* L'Amérique dans les têtes *(1986) and published* Le système politique des États-Unis *(1987).*

FOR many Americans, France is the epitome of anti-Americanism, a little country—better known for its cheeses and fashions than for technological advances or economic power—that has the gall to criticize the United States and thwart its foreign policy. The most recent example of this unfortunate and somewhat ridiculous state of affairs was the French refusal to let American aircraft overfly French territory on their way to retaliate, for the common good of the West, against Libya and its terrorist leader Muammar el-Qaddafi. American public opinion responded immediately. French Beaujolais once again went down the gutter. After all, small countries protected by American military might are supposed to, at the very least, go along with American policies. And French resistance is all the more incomprehensible in that the two countries are supposed to be old allies. France's attitude seems to be nothing more than pique over not being a world power any more and over seeing the United States, a country that had originally been its client, replace it on the world scene to become its benefactor—via the Marshall Plan—and protector.

Of course, Americans who feel this way forget that France is these days rather less anti-American than most of its neighbors, including Britain and Germany. Indeed, most French are fascinated, even enthralled, by what has been called until recently the Reagan model. Those French who dared to say that American economic trends might be a bit worrisome were simply called anti-American—by their own countrymen; it was somehow improper to question American policies.

There is no doubt that French feelings toward the United States are often ambivalent and, at times, downright anti-

American. Nor is there any doubt that these mixed feelings are grounded in pique and deeply rooted in history. The French, even if not always as well-versed in historical matters as they would like to think, are historically minded. Although they may not realize it, their feelings go back a long way indeed, to the aftermath of American independence. They dreamed then of a special relationship with the United States. They had, after all, been instrumental in the achievement of American independence, albeit for reasons of their own given that the defeat of Britain was a concern of France as much as of America. But it was defeated Britain that secured the special relationship with its former colonies while France was left resentful in the cold. The relationship between the former allies deteriorated to a point of quasi-war in the period 1798-99, something the French could not understand. Even though those events are long forgotten, the French dream to this day of a special relationship and have not understood why their love remains unrequited.

What have they done wrong? They have forgotten that they often appeared too radical for American tastes, or not reliable enough, or even chose the wrong side, as in the American Civil War. But they have not forgotten that the United States has also done them wrong—the debt problem after World War I—or that Roosevelt supported Petain against de Gaulle and even thought briefly of making France an occupied territory after World War II.

Misunderstanding thus appears to be the basis of the peculiar attitudes of the French toward the United States and the Americans. Conversely, one could also say that the French feel misunderstood by the Americans and deeply regret the fact. In French anti-Americanism there is just as much love as hate toward America. This ambivalent attitude is the source of recurring swings between frustration and admiration, resentment and fascination, which make it very difficult to define permanent structures in pinpointing who loves and who hates the United States and when and why. Perhaps one could get a hold on this French unpredictability and volatility by realizing that the great divide between pro-American and anti-American is inside each and every Frenchman. As Denis Lacorne and Jacques Rupnik have written, "One can hate Reagan while being in love with American jazz; one can disagree with the Grenada invasion and wear blue jeans."[1] Such contradictory feelings coexist within each individual and may at any moment divide his or her judgment—not to mention the fact that these feelings change over time, according to changing circumstances. Anti-Americanism may not be the most appropriate concept for analyzing reality and the fluctuations of public opinion.

What then is anti-Americanism? If defined as a full-blown contempt for anything American or a systematic and permanent opposition to everything American, a total rejection of the United States, I submit that, in those very restricted terms, anti-Americanism does not exist. Even Jean-Paul Sartre, who wrote after the execution of the Rosenbergs that America was a "mad dog" (*L'Amérique à la "rage"*) with which relations had to be broken, loved American literature, American movies, and American jazz.[2] Americans tend to forget that anti-Americanism is a very mixed attitude.

However vague the concept, it is undeniable that there are changes in the amount of anti- and pro-Americanism that one can detect in France. Those variations affect the various groups that make up French society, leading to unexpected shifts and strange alliances. Moreover, reputations are often wrong. On the political front, for instance, Americans expect the French Left to be anti-American and the Right to be pro-American. There is some truth to this statement, but it lumps together as bedfellows those whose attitudes are fundamentally different. For instance, while one can say that the French Communist Party is basically opposed to American policies, the same cannot be said across the board for the Socialist Party. During the Fourth Republic, the Socialists were considered so profoundly pro-American that they were called "Atlanticists," a code word with pejorative connotations. And the Reagan model has tempted some leaders of the Socialist Party to sound themes quite unfamiliar to the French Left: the rehabilitation of the ideas of market, profit, entrepreneurship, and deregulation. It was Finance Minister Pierre Beregovoy who modernized the French stock market along American lines.

Conversely, until the extreme Right in France became more pro-American in the early 1980s, it had been quite anti-American under the influence of Charles Maurras, who was highly critical of American plutocracy and of Theodore Roosevelt's imperialism. The Gaullists, too, have been somewhat unfairly criticized for being anti-American. De

1. Denis Lacorne, Jacques Rupnik, and Marie-France Toinet, eds., *L'Amérique dans les têtes* (Paris: Hachette, 1986), p. 12.

2. See Marie-Christine Granjon, "Sartre, Beauvoir, Aron: Les passions ambigues," in *L'Amérique dans les têtes*, ed. Lacorne, Rupnik, and Toinet, pp. 144-64.

Gaulle was utterly convinced that it was in the interest of France to be independent from what he called the two "hegemons"—the United States and USSR—but he always sided with the American ally when the situation was critical and when circumstances compelled France to choose sides. The clearest example was the missile crisis of 1962, when he supported President Kennedy's policy lock, stock, and barrel. One should also not forget, as Michael Harrison has written, that de Gaulle is responsible for making France less anti-American. "De Gaulle is the psychologist who has so well cured France from its anti-Americanism that this nation can now have 'normal' relations with the United States, grounded on reasonable perceptions of common and conflicting interests."[3]

THE INTELLIGENTSIA

It is not possible to review the attitudes of each and every group in France, but one group's evolution has been particularly striking in recent years: the intelligentsia. This is, of course, a very nebulous group; who is and who is not an intellectual? In France, the intelligentsia includes more people than it would in other countries—for example, high school teachers—and it is quite influential and vocal. It appears often in the media and consequently is a highly visible part of the intellectual debate.

Intellectuals used to be quite critical of the United States, and because they set the fashion, their phobia toward what they perceived America to be—a very uniform conformist society where to be individualistic and different was

3. Michael Harrison, "La solution gaulliste," in L'Amérique dans les têtes, ed. Lacorne, Rupnik, and Toinet, p. 217.

on the verge of being unacceptable to the overwhelming majority[4]—created distrust of the United States not only as a cultural entity but also as a superpower that might try to impose its views on the rest of the world, its allies in particular. Be it their disappointment with the Soviet model or with the Socialist government of France, or their feeling that the old ideological recipes were no longer suitable, or their perception that America itself had become engrossed in the individualism that they held dear, or whatever reason, intellectuals in the early 1980s became fascinated and enthralled by things American. Reaganism became the model of a new liberalism—in the French sense of the word—the symbol of the revolt against l'état. Of course, this about-face was highly ideological and could swing just as rapidly in

4. It is amusing to see what Auguste Bartholdi, the designer of the Statue of Liberty, wrote after his trip to the United States: "The individual lives like a drop in the torrent without the power to isolate himself on a blade of grass." Marie-France Toinet, "Le statut des libertés: De Tocqueville à Reagan," Le point, 30 June 1986, p. 44. Paradoxically and surprisingly, Tocqueville did not think much differently: "I know of no country where there is so little independence of mind and of real freedom of discussion as in America. . . . There is no country in Europe so subdued by any single authority as not to protect the man who raises his voice in the cause of truth from the consequences of his hardihood. . . . In America the majority raises formidable barriers around the liberty of opinion; within these barriers an author may write what he pleases, but woe to him if he goes beyond them. Not that he is in danger of an auto-da-fé, but he is exposed to continued obloquy and persecution. . . . Every sort of compensation, even that of celebrity, is refused to him . . . . those who blame him criticize him and those who think as he does keep quiet and move away without courage. He yields . . . . and subsides into silence, as if he felt remorse for having spoken the truth." Alexis de Tocqueville, Democracy in America, ed. Richard D. Heffner, (New York: New American Library, 1965), pp. 117-18.

the other direction. Will Gorbachev succeed Reagan as the new idol of the French intelligentsia?

What is particularly striking is how quickly intellectual fashions come and go—but also how deeply they may affect the serious debate. The dispute over more or less state (*état*), which lies deeply embedded in the Reagan intellectual revolution, seems, but only seems, to have resulted in less public intervention. One intelligent guess is that we will not go back to more state but will shift to a debate about the method of begetting a better state. Signs are pointing in that direction already. But the entire discussion about intellectual fashions and changes shows one very important thing about the French fascination and rejection of Americanism: the French are not so much holding a debate about the United States but about themselves, about their society, their goals, and their methods. It is, so to say, a Franco-French debate, where American arguments—often half-baked—are just an excuse or a pretense. The French hold the United States up as a mirror to look, in fact, at themselves.

AMERICAN SELF-DOUBT

One subgroup that stands somewhat apart among the intellectuals is what I would call the experts, the social scientists who study the United States. Their collective attitude toward their subject is useful in that it enables us to get at another facet of anti-Americanism, what can be called the American component. Even though they cannot be considered anti-American in general, they are often characterized as such, both in the United States and in France. In other words, a professional but critical view of American things, realities,

policies, ideas, and features is easily taken for the expression of anti-American feelings, even when it is interwoven into a basically favorable outlook. The particular becomes the whole, criticism becomes hostility, assessment is anti-American. In the end, doubts about a policy or an aspect of the system are often seen as calling into question the United States in its entirety: love it whole or leave it alone; mixed feelings are no better than hostile ones. In other words, it is nearly impossible to be considered as an objective observer of the United States. Tocqueville, again, noted as much in his time along with many other foreign observers:

The Americans, in their intercourse with strangers, appear impatient of the smallest censure and insatiable of praise. The most slender eulogium is acceptable to them, and the most exalted seldom contents them; they unceasingly harass you to extort praise, and if you resist their entreaties they fall to praising themselves. It would seem as if, doubting their own merit, they wished to have it constantly exhibited before their eyes.[5]

In this last sentence, Tocqueville has pinpointed precisely the source of those phenomena that are called anti-Americanism and un-Americanism. There is no nation but the United States where, *mutatis mutandis*, external hostility is called anti-American and internal hostility called un-American. There is nothing called anti-Italianism or anti-Germanism. There has never been an un-Australian or un-British activities committee; only the Philippines has managed an Anti-Filipino Activities Committee, but that was a congenital problem. Americans are both self-satisfied and self-doubting. They are convinced

5. Ibid., p. 252.

that the United States is the best nation on the face of the earth, the most democratic politically, the most successful economically, the fairest socially, and the freest. Yet at the same time, they are deeply worried about the sturdiness and the durability of what they have achieved. They are wrong on both counts. Italy is more democratic, Japan more successful economically, and Sweden fairer socially; yet what Americans have achieved is remarkably durable, their political system above all. This matters little; what counts is the conjunction of both convictions, which leads Americans to believe that foreign or domestic criticism undermines the strength of American society, cracks the indispensable consensus, and erodes the national image. In the end, they take criticism too seriously and hence refuse to hear it. They are deeply ethnocentric, but at the same time they are very sensitive about foreign criticism and, therefore, resent it. They would love to be loved—and only to be loved.

A French ambassador—Ambassador de Rose, I believe—recounts the story of what an American friend told him when he first arrived in the United States: "Americans believe that the French hate them and they are wrong. The French believe that Americans love them and they are wrong too." Americans often believe that the French are anti-American because their behavior is rude. There is no doubt that many—not all, I hope!— French, especially Parisians, are rude, unpleasant, and arrogant. But that is not anti-Americanism, for they can be and are just as unpleasant to Italians or Norwegians, not to mention Algerians. In fact, French public opinion, when measured in polls, shows the French to feel particularly close to the United States, which is always the place where French would prefer to emigrate—if they had to. Public opinion may entertain very stupid, naive, or misinformed ideas about the United States, but it has been more pro-American than anti-American, much more so than some individual components of French society such as intellectuals.

Of course, French public opinion can be opposed to some American policies, particularly in foreign affairs, although it has often been more hostile to French than to American policies. For instance, at the beginning at least, public opinion was not favorable to de Gaulle's decision to leave the North Atlantic Treaty Organization's military organization. Nor was it favorable to the French government's decision not to let American bombers overfly French territory on their way to Libya in 1986. This does not mean that it cannot be critical of any particular American president. It showed quite a bit of skepticism about Jimmy Carter toward the end of his tenure, and it showed enthusiasm about Ronald Reagan at the time of his reelection. The so-called switch from pro- to anti-Americanism that many observers have detected in France lies in these variations in presidential popularity. But Reagan's popularity could slip in France following the stock market crash of 1987, and that would not mean a surge of anti-Americanism in French public opinion.

There is also no correlation between French attitudes toward the United States and those toward the Soviet Union. These are discrete variables. Both countries can stand high or low at the same time in French opinion. They can also be at different ends of the spectrum. Their respective positions are a reflection both of the state of French society and of their own separate policies.

Policies also have an impact on the ambiguous ways in which one society—here, the French—regards another—the American. There are crosscurrents and cross-pressures that, once again, make it very difficult to generalize broadly. The intellectuals may fall in love with American economic policy but at the same time resent American mass culture. The general public may regret a specific foreign policy decision of the United States—for example, its pulling out of Lebanon in 1984 without warning it allies—but dote on *Dallas* or Madonna. In whatever field, it is clear that the divergence or convergence of interests and the intensity of a real or proxy competition will have a definite impact on reciprocal images. But we are talking about images and not about realities; perceptions are very important in shaping those images and then in defining actual realities, in the real world.

FASCINATIONS: FOREIGN POLICY AND CULTURE

Foreign policy and culture are the areas where French fascination with the United States is at its peak, for it is in those areas where American *puissance* ("power") and *modernité* ("modernity") are seen at their apex. I have purposely used those two words in French because they literally sustain and support French images of the United States. The French hate to be considered backward or weak—quaint!—and resent what they see as American condescension toward them. They feel that they are taken for granted because they are no longer a first-rank power. Yet all the while, they are convinced that they have achieved a great deal: transforming a rural society in less time than any of their neighbors without great social convulsions, and becoming

in the process a very proficient agricultural, industrial, and technological nation. They regard the American model not for its short-term, even daily, metamorphoses but for its durable tendencies: American inventiveness, originality, creativity, incredible vitality, and extraordinary capacity to rebound from setbacks. They wish to be considered if not equal partners at least not as a lesser nation. They dream of being reliable partners who, in crucial matters, might be usefully consulted. They forget, of course, that they behave in the American way in dealing with a client-ally, for example, in Africa: "Don't do unto me what I do unto others." Americans feel unappreciated, but most certainly are not and the French feel the same way—and are probably right. This is probably at the core of many misunderstandings and frictions that give the appearance of anti-Americanism among the French.

Foreign policy and culture are two perfect though opposite examples of touchy areas: perfect because they show exactly how the French react and opposite because France has realized it is now a secondary power on the world scene, where it considers itself still a cultural giant.

Ironically, France was probably more anti-American under the Fourth Republic when it clung to the idea that it remained a major power that counted in the world because of its large colonial empire. Now anti-Americanism is less, because France has admitted the fact that it is only an average nation—and is rather pleased with this state of affairs. The French believed earlier that the United States was trying to compel them to shed their colonial extensions and resented this all the more because the United States had extensions of its own. Decolonization was a bloody and fratricidal process that was terribly costly not only in human lives but also financially and even morally. But it left the country leaner, more eager to engage itself in the modern world. France is actually more independent than it was before because it is no longer vulnerable to accusations of imperialism.

Independence is a stronger yearning now that France is less important. It sharply defines French attitudes to each and everyone, including the United States, and if there is a foreign policy consensus in France, it is that the country can and must decide independently what is to be done by France in the world, with its friends and against its foes. Of course, this newfound independence, reinforced by the institutional strength of the Fifth Republic—paradoxically the most American institutions France has ever had—has made the French "surer of themselves and more domineering,"[6] especially under de Gaulle. Having nothing more to lose, the French could indulge in their favorite pastime: the arrogant pleasure of inflicting advice on all sides. And the United States was a favorite target: why were the Americans not following the sound policies we were suggesting from Vietnam to Beirut, from the Middle East to Nicaragua? Still, in being something of a pain—albeit correct occasionally—France was also becoming a stronger and hence a more reliable ally. And in any event, its bark was much worse than its bite.

Americanophobia in France, whatever its depth, is always accompanied by the fear of loss of the French identity. This is, of course, particularly strong in cultural matters, especially the language problem. The French appear to be very defensive about their language, and they are. This can lead to the excessive or even the ridiculous. Who cares if the French say "weekend," "leader," or "football" or use words that they think are English but that Americans cannot understand: *smoking* ("tuxedo"), *waters* ("lavatory"), *un flipper* ("pinball machine")? Do not Americans talk of "entrées," "détente," and "quiche"? Have not both languages been permeated by each other for centuries? After all, a language lives and has always lived by borrowing from others, and it is no problem except for French chauvinists—another French word—if English is the universal language, the lingua franca.

If I may be allowed to intrude personally here, what I have in mind is somewhat different. Even though I take great pleasure in a certain mastery of the English language, I will never be as fluent in that marvelously supple language as is a native speaker. I will always be in an inferior position. Even worse, languages are not neutral. The same words can convey very different meanings, as do, for example, "liberal," "quid pro quo," "alternatives," "pique."[7] Conversely, it is no accident that the same concept is described in different words conveying different attitudes and cultural differences. Thus Americans say "nonvoting," offering the idea of a nonact, nonperformed perhaps by a nonperson, while the French—and British—say "abstention," which means holding oneself far from the polls, the choice by a voter to refrain from making a political

6. This is how de Gaulle described the Israelis on 22 November 1967, after the war. The comment was considered derogatory. I am convinced that it was not. He certainly wished the French, whom he had once called "clods" *(des veaux)*, to be the same.

7. In French *quiproquo* is a misunderstanding; *pique* is a cutting remark.

choice. And in each French election, the amount of abstention is clearly presented and openly discussed, while in the United States the percentage of nonvoters is very difficult to find. Words are not neutral; they carry a certain way of looking at things, the essence of identity, and I, for one, fear losing it. I resent the idea of having to publish only in English—as has already happened in medical research, for instance—of being coerced into this nonchoice, sometimes by Americans themselves who, being dominant, forget how sensitive and central the issue is to our problem.

Language is the essence of identity and of culture, and culture is at the heart of Franco-American misunderstandings and conflicts. Both countries believe they have universal values to offer to the rest of the world. The French call it civilization—French, of course—and the Americans call it democracy—American, of course. But whatever they are called, they imply competition and breed

incomprehension between the two nations because each nation believes its values are superior, more universal, and worth exporting to or imposing upon the rest of the world. The root of any anti-Americanism as well as anti-French sentiment—if there are such things—lies in that competitive and compulsive feeling of each nation that it has something unique to offer to humankind. Each fears that this unique contribution is threatened by the other. The Americanization of France is seen as destroying the essential values of French civilization. French criticisms of American foreign policy, on the other hand, are seen as undermining the credibility of its democratic rationale. The unequal competition between France and the United States is based on very moral perceptions that each nation has of itself and of the other. In that respect, a variable mixture of fascination and rejection will always characterize French perceptions of the United States and vice versa.

ANNALS, *AAPSS*, **497**, May 1988

Anti-Americanism in China

By DAVID L. SHAMBAUGH

ABSTRACT: Anti-Americanism in China has a history of more than a century; however, it is only part of a general ambivalence that is manifest in both pro- and anti-American images and behavior. This ambivalence is rooted in the differing value systems of Chinese and Americans, but it has also been stimulated by Sino-American interactions historically. With the seizure of power by the Communist Party in 1949, anti-American images became de rigueur in the official media and academic circles. Demonstrable anti-American behavior by the Chinese public was also evident during the first 25 years of the People's Republic. Since the 1970s, however, anti-Americanism has progressively declined at all measurable levels. In its place have arisen more nuanced images that take account of American pluralism. Chinese government policies toward America have both driven and reflected these evolving images over time.

David L. Shambaugh is currently program associate of the Asia Program, Woodrow Wilson International Center for Scholars, Washington, D.C. He is also a doctoral candidate in political science at the University of Michigan, where he previously taught. He holds an M.A. in international relations from the School of Advanced International Studies, Johns Hopkins University, and a B.A. in East Asian studies from the George Washington University. He is author of The Making of a Premier: Zhao Ziyang's Provincial Career *and numerous articles on contemporary Chinese affairs.*

C HINESE have always had mixed feelings about America. Over the last two centuries, the United States has been an object of alternating amity and enmity for both the governments and the people of China. Such has also been the case in American images of—and relations with—China.[1] A consistent balance of constructive relations between the two countries has been elusive as mutual images have swung through successive love-hate cycles. In this article, we will explore some of the reasons for this oscillation.

As in many other developing countries, anti-Americanism in China is rooted in a deeper ambivalence about the West as both model and threat. The key intellectual, economic, political, cultural, and spiritual attributes of Western nations have been the object of both emulation and rejection. Many Chinese have held sharply conflicting images of these facets of Western society since the late eighteenth century. Thus Chinese images of America—pro and con—have often been filtered through the broader perceptual screen of the Occident writ large. Any consideration of anti-Americanism in China as a discrete phenomenon must, therefore, take account of the role that America played in the greater Western challenge to China.

In this article, we are primarily concerned with the negative dimension of these ambivalent images, the so-called anti-American component. Yet lest the reader be left with the false impression that there has been no pro-Americanism in China, this article begins with a historical discussion of the evolution of these ambivalent Chinese images of America, with an accent on the positive.

1. See, for example, Harold Issacs's classic study, *Scratches on Our Minds* (Armonk, NY: M. E. Sharpe, 1980).

PRO- AND ANTI-AMERICANISM
IN CHINA IN
HISTORICAL PERSPECTIVE

Historically, Chinese intellectuals and government officials have not perceived the United States merely as a large and powerful nation on the opposite side of the Pacific Ocean that warranted their attention by sheer presence. Rather, these Chinese have generally viewed America in light of their own country's quest for modernity, territorial integrity, national dignity, and international respect. Over time, America has been evaluated on the basis of what it did to facilitate or hinder the realization of these goals. To a significant extent, China's America policy has fluctuated in accordance with this evaluation. The more the United States was prepared to contribute to the attainment of these goals, the more positive Chinese images of America became, and concomitantly, the more cooperative a partner China was for the United States. Conversely, when the United States was perceived as either directly or indirectly frustrating realization of these ambitions, America was perceived as China's enemy.

Early contact

North America was a nonentity to most Chinese until the latter half of the eighteenth century, when the United States arrived in China along with Britain and other foreign powers. Direct contact between the two countries was initiated with the arrival in Canton (Guangzhou) of the American merchant vessel *Empress of China* in 1784. Thereafter, Chinese images of America were largely derived from comparisons of the British and Americans in the Canton trade. These initial images were rather unflattering. Americans were considered to be a subgroup of the British tribe (*zu*). From the Chinese perspective, Americans and British spoke the same language, fraternized with each other, shared the same physical appearance of hairy barbarians (*mao yi*), and seemingly sought the same commercial ends in China.

After learning more about the American struggle for independence from American traders and Jesuits in China, Chinese writings about the United States began to reflect the fact that America was a country at odds with the British. Chinese writers praised Americans for demonstrating martial valor and strategic ability in fighting the war of independence. By fashioning a less regal political system than the British, Americans demonstrated their concern for the plight of the common man.

In the wake of the first Opium War with Britain, several Chinese books appeared that presented the first coherent picture of America. They all painted an admiring portrait of America as a benevolent power possessing resourceful people and virtuous leaders, a society of responsible citizens, a government of decentralized power, and an economy of agriculture, technical prowess, and commercial dynamism. In many respects, Chinese images of America at this time mirrored what they valued in their own society.

The late Qing dynasty

These superficial images of America endured until the mid-nineteenth century, when "understanding the barbarians in order to control them" became a vocation among Chinese scholar-officials. The Qing state established a special bureau for dealing with the United States and Europe, Barbarian Affairs

(*yi wu*), and those literati who staffed it were among the first to articulate distinct images of America. During the westernization movement of the 1870s, the policy decision was made to learn explicitly from America. In 1872, Qing rulers Zeng Guofan and Li Hongzhang dispatched 120 students on the first educational mission to America. The program, however, was aborted nine years later, due primarily to the upsurge of anti-Chinese racism in California. As news of the anti-Chinese riots and the Exclusion Laws of 1882 trickled back to China, the positive images of the previous century began to erode.

A more complex and critical set of images began to replace the previous admiring image. This was reflected not only in the writings of intellectuals and scholar-officials but also increasingly in the visual arts and popular media. Publications such as the popular Shanghai magazine *Tianshizhai huabao* portrayed Americans as prone to various vices, particularly drinking, opium, sex, and public exhibitionism. As the physical presence of Americans in China dramatically increased during the last two decades of the nineteenth century, these negative images of American society were coupled with the proto-Leninist view that the United States was a threatening imperial power competing not just for a piece of the China market but of China itself.

Partition was the most pressing issue in China during the first decade of the twentieth century. The stated American policy opposing partition and in favor of free trade as embodied in John Hay's Open Door Notes was generally welcomed in China at the time, but in Chinese eyes, American rhetoric and reality increasingly began to diverge.

The inconsistent policies and apparent condescension of the McKinley, Roosevelt, and Taft administrations began to give Chinese cause to question their previous faith in American benevolence. American participation in the Boxer expedition of 1900-1901 greatly fueled this apprehension. The U.S. Navy dropped anchor in the Shanghai harbor and American troops fought on Chinese soil for the first time. A few years later, the Chinese responded with the anti-American boycott of 1905, which was undertaken ostensibly to protest Congress's move in 1904 to exclude Chinese immigration to the United States permanently, but it also took place against the backdrop of increased acts of xenophobic violence against Americans in China, including the random murders of a number of missionaries. Chinese boycotted American goods and refused to serve Americans, and anti-American invective was prominent in the media.

Modern Chinese nationalism was awakened. Anti-foreignism in general—and anti-Americanism in particular—spread rapidly. The United States became the target of not only boycotts and diplomatic representations but also stinging criticism from intellectuals like Liang Qichao who had once been laudatory of America. Of significance in these criticisms was the description of American behavior as imperialist. While imperialism had not yet taken on a Leninist theoretical cast, the Chinese did describe it as the phenomenon of economic and military expansion overseas by the Western powers. In the mind of Liang Qichao and other prominent intellectuals, the Monroe Doctrine and Theodore Roosevelt's naval buildup were a blueprint for world domination by the United States. In the eyes of many Chinese intellectuals, the Spanish-American War had in-

augurated the era of American imperialism. The annexation of the Philippines was seen as proof positive that the American imperial threat had crossed the Pacific and was nearing Chinese shores.[2]

The Nationalist period

Following the 1911 Revolution, many Chinese intellectuals' critical images of American imperialism persisted, but at the same time, a more admiring image reemerged among reform-minded nationalists. Sun Yatsen led the way in articulating the view that America represented a model for China's own development. He praised America's social vitality, political stability, technological prowess, and economic efficiency. Sun and other leaders of the new republic believed that America was progressive and benevolent. Woodrow Wilson helped to restore Chinese belief in this image briefly. Then came the Versailles Conference of 1919, where the Western powers, Wilson included, ceded German interests on the Shandong peninsula to Japan. The May Fourth Movement erupted.

The May Fourth Movement and its aftermath composed an epic period in modern Chinese history. The movement was a patriotic one with strong political and social ramifications, but perhaps most important in retrospect, the May Fourth Movement was an intellectual watershed. Marxism-Leninism began to germinate in China, and the Chinese Communist Party was founded in Shang-

2. Anyone interested in learning more about Sino-American interactions and mutual images prior to World War I should consult Michael Hunt's classic study, *The Making of a Special Relationship: The United States and China to 1914* (New York: Columbia University Press, 1983).

hai in 1921. From that point onward, an entirely new critical interpretation of the United States began to evolve in China— the Marxist-Leninist image—which competed with the more admiring liberal image articulated by the likes of Hu Shi and other intellectuals who had studied in America or in missionary colleges in China.

The American impact on the Chinese intelligentsia during the Nationalist period was substantial. An estimated 20,000 Chinese pursued collegiate studies in the United States and returned to China during this time.[3] The American missionary presence in China reached several thousand. Together with private American foundations and philanthropists, missionaries played a leading role in establishing Chinese educational and scientific institutions based on the American model. These American efforts resulted in institutions such as Peking Union Medical College, the Geological Survey of China, Academia Sinica, and a dozen Jesuit universities including Nanjing University, Yanjing and Qinghua in Beijing, Nankai in Tianjin, St. Johns in Shanghai, and Lingnan in Guangzhou. An estimated 6500 students graduated from these universities.[4]

While the total American effort in China during these years was quite significant in terms of institution building and educating thousands of young intellectuals in the scientific method and American liberal arts tradition, the fate of liberalism in China was closely tied to the educational realm and did not take

3. John K. Fairbank, *Chinese-American Interactions: A Historical Summary* (New Brunswick, NJ: Rutgers University Press, 1975), p. 68.
4. John K. Fairbank, Edwin O. Reischauer, and Albert M. Craig, *East Asia: Tradition and Transformation* (Boston: Houghton, Mifflin, 1973), p. 795.

root in society at large. Pro-Americanism remained an elite phenomenon. For the broad masses of Chinese, to the small degree that they contemplated the United States, images of America were largely defined through the U.S. commercial and military presence in China and the increasing perception of the Chiang Kai-shek regime as an American puppet—all of which contributed to very negative, anti-American sentiments among the populace.

Anti-Americanism in the People's Republic of China

The liberal image and the Marxist-Leninist image continued to be the two predominant and rival images of America until the Communists' victory in 1949. The triumph of the Communist Party and collapse of the Guomindang not only brought intellectuals committed to Marxism-Leninism to the fore, but the Marxist-Leninist image of America similarly triumphed over the liberal image.

Mao returned from Moscow in February 1950 with more than just a treaty of friendship and aid package. He also returned with a commitment to the Soviet model of education and research. The near-total adoption of Soviet textbooks and categories of analysis had a lasting impact on the ways in which Chinese intellectuals looked at the world— including the United States. The ideological orthodoxy inherent in the Stalinist worldview dominated Chinese images of America for the next 30 years.

Most Chinese intellectuals accepted the doctrinal interpretation of the world put forward by Stalin and his polemicists in its totality during the 1950s, and they only marginally modified it during the 1960s and early 1970s. This included the view of the world as divided into two camps, socialist and capitalist, with the United States as the leading imperialist power. By identifying America as imperialist, this interpretation was a commentary not just on its foreign policy but also on the domestic political-economic environment inside the United States that gave rise to an aggressive foreign policy.

This view emanates from Lenin's treatise *Imperialism, the Highest Stage of Capitalism*, which argues that when capitalism reaches the monopoly stage of development it is a qualitatively new stage characterized by a dominant financial oligarchy. In this stage, the monopoly capitalists work in close collaboration with and, in Stalin's view, control the state apparatus. As proclaimed by Lenin and Stalin, and accepted a priori by Chinese analysts, this is capitalism's moribund stage, that is, a giant economic crisis worse than the Great Depression will imminently arise that, in turn, will stimulate socialist revolution.

This was the dominant image of America articulated in the Chinese media and scholarly publications until the late 1970s. During this 30-year period, China's professional America watchers spent their time trying to document the changing financial, and hence political, power of different families and regional monopoly groups within the financial ruling strata; the severity of different economic crises; a society beset with class struggle; and the rising militancy of the American proletariat. The earlier Chinese image of America as a model of science and democracy was replaced by an image of a greedy and violent nation struggling to remain the wealthiest and strongest on earth, yet racked by internal class contradictions.

Revolution in America, along with the collapse of U.S. imperialism abroad, was deemed imminent.

Throughout the Maoist era, these negative images in the Chinese Communist media were paralleled and reinforced in society at large. Numerous propaganda campaigns (*yundong*) against America were carried out, and the United States became the target of Chinese ire in forums ranging from small-group (*xiaozu*) criticism sessions to massive public demonstrations.

The Communists had not been in power a year when the first of these campaigns was launched. The "Resist America, Aid Korea" Campaign (*kang Mei yuan Chao*) was waged nationally during 1950-51. The campaign was significant not only for its anti-American invective but also because it offered the Communists the first opportunity to erect an extensive propaganda apparatus in urban centers. Denunciations of America were carried out at the municipal, district, ward, neighborhood, enterprise, factory, and shop-floor levels.[5] During the Korean War, many Americans who had elected to remain in China following the revolution were imprisoned as spies.

Similar anti-American campaigns were waged—albeit of shorter duration and intensity—during the 1954 and 1958 Taiwan Straits crises. Throughout the 1950s and 1960s, calls to "liberate Taiwan" were coupled with harsh criticism of American support for the Guomindang government on Taiwan. American-trained intellectuals also became specific targets of the 1957 "Anti-

5. For a discussion of how this campaign was carried out in one northern Chinese city, see Kenneth G. Lieberthal, *Revolution & Tradition in Tientsin, 1949-52* (Stanford, CA: Stanford University Press, 1980), chap. 6.

Rightist" Campaign. Many were severely criticized for their "bourgeois American outlooks" and were banished to labor camps or consigned to menial jobs. There was also a brief campaign in 1960 against support from the Central Intelligence Agency for exiled Tibetan resistance groups.

By far the most vituperative anti-Americanism of the Maoist era came during the American involvement in the Vietnam war, much of which coincided with the Great Proletarian Cultural Revolution. In 1965, the populace girded for an expected American attack on China as U.S. bombing of North Vietnam intensified. The United States was deemed the nerve center of global imperialism in Marshal Lin Biao's famous tract "Long Live the Victory of People's War!" "Combat American imperialism" (*Fan Mei di*) became a national rallying cry as Red Guards besieged the capital with mass demonstrations from 1966 to 1969. Uncle Sam was burned in effigy with regularity. Officials and intellectuals with any connection to the United States were persecuted with particular zeal. These individuals were routinely brought before mass criticism sessions with placards around their necks identifying them as "agents," "lackeys," or "running dogs" of the United States before being "sent down" to May Seventh Cadre Schools in the countryside for rustication. Many of the few American expatriates remaining in China were also imprisoned. With no American embassy against which to vent their anger, the Red Guards unleashed their wrath on the next best substitute and burned the British mission to the ground in August 1967. While anti-Americanism was rampant during the Cultural Revolution, it was, to be sure, not isolated. All foreigners, but particularly Westerners, bore the wrath of Chinese xenophobia.

As the Cultural Revolution wound down so, too, did overt anti-Americanism. With the visits of Henry Kissinger in 1971 and President Nixon in 1972, strident denunciations of the United States in the Chinese press were toned down and Uncle Sam was no longer vilified in public. Soviet "revisionism" and "social imperialism" had now replaced "American imperialism" as "the number one enemy of the Chinese people." An elaborate system of bomb shelters was built beneath Chinese cities in preparation not for an American attack from the south but for a Soviet attack from the north.

Beginning in the late 1970s, media images of the United States derived from the canons of Marx, Lenin, Stalin, and Mao began to be replaced by more objective and nuanced analyses. During the past decade, rabid anti-Americanism has gradually given way to cautious pro-Americanism in the general Chinese media and specialized professional publications. This has not been a zero-sum transformation, however. Rather, it has been a shift of degree whereby more positive and objective images of the United States have emerged to coexist with the negative and subjective images. Chinese commentaries on the United States during the 1980s contain both types of images, although pro-American images have grown more salient over time. The ambivalence has returned.

The reemergence of pro-American images in the Chinese media since the late 1970s is primarily attributable to two principal factors. First, the reestablishment of contact between the United States and China in 1972 and the normalization of diplomatic relations in 1979 have opened multiple channels of learning about the United States for all Chinese. Second, a community of professional America watchers has emerged in China during this period who, through classified channels, interpret the United States for the top leadership and concerned elites and, through the popular media, for the general populace.

During this period, the U.S. government, academic community, public affairs organizations, and private foundations have all contributed substantial funds and manpower to improving the general level of understanding about the United States among Chinese. For example, the Fulbright program in China is now the largest in the world. American scholars, teachers, and students now populate Chinese campuses, and joint training programs have been established in Beijing, Nanjing, Dalien, and other cities. Voice of America has a listenership of several hundred million daily for news and features about American society as well as English lessons. American films are shown in Chinese theaters. Central China Television airs more than 200 hours of programming from the Columbia Broadcasting System per year, and satellite feeds from American networks run on the evening news. Translations of American articles and books fill Chinese periodicals and bookstores, respectively.[6] A web of sister-city and state-province relationships now tie the two societies together. More than 20,000 American tourists visit China annually.

While the efforts of concerned American organizations have been impressive, they will never completely satisfy the insatiable appetite for things American among the Chinese public, particularly among young people. In this respect, it may be concluded that 30 years of unremitting anti-American propaganda has had an effect on the Chinese public opposite of what was intended. Starvation and force-feeding have greatly stimulated the appetite.

In addition to the substantial number of programs undertaken in China, a key component of the total American effort has been to bring select Chinese to the United States for short-term visits and long-term research and study. Hundreds of Chinese visit the United States annually on delegations, and the number of those staying for longer-term research and collegiate study total nearly 20,000 today. Through direct exposure to the United States and through programs run in China, overall knowledge about America has vastly increased and the objective quality of the analysis of the United States in the Chinese media has markedly improved.

The professional America watchers in China have probably benefited most from this exposure, and through their writings they have had a profound impact on what the average Chinese learns about the United States. Chinese newspapers and periodicals now regularly carry features about America, many of which are dispatches from correspondents posted in America. A large portion of this commentary is rather straightforward reporting of events in the United States, much of which is rewritten from the American press. Thus a kind of double-mirror effect is taking place; Chinese are increasingly interpreting the United States as Americans interpret it.

Keeping in mind that more positive

6. For an analysis of the content of these writings, see David L. Shambaugh, *Coverage of the United States in Key Chinese Periodicals during 1984* (Washington, DC: United States Information Agency, Office of Research, 1985); idem, *Books on the U.S. in the P.R.C.* (Washington, DC: United States Information Agency, 1988).

pro-American images have become dominant in the Chinese media during the 1980s, let us now consider anti-Americanism in the Chinese media such as it exists during this period. These anti-American images usually find expression in the terminology and categories of analysis of Marxist-Leninist political economy.

IMAGES OF THE
AMERICAN ECONOMY

No aspect of the United States is analyzed more extensively in the Chinese media and professional publications than the U.S. economy. A larger cadre of America specialists is devoted to this pursuit than any other. Negative images of the American economy are usually associated with the Marxist image of economic "crises," the Leninist image of imperialism, and the Stalinist image of state-monopoly capitalism.

Marx put forth the view that capitalist economies are intrinsically afflicted with repetitive "partial" crises characterized by underconsumption, depressed demand, inflationary prices, stagnant production, rising unemployment, lower wages, higher surplus value, and a falling rate of profit. Supposedly each "partial" crisis becomes more intense and brings the capitalist economy closer to a "general crisis," which will precipitate the collapse of the capitalist system and stimulate social revolution. According to Chinese Marxist political economists, the United States has undergone seven such economic crises (*jingji weiji*) since World War II: 1948-49, 1953-54, 1957-58, 1960-61, 1969-70, 1973-75, and 1980-82. With each crisis, the American bourgeoisie has tightened the noose further around the neck of the proletariat, and the economy has become increasingly beset with structural "contradictions"

for which the American ruling class has no solution.

Yet somehow a "general crisis" like the Great Depression has not occurred, and the American economy has not collapsed as an imperialist economy should according to Lenin's theory of imperialism. The refusal of the U.S. economy to cooperate with its projected demise befuddled many Chinese analysts who, beginning in 1978, began to reevaluate Lenin's core assumption of imperialism's certain collapse. A vigorous and prolific polemic was waged among Chinese Marxist theorists on the validity of this premise—particularly regarding the United States—from 1978 to 1982. It was generally concluded that American imperialism still "exhibited some vitality," in the words of one analyst, and, while "moribund," as Lenin had termed it, was not in danger of dying any time soon. It was concluded by many that imperialism was a "long-term historical stage" that could last well into the twenty-first century before the full transition to socialism was achieved in the capitalist world.

Relatedly, Stalin's thesis that the imperialist stage of capitalist development was characterized by the "subordination" of the state apparatus to the financial oligarchy was also reevaluated. Chinese Marxist theorists concluded that this interpretation was an overly dogmatic reading of what Lenin and Hilferding had originally argued was a relationship of "coalescence" between the apparatus of state and the monopoly bourgeoisie. Thus the political superstructure in capitalist societies is now viewed by many Chinese Marxist theorists as not a total function of the economic base. Rather, politics is now recognized as a semi-independent sphere of activity.

What these theoretical debates meant for specific analyses of the American economy was a shift from the bifurcated bourgeoisie-proletariat emphasis to analyses that are concerned not with issues of political economy but rather with economic trends and methods of fiscal adjustment. Articles depicting the big capitalist tycoon (*da zibenjia*) wringing every last drop of surplus value from the "impoverished" (*chongkunhua*) American worker now appear less and less frequently in the Chinese press. To be sure, the phenomena of widespread unemployment, spiraling inflation, public and private debt, capital concentration in the hands of a financial oligarchy, and other characteristics deemed endemic to the American economy are all reported at some length. But, increasingly, Chinese analysts focus their attention on statistical trends in investment, savings, consumption, national budgets, industrial and agricultural productivity, trade and capital flows, tax policy, and the like.

For many, the subject of greatest intrigue is the "new technological revolution" (*xin jixu geming*) taking place in the United States and other Western countries. Chinese writings on this subject show familiarity and fascination with Toffler's "third wave," Bell's "post-industrial society," Brzezinski's "techtronic era," Nesbitt's "megatrends," and so forth. The Chinese very much want to be part of this revolution and believe that if they are left behind in these new technologies China will never truly modernize and catch up to the West.

IMAGES OF
AMERICAN POLITICS

Anti-American images of U.S. domestic politics are similarly analyzed from an economic determinist perspective characteristic of Marxist-Leninist political economy. The majority of these analyses attempt to trace the ties of big business and banking, on the one hand, to government and private sector interest groups, on the other. The key actors in American politics are so-called monopoly financial groups (*longduan caituan*). All other political actors in the United States are viewed as instruments (*gongju*) of these groups. Chinese analysts of this genre argue that these groups have occupied the pivotal position in American politics at least since the New Deal, when the United States entered the stage of state-monopoly capitalism (*guojia longduan zibenzhuyi*).

Before World War II, these groups tended to be familial, interconnected, and concentrated in the northeastern United States, giving rise to a unitary Wall Street-rules-Washington model of American politics. Since the war, however, these groups have become regionally dispersed, more competitive, and less beholden to a few families.

Chinese analysts note, for example, the declining ability of the Morgans and Duponts to place their "henchmen" in government and the marked ascendance of the southern and western financial groups vis-à-vis the traditional northeastern groups. They point to the election of every president since Kennedy as proof of this fact. Johnson owed his allegiance to the "Texas petroleum clique," Nixon and Reagan to the "west coast war industries faction," Ford to the "midwest commodities clique," and Carter to the "Peach Street Gang." Some Chinese analysts stress, however, that the northeastern financial group—particularly the Rockefellers—remains very influential behind the scenes.[7] These

7. See, for example, Zhang Jialin, "The New Composition of the Eastern Financial Group"

observers assert, for example, that Nixon was forced from office following the
Watergate affair (*shuimen shijian*) because "the economic base of his political
power infringed upon (*weifan*) the interests of the Wall Street oligarchy."[8]
That is, there were too many westerners
on the White House staff and in his
cabinet, the Defense Department was
giving too many contracts to southern
and western defense industries, and his
policy of détente with the Soviet Union
was not in the overall interests of the
military-industrial complex.

This unitary image of American politics as dictated by elements of the monopoly bourgeoisie still finds expression in
the media and scholarly writings, but in
recent years Chinese analysts have found
greater virtue in the American political
system as they have become familiar
with the separation of powers, feder-
alism, and electoral democracy. Previously they only articulated the view that
American elections were futile exercises
because both parties represented one
class—the bourgeoisie—and hence American democracy was "sham bourgeois
democracy." As they have begun to
follow the U.S. electoral process more
carefully in the 1980s, the America watchers have developed a greater appreciation of the process of campaigning
and now assert that all classes can
participate in the electoral process.

Similarly, they formerly believed that
the executive branch ran roughshod
over the rest of government, but they
have now come to see fact and merit in
institutionalized centers of competing

political power. Congress's increasingly
assertive role in the foreign policy arena
in general, and Sino-American relations
in particular, has stimulated this shifting
image. Even within the executive branch,
China's America watchers, not unlike
the American media, now identify competing factions and power struggles. In
fact, many of their sources for this
analysis are the American media. We,
therefore, again see a double-mirror
image.

Perhaps the greatest revelation to
Chinese analysts has been the multiple
roles of interest groups and other non-
government actors in society. Instead of
trying to link X lobby to Y element of
the financial oligarchy, Chinese analysts
are now more concerned with the substance of a particular organization's
position and how the organization press-
es its constituency's demands.

In other words, the focus of Chinese
research on American politics has expanded from a unitary state to a disaggregated federal bureaucracy, Congress, state and local government, and a
multitude of private sector actors. A
multiple-actor approach has replaced
the unitary-actor approach. In the process, implicit and explicit anti-American
sentiments have given way to more
objective and implicitly pro-American
images.

Such has not been the case when
Chinese analyze domestic American society or American foreign policy. Both
aspects continue to come in for sharp
negative commentary with anti-American invective.

[Dongbu caituan de xin zhuhe], *World Economic
Herald* [Shijie jingji huabao], 1 Aug. 1983, p. 5.
    8. Fudan University Capitalist Countries' Eco-
nomic Research Institute, ed., *American Monopoly Financial Groups* [Meiguo longduan caituan]
(Shanghai: People's Press, 1975), p. 51.

IMAGES OF
AMERICAN SOCIETY

Fundamental to Chinese images of
U.S. society are the issues of class, race,

and welfare. Class antagonism, racism, and gross inequities in the standard of living are prominent features of a degenerating society. The Chinese media continually present written and visual images of such social decay: the prevalence of divorce and the decline of the nuclear family; neglect of the elderly; gambling, pornography, prostitution, drugs, alcoholism, vagrancy, illiteracy; premarital sex; youth gangs; rock music and modern art; counterculture movements; rampant crime; and the need for religion, which reveals the spiritual void in the lives of most Americans. Such phenomena are frequently pointed to by the Communist Party-controlled media as proof of the "superiority of socialism" and have been used as negative examples of the 1984 campaign against "spiritual pollution" and the 1987 campaign against "bourgeois liberalization."

Despite the prevalence of such negative images of American society in the Chinese press, more admiring images do appear on occasion. Yet even when a more positive portrait is offered, it is often coupled with a corresponding reproof. An example par excellence was an article published in the popular journal *Around the Globe* in December 1984. In "America: A Country Full of Contradictions," the leading Washington correspondent of the New China News Agency presented a series of "contradictions" in American society:

America is so rich, yet has so many poor people. . . . This country's education is so highly developed, yet 26 million Americans are illiterate or semi-literate. . . . America's science and technology is so advanced, but religious superstition is so prevalent. . . . There are a large number of unemployed persons in America, yet each year as many as a million foreigners try by every means to migrate to America. . . . America's medical

profession is so advanced, but the cost of medical treatment is so high that if a person needs an operation it is better to spend the money on airfare to Europe and go into hospital there. . . . Americans put a lot of stress on keeping fit, yet so many people become addicted to drugs and do not hesitate to destroy themselves. . . . America is a country that is particular about its legal system, yet there are so many people who after they commit a crime are able to escape the law's punishment. . . . America is the world's biggest lender, but is also the biggest debtor nation.[9]

The author goes on to contrast bountiful harvest with high levels of malnutrition, affluent suburbanites with urban vagrants, the claim of equal opportunity with racial inequality, and so on.

The article just cited reflects not only the ambivalence in Chinese images of American society but, more important, the negative image that the Communist Party-controlled media feel compelled to present to the Chinese people. The discussion of positive aspects is mere recognition by the authorities that these are the predominant images in the public mind, but the negative commentary reveals what the Communist Party wants the public to believe about capitalist society. The Communist Party has a vested interest in promoting the "superiority of the socialist system" and, therefore, cannot condone its antithesis.

IMAGES OF AMERICAN FOREIGN POLICY

Nary a word of explicit support for U.S. foreign policy objectives or actions is offered in the official Chinese media. The United States is portrayed as locked

9. Li Yanning, "America: A Country Full of Contradictions" [Meiguo: Yige chongman maodun de guojia], *Around the Globe* [Huanqiu], no. 12, pp. 2-5 (1984).

into interminable struggle for global hegemony with the Soviet Union on the one hand and imperialist exploitation of the developing countries on the other. The United States is portrayed as a leading contributor to world tension. Further, under the Reagan administration, the United States has demonstrated an increased willingness to employ military power for political gain. As a result, the country has increasingly meddled in Third World conflicts and has generally become more isolated from these countries.

The United States is portrayed as the prime source of instability in Central America, the Middle East, and southern Africa. During the 1980s, it is argued, the United States has been shifting its meddlesome attention to Asia. U.S.-West European relations are also believed to be increasingly disharmonious, due to nuclear and financial issues.

Sino-American relations have progressed but are plagued by the irresolution of the "Taiwan problem." From the Chinese perspective, the United States is always at fault when an issue of contention arises in bilateral relations, be it perceived intransigence on Taiwan, trade protectionism, export controls, or defections, for instance. On international issues where the United States and China find themselves in agreement, the Chinese media will generally show its approval of American policy by remaining silent, rather than unleashing its usual salvo of criticism.

The critical treatment of American foreign policy in the official Chinese media reflects the continuing sensitivity of the American connection among leadership circles in Beijing. Those who favor a strong Sino-American relationship and support American pressure on the Soviet Union cannot openly say so because they would leave themselves open to criticism from more neutralist or pro-Soviet factions. By not praising U.S. actions, those who control the media—generally hard-line, orthodox Marxists in the Chinese Communist Party's Propaganda Department who are wary of the impact of the West on China—play to a more nationalistic sentiment in their audience, thus leaving open the possibility of a policy reversal.

Such is the portrayal of anti-American attitudes in the Chinese media today. Anti-Americanism is indeed manifest in the press but should not be overstated. Since the 1970s, it has declined markedly in sheer volume and its vitriolic tone has also diminished. The Chinese press remains, however, the place where anti-Americanism is most readily apparent in post-Mao China.

ANTI-AMERICANISM AT THE
MASS LEVEL

Measuring anti-Americanism at the level of the mass populace in China today is presently impossible. No survey research measuring Chinese public attitudes toward the United States has yet been undertaken by Chinese or American researchers. Indications of the Chinese public's images of America are, therefore, impressionistic and anecdotal. These impressions generally reveal pro-Americanism, while anti-American attitudes are usually part and parcel of broader xenophobia.

Visiting Americans frequently return from China recalling euphoric stories of the friendship extended to them as Americans during their trips. Such expressions of amity are not merely the product of well-orchestrated hospitality designed to impress visiting Americans.[10] My

10. For a discussion of the art of political hospitality, see Paul Hollander, *Political Pilgrims*

personal experience from living in China for more than two years indicates that a rather deep reservoir of pro-Americanism does indeed exist at the mass level. America is seen as a land of wealth and opportunity, advanced technology, democracy, friendly and honorable people. Americans are routinely praised for their extroverted and friendly nature, wealth, mobility, industriousness, and lack of the condescension that characterizes the attitudes of other Westerners toward Chinese. In short, Chinese public images of America reveal a pro-Americanism informed much more by direct contact with Americans and the grapevine through which overseas Chinese transmit their stories of America back to China than by the more critical images of the United States presented in the official media.

This reservoir of pro-Americanism among ordinary Chinese was very evident during President Reagan's 1984 state visit to China. Throngs of urban residents in Beijing and Shanghai packed the streets—10 to 20 deep—to get a glimpse of the American president. These crowds were spontaneous. Times of arrival and motorcades were intentionally not announced ahead of time for security reasons, yet hundreds of thousands struggled to get their first glimpse of an American president. Such is never the case for other visiting heads of state.

The point here is that while attitudes of the Chinese mass public toward the United States are difficult to gauge, there does appear to be a great curiosity about, and genuine friendship toward, America and Americans. To find anti-Americanism, one must look to the official Chinese Communist media.

(New York: Harper Colophon Books, 1981), chap. 8.

SUMMARY REFLECTIONS ON ANTI-AMERICANISM IN CHINA

Anti-Americanism in China is essentially rooted in the more general xenophobic impulse in Chinese society that views all foreigners outside the realm of the traditional Chinese tribute system as barbarians. Thus, on one level, Americans have been discriminated against no differently from other Westerners. Yet, as we have noted, Americans have been singled out as the targets of boycotts, demonstrations, political campaigns, public ridicule, scholarly critiques, and media attacks with some regularity during the twentieth century, particularly since 1949.

While these actions are important indicators of manifest anti-Americanism in China, it must be remembered that they are largely events orchestrated by the government to serve political purposes. Participation in these events is virtually mandatory. Therefore, the depth of true anti-American sentiment among the mass populace of China remains an open question. Indeed, as we have noted, the 30 years of harsh anti-American invective seems to have produced, if anything, the opposite of the effect intended. There does appear to be a deep reservoir of pro-Americanism at the mass level today.

It has been the intelligentsia and the bureaucracy that have been the most critical of the United States from Confucian to Communist times. Yet it is precisely among these Chinese where the images of America as a model of science and democracy and as a model of a morally decadent society and aggressive nation abroad coexist. This dichotomy has been operative in the minds of many influential Chinese for more than two centuries since the two nations first came into direct contact, and it is most likely to continue into the foreseeable future.

This ambivalence about America reflects the fundamentally different value systems in the two societies. There are fundamental differences in basic beliefs about the nature of man and society that make it difficult for Chinese to understand America and vice versa.[11] We have seen that some of the Chinese beliefs are derivative from Marxism-Leninism, but most are just rooted in traditional Chinese thought. For example, the Chinese perception of the self as an integral part of a larger network of human relationships is quite different from the American belief in the natural rights of man. Viewed in this light, it is not surprising that the American concerns for privacy, private property and enterprise, and civil and human rights are often misinterpreted by Chinese as narcissistic and "bourgeois." The idea that personal life-style is separable from public duty has never been fully elaborated in Chinese philosophy.

Similarly, the concept of law in a constitutional democracy is quite alien to the Chinese experience. The very idea that civil and economic behavior should

11. These themes are developed at greater length in Tu Wei-ming, "Chinese Perceptions of America," in *Dragon and Eagle*, ed. Michel Oksenberg and Robert B. Oxnam (New York: Basic Books, 1978), pp. 87-106.

be codified and regulated by the external authority of the state strikes many Chinese as unnecessary given Confucian traditions of civic duty and self-discipline. If the social contract already exists de facto, these Chinese would argue, why codify de jure?

The traditional Chinese preference for clearly defined hierarchical relationships and roles and functions in society lies at the very heart of why the American commitment to pluralism in every sphere of life confounds most Chinese. Chinese have repeatedly interpreted American pluralism as a sign of the disintegration of the social order rather than as a sign of the internal dynamism of the system. Chinese do not generally view conflict, competition, and pluralism as having intrinsic merit.

With these psychocultural lenses filtering information about America in the Chinese mind-set, it is no wonder that images of the United States have frequently taken on a negative, anti-American cast. Thus, despite the political expedience of anti-Americanism in public and in the press, in the final analysis anti-Americanism in China is a cultural phenomenon. It is one side of an ambivalent set of images that have persisted for two centuries. As such, anti-Americanism in China exists irrespective of the regime that holds political power in the Middle Kingdom.

ANNALS, *AAPSS*, **497**, May 1988

The Changeable
Soviet Image of America

By VLADIMIR SHLAPENTOKH

ABSTRACT: Perceptions of America in Soviet society are very change-able under the influence of domestic political developments, even if cultural traditions exert significant influence on them. In the 1970s, the image of the United States in the Soviet Union was strongly influenced by Russophile ideology, which held the upper hand over liberal ideology and which coalesced with the official ideology in its attitudes toward the United States. Unlike the previous period, in the 1970s and the first half of the 1980s, the focus was not so much on the capitalistic nature of American society but on the American style of life. The average American was portrayed as completely absorbed with material interests and as insensitive to cultural values and the plight of others. Denouncing Americans for consumerism and vanity, the Soviets during this period themselves demonstrated a growing interest in material comfort and prestige. The image of Americans became a part of the mythological level of the Soviet mentality, which, with the claim to cultural superiority over Americans, was intended to rationalize the growing economic and technological gap between the two countries.

Vladimir Shlapentokh is currently professor of sociology at Michigan State University in East Lansing. He was previously senior fellow in the Sociological Institute in Moscow, where he conducted the first national survey of public opinion in the Soviet Union. He has published numerous books and articles on the subject of sociology in general and Soviet sociology in particular.

THE influence of foreign countries in the life of the Soviet people is immeasurably greater than their influence on Americans. Developments in the West, especially in the United States, "beyond the mountain" (*za bugrom*), to use the modern Moscow slang, rivet the attention not only of the political and cultural elites and the intelligentsia but also of the masses.

Various surveys, including those I have conducted, show, for instance, that unlike Americans, Soviets are truly obsessed with hunting for information about the West. As surveys conducted for *Pravda* in 1968 and 1977 showed, about 90 percent of all readers more or less regularly read the articles on international issues whereas only 70 percent read those on domestic economic issues, 68 percent on moral and educational issues, and 60 percent on Marxist theory. The same pattern was typical for the readers of all other central newspapers. Even the readers of local newspapers preferred international issues to local materials.[1]

1. Vladimir Shlapentokh, *Sotsiologia dlia vsekh* [Sociology for all] (Moscow: Sovietskaia Rossiia, 1970), p. 170; Boris Evladov et al., "Chetyre tysiachi i odno interviu" [One thousand and one interviews], *Zhurnalist,* 10:34-37 (1969); Nina Chernakova, "Informatsionnyie potrebnosti auditorii gazet, radio i televideniia" [The information needs of the mass media audience] in *Sotsiologicheskiie problemy obshchestvennogo mneniia i deiatel'nosti sredstv massovoi informatsii,* ed. V. Korabeinikov (Moscow: Institut sotsiologicheskikh issledovanii, 1979); Vladimir Shlapentokh, "Metodicheskiie problemy sopostavleniia pokazetelei v sotsiologicheskom issledovanii" [Methodology of comparisons of indicators in sociological research], in *Sotsial'nyie issledovaniia: Postroieniie i sravneniie pokazatelei,* ed. E. Andreeiv, N. Blinov, and V. Shlapentokh (Moscow: Nauka, 1978), p. 262; Boris Grushin and Lev Onikov, eds., *Massovaia informatsiia v sovietskom promyshlennon gorode* [Mass information in a Soviet industrial city] (Moscow: Politizdat, 1980), pp. 228-39.

It is obvious that under *glasnost*, with Soviet mass media replete with muckraking materials about various flaws in Soviet life, the interest of Soviet people in domestic information has increased significantly. This eruption in Soviet history, however, is unlikely in the long run to reduce significantly the deeprooted interest of Soviet people in Western life. In fact, the preoccupation of Soviet people—especially the intelligentsia—with Western culture and lifestyle has increased during Gorbachev's regime. The total infatuation of Soviet youth with rock music in this period is only one of many signs of this trend.

This deep interest in the West has been characteristic of Russia since the period when its leaders and intellectuals became aware of the backwardness of their country in standard of living, technology, and science and to some degree also in political culture. The struggle between westernizers, who regarded the West as the model for Russia, and their opponents, who praised Russian exceptionalism, has been an important factor in Russian history in the last two centuries. The October revolution can be regarded as an important episode in this struggle because Bolsheviks, as westernizers, saw as their goal the termination of Russia's status as a developing country.

Russians have always singled out one Western country to be either a model for imitation or a model for rejection. In the late eighteenth century and in the first half of the nineteenth century, it was, of course, France. In the next period up to the Revolution, it was England and to some degree Germany. Since the creation of the Soviet state, and especially after World War II, however, it has been the United States that has captured the imagination of the Soviet people and that has become the symbol of the West in the Soviet mind.

It was Josef Stalin himself who in 1925 presented the "American business-like approach" as no less important for the future of the country than was the "Russian revolutionary style."[2] The most popular book on a foreign country published in the USSR before the war was Il'ia Il'f and Evgenii Petrov's *One Storey America* (1936).[3] The prestige of America grew enormously during the war against Hitler. Following the war, U.S. dominance almost completely replaced all other Western countries as a point of reference for Soviet people until Japan reemerged as such in the 1970s.[4] Therefore, the images of the United States and the attitudes toward this country in the USSR represent the stance of the Soviet people toward the West in general.

INSTABILITY OF SOVIET PERCEPTIONS OF AMERICA

The stability of perceptions of foreign countries is quite uneven. It can be asserted that Soviet attitudes toward India, Africa, or even France hardly underwent serious oscillations during the last several decades. This is not the case, however, with America. Though retaining a strong interest in this country for 50 years, Soviet people have changed their views on America very significantly, focusing at various times on different traits ascribed to the United States. This does not imply that cultural traditions stemming from as far back as the nineteenth century do not maintain their influence on Soviet images of America. The present political, economic, and social developments in the USSR have affected these images so strongly, however, that even within a generation there have been different phases in the attitudes of the Soviet people toward the United States. The changes in the flow of so-called objective information about America—such as data on national income, standard of living, health care, and so forth—are much less accountable for the evolution of these attitudes than are various social trends in Soviet society.

Such a variation in perceptions of America is possible because these perceptions reside mostly in the mythological level of the Soviet mind, whose goal is not to direct human behavior—that is the function of the pragmatic level—but rather to create psychological comfort and justification of conformity such as allegiance to dominant ideology. It is this mythological level that explains why many Soviet intellectuals in the 1970s, the period of political reaction, so easily replaced in their mind the set of enthusiastic images of the United States with a set with mostly negative pictures.[5]

Such flexibility in the image held of the United States and other countries is achieved by attributing different weights to the elements of the schema used by an individual for the organization of the data about the external world.[6] The

2. Josef Stalin, *Voprosy Leninizma* [Questions of Leninism] (Moscow: Politizdat, 1952). See also Stalin's conversation with Emile Ludwig in 1932 in which Stalin again praised the American style of work as well as democratic traditions in the workplace. Idem, *Sochineniia* [The collected works] Moscow: Politizdat, 1951), 13:114-15.

3. Il'ia Il'f and Evgenii Petrov, *One Storey America* (Moscow, 1936).

4. See, for instance, Vsevolod Ovchinnikov, *Vetka Sokury* [Branch of the Sokura] (Moscow: Sovietskii pisatel', 1975).

5. As an example, see Evgenii Evtushenko, *Iagodnyie mesta* [Berry fields] (Moscow: Sovietskii pisatel', 1982).

6. Ulric Neisser, *Cognition and Reality: Principles and Implications of Cognitive Psychology* (San Francisco: Freeman, 1976); John Anderson, "Concepts, Propositions and Schemata: What

stock of information about the external
world held by the average Soviet individual with education close to the secondary school level contains numerous
supposed facts about the United States
and about Americans. These facts come
from textbooks, the mass media, novels,
films, and other sources.

The various factors that have an
impact on the mentality of an individual
can activate or deactivate single traits
attributed to America and, therefore,
can create different images of this country ranging from very positive to very
negative without causing major disruptions in the individual's mental continuity. This same cognitive mechanism
can explain how different Soviet individuals with the same knowledge about
the United States have opposite perceptions of this country. And, of course,
with a given schema about the United
States at work, whether positive or
negative, groups and individuals tend to
select that information that endorses
their already formed stereotypes about
America.[7]

Are the Cognitive Units?" *Nebraska Symposium
on Motivation* (Lincoln: University of Nebraska
Press, 1980).
    7. About the influence of the cognitive
schema on the selection of information and the
attitudes toward objects, see Myron Rothbart et
al., "Recall of Confirming Events: Memory Processes and the Maintenance of Social Stereotypes,"
Journal of Experimental Social Psychology,
15:343-55 (1979); Abraham Tesser, "Self-Gen-
erated Attitude Change," *Advances in Experimental Social Psychology*, vol. 11 (New York:
Academic Press, 1978); Abraham Tesser and
Christopher Leonne, "Cognitive Schemas and
Thought as Determinants of Attitude Change,"
Journal of Experimental Social Psychology, 13:
340-56 (1977); Abraham Tesser and Paul Dan-
heiser, "Anticipated Relationship, Salience of
Partner and Attitude Change," *Personal Social
Psychology Bulletin*, 4:35-38 (1978).

The major phases of Soviet political
developments after 1953, as well as
before—the 1960s with its post-Stalin
liberalization, and the 1970s and early
1980s with its conservatism—created
their own dominant images of the United
States even if they had common elements
reflecting the deep animosity of Soviet
official ideology toward the capitalist
society and the old traditional xenophobia.

Of course, developments in the United States also have an impact on the
images held in the USSR. The successful
economic growth in the 1960s and the
decline in the 1970s, with their many
consequences, had some impact on the
Soviet image of the United States as well
as on the evolution of international
relations, especially the relations between the United States and the USSR.

HETEROGENEITY OF
SOVIET IMAGES

The idea that it is possible to describe
the image of America held by the Soviet
individual is unrealistic simply because
Soviet society is too heterogeneous to
speak about aggregate perceptions of
the United States. Without the large
middle class found in the United States,
Soviet society is more differentiated
than American society. It is likely that
the variance in American perceptions of
the USSR is much lower than that in
Soviet perceptions of the United States.

Such variables as ethnicity, age, edu-
cation, and place of residence are ac-
countable for the strong diversity of
Soviet attitudes toward the United
States. All other things being equal,
Russians are less favorable toward the
United States and the West in general
than non-Russians, especially non-
Slavs; the same is true about old people

in comparison with young, poorly educated compared to highly educated, and villagers in relation to city dwellers. These correlations were discovered in our and other studies as early as the 1960s and were corroborated by subsequent investigations in the 1970s and later.[8] The difference between groups are so great that we have to speak about many images of America held in the USSR.

Having insufficient space in this article to discuss the images of America held by all the various groups in the USSR, we will concentrate on the perceptions held by the intelligentsia.

The intelligentsia, formally defined as professionals and people with higher education, includes about 20 million people and about 12 percent of all employees in the country.[9] Due to high social mobility, practically every family contains among its members or among their close relatives people with higher education. This makes the intelligentsia a stratum that is strongly intertwined with the masses, and the views of the intelligentsia and their way of life tend to spread gradually among other groups. Our data and the results of a survey conducted by my former Soviet colleagues show, for instance, that workers, peasants, and clerks, with at least elementary school education, follow the pattern of the intelligentsia in monitoring life in the West, in their interest in foreign literature, foreign movies, and so on.

This does not imply, however, that there are no radical differences between the attitudes of the intelligentsia and those of the masses toward various issues, including America. The ideas adopted by the intelligentsia to a considerable degree pave the way for the masses, however, and, therefore, it is reasonable to make the intelligentsia, as the key opinion leaders, the major subject of this study.

IDEOLOGIES AND AMERICA

Among the factors that directly influence the image held of the United States, ideology is probably the most powerful. By "ideology" we mean here the more or less cohesive set of beliefs and values that describe the main goals of a society or group and that establish standards for the evaluation of human behavior.[10]

The various ideologies functioning in Soviet society differ in their attitudes toward the West in general and toward the United States, as the epitome of capitalism, in particular. All three major ideologies that today circulate among the Russian intelligentsia—official, democratic, and Russophile—have quite distinctive images of the United States, even if variations of these images exist within each ideology and although each ideology on the whole tends to change its perception of America over time. Each of these ideologies has been dominant among the intelligentsia in dif-

8. Shlapentokh, Sotsiologiia dlia vsekh; idem, "The Study of Values as a Social Phenomenon: The Soviet Case," Social Forces, 61:403-17 (Spring 1982); Grushin and Onikov, Massovaia informatsiia.

9. Soiuz sovetskykh sotsialisticheskyh respublik, Tsentral'noe statisticheskoe upravlenie, Narodnoie khoziastvo SSSR v 1985 godu [Statistical yearbook of 1985] (Moscow: Finansy i statistika, 1986), p. 27.

10. Clifford Geertz, Interpretation of Cultures (New York: Basic Books, 1973); Clyde Kluckhohn, "Values and Value Orientations in the Theory of Action," in Toward a General Theory of Action, ed. Talcott Parsons and Edward A. Shills (Cambridge, MA: Harvard University Press, 1951); Vladimir Shlapentokh, Soviet Public Opinion and Ideology: Mythology and Pragmatism in Interaction (New York: Praeger, 1986).

ferent periods of Soviet history though all three have always been present to varying degrees in the intellectual community and in the mass intelligentsia.

The official image of the United States and the West prevailed among the Soviet intelligentsia in the first decades after the revolution and especially in the period of mass repressions, when even a single good word for any foreign country—especially the United States, England, or France—could cost the freedom and even the life of an individual careless enough to pronounce it.[11] The official image of America, which carried over from this period to the next, was based on the so-called class approach, which emphasized the life of America's various underprivileged minorities—the unemployed, blacks, the homeless—rather than that of the average American. It also focused on specific features of capitalism—social differentiation, exploitation, monopolies, and mass culture. The American masses, to the extent that ideological writers touched upon them, were described in accordance with this class approach rather positively, as having a hard life and suffering from the precarious character of their life under capitalism, which included uncertain futures and dependence on bank credit.

After Stalin's death, democratic ideology gradually began to take the upper hand among the intelligentsia and with it came a radically different image of America and the West. Releasing themselves gradually from the shackles of official ideology, Soviet intellectuals and after them the mass intelligentsia began in the 1960s to forge an image of Ameri-

11. See Aleksandr Solzhenitsyn, *A World Split Apart: Commencement Address Delivered at Harvard University* (New York: Harper & Row, 1978).

ca as a country that achieved a fantastic level of technological and scientific progress. The landing of Americans on the moon in 1969, in evident contrast to the Soviet failure to do the same, was perceived as the logical demonstration of American economic superiority over the USSR, whose success with Sputnik was seen as merely temporary.

Focusing on America's brilliant economic performance in the 1960s, Soviet intellectuals ascribed it to the country's democratic system and market regulation of its economy. Being absorbed with discussions of institutional aspects of American society, they, like the official ideologues with whom they disagreed, gave relatively little attention to the life of the average American though presenting it in rather positive light. The negative side of the American social system, which was at the core of the official image, was mostly ignored by intellectuals.

The ideological climate in the country significantly changed in the 1970s, after the Soviet invasion of Czechoslovakia and the defeat of the democratic movement inside the Soviet Union. The frustration of the intelligentsia combined with strong political pressure led to a widened influence of Russophile ideology, which had played only a secondary role in the 1960s. This ideology, especially in its aggressive version, advanced the superiority of Russians and Russian cultural and moral traditions over the West. Unlike official and democratic ideologies in the 1960s, with their common emphasis on the economic and political dimensions of America's image, Russophile ideology focused on the life of the average individual, especially its moral and cultural aspects. What is more, in the 1970s, official ideology also gradually began to move in the direction of Russophile ideology, making the superiority of the Soviet style of life over its American counterpart the core of its foreign propaganda and publishing hundreds of books and articles addressing this issue.

One very important development significantly contributed to the convergence of official conservative and Russophile ideology in their attitudes toward America. Until the 1970s, anti-American propaganda was combined with the public recognition of the American lead in economic efficiency, technology, and science. Since the October revolution, America had been in this respect the paragon for imitation, with the exception of a short period of Stalin's paranoiac campaign against cosmopolitanism in the late 1940s, when Russia was proclaimed as being ahead of the whole world in everything.

The strong confidence that the USSR could catch up and even outrun the United States in certain domains tempered to some degree the envy of American well-being felt by officials and those who were under the influence of Soviet ideology. Khrushchev's numerous speeches were the last official speeches to express this optimism, however, and his party program of 1961 was the last official document to do so. With the stagnation of all sectors of Soviet society in the Brezhnev period, both the Soviet bureaucracy and the intelligentsia lost all hope of catching up with the United States. The new party program adopted in January 1986, which reflected the spirit of the previous period though Gorbachev had already been in power a half year, avoided, in clear contrast to Khrushchev's program, all comparisons with the United States.

Under such circumstances, American technological and economic superiority has gradually engendered an inferiority complex among Soviet leaders, intellectuals, and ordinary people. Stanislav Kondrashov, a prominent Soviet journalist who worked in New York for many years, revealed this strong "black" envy of America in his 1985 documentary novel about this country, *In the Alien Element*. He wrote, for example, that "since we are behind in the world of consumer goods and comfort, those who hate us—the bourgeoisie—feel justified in not treating us as equal to them in the world of interstate relations as well."[12] Vera Tkachenko, a well-known *Pravda* journalist, recognized that "the plebian envy of other people born on more warm and abundant land" is a serious problem in Soviet society.[13]

It is remarkable that even the most committed haters of the West and especially of America among Russophiles are convinced of the absolute scientific and technological superiority of the United States, exhibiting a clear tendency to overstate American potential in various spheres. For example, Vasilii Belov, one of the most aggressive representatives of this ideological trend, revealed in his vitriolic anti-Western novel his conviction that the Central Intelligence Agency, with its sophisticated methods, knows much more about present and future Soviet life than does Gosplan, the State Planning Committee.[14]

The loss of optimism with regard to the technological and economic progress of the USSR pushed both officials and Russophiles to the psychologization and

12. Stanislav Kondrashov, "V chuzhoi stikhii" [In the alien element], *Novy mir*, 11:20 (1985).
13. *Pravda*, 21 Aug. 1987.
14. Vasilii Belov, "Vse vperedi" [All is ahead], *Nash sovremennik*, 7:29-106 (1986); ibid., 8:54-110.

individualization of the American image in an attempt to take revenge in the spheres of culture and morals. As all other images of America, the image offered by this ideological alliance was also based on presumably hard facts about American life, but again, as with other images, its specificity lay in the weight attributed to it, that is, in the underscoring of data that fit and the disregarding of data that did not fit the desirable schema.

The dominance of the Russophile component in the image of America that we discuss here manifests in the disregard for a major principle of the class approach to a foreign country—to contrast the ordinary people as good to the capitalists, who are bad. As was the case during the war against Nazi Germany, the clear tendency of Soviet authors in the 1970s and especially in the first half of the 1980s was to express negative attitudes toward the American nation without making serious distinctions between the proletariat and the capitalists.

Grigorii Oganov, an active journalist who writes on foreign life, contends, in defiance of the class approach, that American mass media are successful in controlling the minds of the American people and that the whole American population was "caught by chauvinistic euphoria under the impact of ABC's broadcast of the Olympic Games in Los Angeles."[15]

Kondrashov, who did not spare many disparaging remarks about the American people in general—Americans are, for instance, "boorish"—describes American workers with the same barely hidden disgust with which he treats the majority of other Americans: physically, the

miner as well as his wife, "a pale and uncomely woman,"[16] are repulsive. Only a few authors in the 1980s, such as Iurii Iziumov—"Americans are mostly beautiful people"[17]—have dared to express some sympathy toward the American people or to treat American issues in a mostly traditional Marxist way.

The rise of Russophilism brought another element to the American image— a real novelty in comparison with the 1960s—the role of Jews in the United States. Two schools of thought on this issue can be discerned in the Soviet Union. The first, closer to Marxist analysis, tended to present Zionism and Israel as servants of American imperialism whereas the second, dominated by Russophiles, presented America as being in the grip of Zionists—a code word for "Jews"—or even explicitly of Jews. So, Vladimir Semeniuk and Vladimir Bolshakov, along with many other authors, portray Zionists and American Jews as responsible for American foreign policy, especially that of the Reagan administration.

Even Kondrashov, who is clearly not among the Russophile extremists, expressed negative attitudes toward Jews. Vitalii Korotich, who, as the editor of the weekly *Ogoniok*, later became a leading figure of *glasnost*, filled his book on America with strong diatribes against American Zionists, among whom he included all Jews who are critical of the USSR.[18]

With their strong focus on the life of the average American, both ideologies, especially the official one, retained their

15. Grigorii Oganov, *Pautina* (Moscow: Politizdat, 1985), p. 242.

16. Kondrashov, "V chuzhoi stikhii," p. 84.
17. Iurii Iziumov, *Neofitsial'noe puteshestvie* [An unofficial trip] (Moscow: Moskovskii rabochii, 1983), p. 20.
18. Vitalii Korotich, *Litso nenavisti* [The face of hatred] (Moscow: Sovetskii pisatel', 1985).

critique of American social problems, and the list of these problems was significantly increased in the 1970s to include, along with the traditional flaws of America such as unemployment, poverty, the exploitation of immigrants, and racism, newer problems such as crime, drugs, pornography, and sexual libertinism. America's imperialism—economic, cultural, and political—its aggressive foreign policy and subversive activity against socialist and other progressive countries, its desire to unleash nuclear war, its lying mass media and intoxicating mass culture, and its persecution of progressive people were, of course, absolutely obligatory elements of any writings on America.

Primarily this type of critique rather than a factual description of the American style of life is presented to the Soviet mass audience—workers, peasants, and clerks—which, as some surveys showed, almost completely accepted this vision of the United States. Grushin's study discovered that the average Soviet individual is sure that the standard of living in the United States is much less than in Czechoslovakia—55 percent of respondents named the latter as the more prosperous against 15 percent who pointed to the United States—and that Americans enjoy much less democratic freedom than Czechoslovakians—55 percent versus 19 percent—whereas the United States ranks first in the extent to which political freedoms are suppressed—53 percent versus 16 percent for China and 7 percent for South Africa.[19]

The image bolstered by these two ideologies became dominant among intellectuals and mass intelligentsia in the late 1970s and early 1980s. This image

was carried over to the Gorbachev era and only in 1987 could we witness a growing counteroffensive by democrats and westernizers. It is notable that the same image of American life was generally supported abroad by Alexander Solzhenitsyn, especially in his famous Harvard speech,[20] as well as by other emigrants. Since the mid-1970s, and especially in the first half of the 1980s, the negative image of the American style of life was supported with information brought by disillusioned Soviet emigrants who returned to the USSR from the United States. Books and articles presenting the emigrants' negative impression of the United States became prominent sources of such information.

A circumstance that also contributed very much to the making of the strongly negative American image in the early 1980s was the strong exacerbation of conflicts in the relations between the USSR and the United States. Anti-Americanism in Soviet propaganda began to increase immediately after the Afghan invasion of 1979 and reached its peak in 1983 under Andropov, when the Soviet leadership tried to scare the world about the risks of nuclear war in order to prevent the basing of American missiles in Western Europe. The vituperation against the American government, President Reagan, and America in general was probably unprecedented in Soviet history, even compared to the days of the cold war from 1948 to 1952. The fear of war that spread in Russia for the first time since 1945, combined with anti-American hysteria, largely accounted for the further lowering of American prestige in Soviet eyes.[21]

19. Grushin and Onikov, *Massovaia informatsiia*, p. 312.

20. Solzhenitsyn, *World Split Apart*.
21. Vladimir Shlapentokh, "Moscow's War Propaganda and Soviet Public Opinion," *Problems in Communism* (Sept.-Oct. 1981), pp. 88-94.

SOVIET PERCEPTIONS OF THE
AMERICAN DREAM

The image of American life held by intellectuals consists of three major clusters that describe the major goals of average Americans, their cultural interests, and their human relations.

Americans, as well as Russians and many other peoples, like to think that they are loved by the whole world, at least by objective and honest people in other countries. The reality, however, is quite different. Though many Americans do not realize it, in the early 1980s, their country was hated by a majority of Russians. It is interesting to note that, in the period of *glasnost*, Russians are also being told for the first time that the belief that their country is loved by the peoples of the world is one of many illusions that they have long cherished.[22]

Since the mid-1970s, the average American has been portrayed as a person absorbed with material interests, indifferent to others, and far from real cultural values.

Russophile writer Iurii Davydov, in his work *Etika lubvi i metafisika svoevoliia* (The ethics of love and the metaphysics of arbitrariness), describes the Russian people as "the single carrier of the moral idea" and as the people ready to suffer for the sake of this idea.[23] Another Russophile author, Iurii Seleznev, in *Glazami naroda* (Through the people's eyes), contends that "the Russian national mentality was never bourgeois."[24] Russophiles present Americans as a people completely absorbed with narrow mercantilistic interests and the accumulation of wealth and money. In this view, the "yellow devil"[25]—money—which runs the country, conveys the core of American life.

Gennadii Gerasimov, a leading Soviet foreign journalist who, like Kondrashov, spent several years in this country and who is the main mouthpiece of the Ministry of Foreign Affairs in Moscow, begins a chapter in his book on the United States with the sentence "You can say that people in America speak only about money."[26] Another Soviet author, Vladimir Nikolaiev, begins an article on American life in practically the same say, saying, "[The] dollar—the first and most important symbol of the United States, the second—the automobile."[27]

Only a few of the Soviet authors who continue to adhere to orthodox Marxism—such as Shestakov—are inclined to treat the American dream as more than the hunt for money and affluence, pointing also to "a democratic version" of this dream based on a yearning for social and national equality.

In the Soviet image of America, the passion for money is linked with blatant consumerism and vanity. The relentless desire to replace one model of car with another and the obsession with conspicuous consumption is presented by many authors as an essential part of American life. The purposeful selection of American novels for translation, which includes mainly those that cast a very critical eye on the life of the average

---

22. See *Literaturnaia gazeta* [Literary gazette] (Sept. 1987).

23. Iurii Davydov, *Etika lubvi i metafisika svoevoliia* (Moscow: Molodaia gvardiia, 1982), pp. 270-71.

24. Iurii Seleznev, *Glazami naroda* (Moscow: Sovremennik, 1986), p. 50.

25. Maxim Gorky coined this phrase in 1906.

26. Gennadii Gerasimov, *Obshchestvo potrebleniia: "Mify i real'nost"* [Consumer society: Myth and reality] (Moscow: Znanie, 1984), p. 21.

27. Vladimir Nikolaiev, "Amerikantsky vos'midesiatykh godov" [Americans of the 1980s], *Nash sovremennik*, 9:155 (1985).

American, has helped strongly to buttress such perceptions of Americans among the intelligentsia.

SPIRITUAL AND CULTURAL EMPTINESS

In the Soviet view, the Russian superiority over Americans manifests itself most clearly in the different attitudes of the two peoples toward culture. In the Soviet view, Americans, preoccupied with the accumulation of wealth, with consumerism, and with the desire to keep up with the Joneses, are indifferent to high cultural values. As Gerasimov wrote, "They all embraced absorption with making money and achieving success. Thus, they have neither the time nor the interest for science, literature and the arts."[28]

Iurii Bondarev, one of the most eloquent Russophile spokesmen of the 1980s, put in the mouth of Viasheslav Krymov, the hero of his novel *Play,* the following words: "American ignorance and the madness of money became the invincible legislators of fashion in the world, leading to the degradation of taste in the world."[29] His American friend, also a film director and a supporter of this view of America, came to Moscow in order to find salvation in Russian culture. Vladimir Soloukhin, another representative of Russophilism, is sure that America lacks "clear national originality."[30]

In general, Americans are portrayed as completely immersed in mass culture

and deeply alienated from the high traditions of European culture and from high poetry and prose.

HUMAN RELATIONS AND MORALS

Human relations is another sphere where the Russians can feel themselves superior to Americans. Those who built up the image of the United States in the 1970s and early 1980s considered "jungle individualism" one of the most typical American traits.

According to Gerasimov, "In general, everybody in the U.S. is concerned only about himself, and only God is for everybody. . . . Such concepts as labor collective or civic duties are alien to this country, and the concept of society is treated only as the arena for life's struggle."[31]

With such egotism, Americans are deprived of altruism and compassion and can easily tolerate the poverty and sufferings of their fellow citizens. Nikolai Popov, for instance, asserts that "the average American is educated to believe that the 'lower class' only consumes and does not work."[32] And certainly, Americans with their coldness, mercantilism, and egotism have no real idea about genuine friendship or romantic, self-sacrificing love.

American individualism, as asserted by the architects of this image, is directly accountable for the American love of guns, which results in violent behavior and crimes. What is more, the same individualism combined with affluence makes Americans the most conceited people in the world and strongly self-

28. Gerasimov, *Obshchestvo potrebleniia,* p. 66.

29. Iurii Bondarev, *Igra* [Play] (Moscow: Sovetskii pisatel', 1983), pp. 133, 139.

30. Vladimir Soloukhin, *Kameshki na ladoni* [Pebbles on the palm] (Moscow: Molodaia gvardiia, 1982), p. 84.

31. Gerasimov, *Obshchestvo potrebleniia,* p. 71.

32. Nikolai Popov, *Amerika 80-kh g: Obshchestvennoe mnenie i sotsial'nye problemy* (Moscow: Mysl', 1986), p. 127.

centered. As Kondrashov writes, "America considers the whole world as its appendage, and this self-complacent imperial ethnocentrism cannot lead to good things."[33]

Many Soviet authors—including those who, as consistent Russophiles, claim for Russia a missionary role in the moral rejuvenation of the world or those who, as Marxists, claim such a role for Russia in the creation of the new Communist society—blame Americans for their pretensions to appropriate precisely this exceptional role in the world. The critique of American exceptionalism is thus a leading theme in many publications on the United States.

According to the authors of the late 1970s and early 1980s, American self-confidence and conceit is often combined with hatred of other people, Russians most of all. This idea was a leading one in Gerasimov's book *Society of Consumption* (1984) and also in Vitalii Korotich's book *The Face of Hatred* (1985).

ONLY ONE POSITIVE TRAIT

Presenting a very unpleasant portrait of the average American, Soviet authors of the 1970s and 1980s have had positive words for only one quality: American labor ethics, whose level they may in fact have overestimated. Of course, not every author has been ready to utter something positive about America, and a survey of textbooks on social issues published from 1970 to 1985 provides a convincing example. [34] Writers such as Kondrashov, Vitalii Korotich, or Iurii Iziumov, however, who preserved some autonomy of

judgment, could articulate something about hardworking Americans, revealing in this way to their readers that American well-being is not 100 percent attributable to the exploitation of blacks and the Third World.

THE CONSPICUOUS DISREGARD OF TWO PHENOMENA

Presenting American life as deeply flawed and corrupt, those who managed this issue in the 1970s and the first half of the 1980s generally preferred to avoid addressing the role of religion in American society. Religion's role in the United States is many times greater than it is in the USSR. It is almost impossible to find diatribes against the pernicious influence of the church on the mind of Americans, something that could be expected from intellectuals brought up on atheism and contempt for "the opium of the people" and especially from official propagandists who are eager to add to the list of flaws in American society. Authors such as Gerasimov, Kondrashov, and Korotich almost completely skirt this issue, however, making an exception only for Judaism. Only Nikolai Iakovlev, an author despised inside as well as outside the USSR and notorious for his nasty publications attacking Sakharov, Jews, and the United States, published a book, *Religion in America of the 80s*, citing data on the religious beliefs of Americans, which he interpreted in a primitive Marxist way.[35]

The cause of this strange reticence of many Soviet authors to criticize the religiosity of Americans lies again in the fact that in the 1970s it was Russophiles who held sway among intellectuals and

33. Kondrashov, "V chuzhoi stikhii," p. 23.

34. Piotr Fedoseiev, ed., *Nauchnyi kommunism* [Scientific communism] (Moscow: Politizdat, 1985).

35. Nikolai Iakovlev, *Religiia v Amerike 80-kh g* (Moscow: Politizdat, 1987).

who also very much influenced official ideology. Religion, even if mostly Orthodox, is a very important element of Russophile ideology. To recognize the strong religiousness of Americans is thus to credit them with a very important virtue that Russophiles want to flourish in their own country. In their inclination to avoid blaming America for its religiousness, Russophiles could find support even among their major adversaries—liberals and westernizers—who, though generally not regarding religion as the salvation of Russia, nevertheless, in defiance of Marxist ideology, demonstrated their respect for religion and their recognition of its positive role in society.

If intellectuals touched upon the religiousness of Americans, they did so mostly to point out the secularization of the population, especially the youth, the hypocritical character of American allegiance to religion, or the spread of so-called nontraditional religions such as Moonism, transcendental meditation, various types of Oriental religions, different sects, and so on.

Soviet intellectuals in the 1970s and early 1980s also tried to ignore the political freedoms enjoyed by Americans in their presentation of American life. Purely hack writers who flaunted their political cynicism, of course, simply denied the existence of real democracy in the United States. American mass media and pluralism are the most frequent objects of criticism in the derogation of democracy in the United States. It is typical for these authors to avoid crediting American democracy and mass media for the discovery of the Watergate affair and the impeachment of Nixon. Instead, they present this affair as having nothing to do with public opinion and as instigated by the monopolies that had come to view Nixon's foreign and domestic policy as dangerous for the dominant class.

Authors, usually with Russophile tendencies who pretend to address the intelligentsia but who are mainly concerned with their reputation and do not want to resort to straight lies, however, usually try to avoid this subject or at least to downgrade as much as possible the importance of democracy for the average American. It is thus not surprising that Russophiles, largely ignoring the role of political freedoms in American life, are rarely successful in understanding the essence of American society, especially American individualism and self-respect and even the American yearning for wealth as a condition for independence.

SOVIET BEHAVIOR AND
AMERICAN IMAGES

There is no question that the image of Americans held by the Soviet intelligentsia reflects the cultural difference between the two societies and that many Russian professionals look down on Americans for their individualism, weak social bonds, and relatively moderate interests in literature, as well as for their complacency toward poverty, unemployment, crime, and other problems attributed to the United States.

As is the case in all other countries, however, the image of the United States in the 1970s and early 1980s was strongly influenced by domestic ideological and political conflicts and by various emotions among which envy was often especially important. This image served not so much as a crystallization of information about the United States, but more as an important component of the mythological level of mentality.

Among other things, this helped people to preserve psychological comfort in relation to a country that was beyond reach in the economic and technological spheres and whose freedoms and democracy were also impossible to imitate.

For just this reason, the image that was just described contains elements that have nothing to do with the real material behavior of the Soviet intelligentsia and that can be considered a product of mythological activity. The hypocritical character of the Soviet image of America reveals itself especially clearly in the castigation of Americans for their materialism and consumerism. Soviet mass media—the speeches of Gorbachev and other Soviet leaders as well as novels and films—depict Soviet people as in many ways even more absorbed with enrichment, with the acquisition of consumer goods, and with conspicuous consumption than Americans. Describing present Soviet society, Alexander Iakovlev, a secretary of the Central Committee, writes about "social passivity and corruption, irresponsibility and moral libertinism, careerism and consumerism" as typical phenomena of Soviet society.[36]

The quest by Soviet people, especially the intelligentsia and the most refined intellectuals, for foreign, particularly American, goods long ago became a fixture of Soviet life. Soviet novels and films colorfully depict this passion of Soviet people for foreign clothes, cars, electronics, videotapes, discs, and so on. A number of surveys conducted in the USSR also confirm the growing consumerism of Soviet people and their

absorption with the Western style of life.

Accusing Americans of individualism and indifference to the lives of others, the creators of the dominant image of the United States manifest blatant disregard for elementary facts of Soviet life that have become known to everyone in the USSR—the alienation of Soviet people from their collectives and from the state, and the growing callousness of Soviet people toward their colleagues, neighbors, and even friends. Soviet novels and films describe Soviet individuals as completely absorbed with their private lives and completely indifferent to any forms of public life. The works of some of the best Soviet writers—such as Iurii Trifonov, Iurii Bondarev, and Georgii Semenov, who portrayed urban life, and Valentin Rasputin, Vasilii Shukshin, and Viktor Astafiev, who described rural life—leave no doubt about the dominance of private interests in the life of the Soviet people and their deep indifference to collective forms of life.

What is more, even in the sphere of literature and the arts, where the Soviet intelligentsia felt itself so superior to Americans, many trends reveal a growing embrace of American habits: for example, the increasing emphasis on television and video recorders, the decline of reading, and many other similar developments. While portraying America darkly, Soviet intellectuals and the mass intelligentsia avidly imitate it in various ways, a phenomenon that is rather universal,[37] whatever our judgments about this process.

36. Alexander Iakovlev, "Dostizheniia kachestvenno novogo sostoianiia obshchestva i obshchestvennye nauki" [Achievements of a new stage of social development and social sciences], *Kommunist*, 8:7 (1987).

37. About the attitudes toward America in Western Europe, Asia, and Africa, see Alvin Z. Rubinstein and Donald E. Smith, eds., *Anti-Americanism in the Third World: Implications for U.S. Foreign Policy* (New York: Praeger, 1985).

CONCLUSION: GORBACHEV'S *GLASNOST* AND THE AMERICAN IMAGE

The new stage in Soviet political history initiated by Mikhail Gorbachev has not yet, at the end of 1987, affected the image of America described in this article. Gorbachev's report at the twenty-seventh party congress was extremely hostile toward the United States, and, in 1985 and 1986, Russophiles and their allies from Brezhnev's times were able to continue propagating their view of the United States as shaped in the previous period.

By 1986, however, it had become possible to publish books with balanced and relatively objective views on America, mostly with Marxism as a theoretical framework. But it was only in 1987 that liberal intellectuals could begin to offer a cautious critique of the image of the United States that had been dominant in Brezhnev's period. The leading periodicals of *glasnost* such as *Literaturnaia gazeta* (Literary gazette), *Sovietskaia kul'tura* (Soviet culture), *Moskovskiie novosti* (Moscow news), *Ogoniok* (Little light) were also among the vanguard in this process.

Gennadii Malmin, writing in *Sovietskaia kul'tura*, attacked the stereotype that Soviet society was in all respects better for children than American society and reported that after his trip to the United States it was necessary to revise the concept that "our children's theatre is the best in the world." Malmin found that American children's theater is professionally far superior.[38] Mikhail Roshchin, a famous dramaturgist, indirectly rejected another important element of the dominant image—the cultural backwardness of Americans—describing the intensive activity and high professional level of American cultural institutions.[39]

If Gorbachev's regime persists and the process of liberalization continues, the westernizers will enhance their position among the intelligentsia and this will lead to the gradual improvement of the American image in the Soviet Union. The intensification of cultural and human exchange between the two countries will also favor this tendency.

38. *Sovietskaia kul'tura*, 7 July 1987.
39. *Moskovskiie novosti*, 21 June 1987.

Book Department

PAGE

INTERNATIONAL RELATIONS AND POLITICS

DAMASKA, MIRJAN R. *The Faces of Justice and State Authority: A Comparative Approach to the Legal Process.* Pp. xi, 247. New Haven, CT: Yale University Press, 1986. No price.

The vast majority of the world's formal legal structures and activities are dominated by three traditions—civil law, common law, and Islamic law. This book is a comparative study of the first two of these, and of the political and administrative systems in which they are embedded. Following Max Weber and other legal and political scholars, Damaska derives an ideal type from each legal system and its political parent. Organizing his analysis along two dimensions—the role and scope of the state, and differences in legal procedure—he sets out a scheme that he hopes will have greater heuristic powers than the many previous studies of comparative legal procedure that have proceeded along variously piecemeal lines.

Damaska translates his abstraction of the Anglo-American tradition of politics and public administration into what he terms the "reactive state"; the Continental counterpart he describes as the "activist state." Each political tradition tends to a form of justice appropriate to its political canons and culture: the Anglo-American to conflict-solving and the Continental to policy-implementing justice. There are matching conventions in public administration. The Anglo-American approach necessitates what Damaska calls a coordinate organization of authority, with distinguishing features such as the use of rotating and lay officials, a horizontal distribution of powers, and an urge toward substantive or equitable judgments. Continental public administration, by contrast, is hierarchical and professional and tends in decision makeup toward technical rather than substantive or equitable standards.

These are the barest of the bones of Damaska's schema. As with all formal analysis, success depends entirely on the credibility of application. Damaska does not claim originality for the insights upon which he draws but rather for the way in which he combines and applies them. The novel part of the study is the linkage between details of legal procedures and the differing spirits of the state and styles of officialdom.

In its range and use of historical, political, philosophical, and legal materials, this study is impressive and is a valuable addition to comparative scholarship. Damaska largely succeeds in his objective of integrating disparate insights and providing a convincing analytical framework upon which more individualized studies might be modeled. The critical question, of course, is whether alternative methods of integrative analysis would yield deeper insights and cover more ground.

To political and legal modes one must add intellectual traditions in our comparative understanding of the life of nations, and readers will doubtless find additional support for Damaska's persuasive contentions about the sources of differences and distinctions in his pleasing adherence to the stringent forms and conventions of central European scholarship.

SEAN McCONVILLE
University of Illinois
Chicago

GILDERHUS, MARK T. *Pan American Visions: Woodrow Wilson in the Western Hemisphere, 1913-1929.* Pp. xiii, 194. Tucson: University of Arizona Press, 1986. $25.95.

SMITH, WAYNE S. *The Closest of Enemies: A Personal and Diplomatic History of the Castro Years.* Pp. 308. New York: W. W. Norton, 1987. $19.95.

Perhaps the most telling observation made by Wayne Smith in his personal history of U.S. diplomatic relations with Cuba concerns Jimmy Carter.

Worst of all, Jimmy Carter presided over the death of idealism. He wrapped himself in the banner of good causes—human rights, sympathy with democrats more than with the dictators in the Third World, promotion of peace in the Middle East, and a serious effort at arms control. His failure as president raised doubts about the causes themselves. In effect, Carter took the banners with him. That was his legacy to the nation.

To some degree this failure is similar to that recounted in Mark Gilderhus's painstaking account of Woodrow Wilson's conviction that Pan Americanism and the League of Nations would be built upon putative natural harmonies existing among nations that could form the basis for hemispheric and world order and prosperity.

In his meticulous study based largely upon diplomatic correspondence with particular reference to Brazil, Argentina, and Chile, Gilderhus chronicles the fact that relations with Latin America were of major concern to Wilson and his adviser, Colonel Edward M. House. Wilson believed the economic concessions sought by European nations threatened the right of self-determination of Latin America, and he promised U.S. support to emancipate them, at the same time pledging that the United States would "never again" acquire "territory by conquest."

The mechanism by which the Wilson administration sought to gain regional cooperation was a Pan American Treaty that through "collective security and compulsory arbitration" could achieve a "multilateral definition" of the Monroe Doctrine. The proposal included provisions for "mutual guarantees of political independence under a republican form of government" and of "territorial integrity." Regulation of arms trade was also envisioned. For Wilson, this would also provide a model for peace among Europeans.

The war itself interrupted European commerce and provided the United States with the opportunity to expand trade within the hemisphere. The U.S. government promoted the facilitation of commerce through the extension of credit by U.S. foreign branch banks made possible under Wilson's Federal Reserve Act of 1913.

The Pan American Pact pursued through diplomatic initiatives by Wilson's ambassadors over a two-year period foundered on his Mexican policy, a topic explored more fully by Gilderhus in his *Democracy and Revolution: U.S.-Mexican Relations under Wilson and Carranza.* The Pershing expedition of 1916 and the refusal to accept offers of good offices from other Latin American nations renewed suspicions about U.S. good faith in multilateral processes. It was in relation to Mexico that Colonel House had earlier recorded thoughts in his diary displaying the paternalism that characterized hemispheric relations of the period. "If a man's home was on fire he would be glad to have his neighbors come in and put it out." Therefore, Mexico "should not object to our helping adjust her unruly household." It was apparent to Latin American leaders that the natural-harmony theory masked a threat of hegemony that made participation in U.S.-dominated political schemes a risky business. The minor role to which they were relegated in postwar deliberations confirmed their reservations.

Gilderhus's book is a work for specialists. Gilderhus rarely departs from his detailed narrative of complicated events to give an overview or interpretation. For the most part he relies upon parameters established by the writers of the diplomatic correspondence or the contemporaneous bulletin of the Pan American Union. Why, for instance, in appraising the basis for Argentina's posture toward the war does he give primacy to competition with Brazil and the impact of German influence but make no reference to the historical relationship with Great Britain?

In contrast to this dense and demanding account, Wayne Smith's book is a good read. Drawing on his personal experience, and full of his judgments, Smith's work is a provocative and important book. It demonstrates how often the United States has failed to take advantage of opportunities for easing tensions with its nearby island neighbor. The current impasse, which led to Smith's early retirement from the foreign service, is clearly ideological. What is more disturbing is that the pragmatism of the Carter period was equally ineffective in achieving a *modus vivendi*. Carter began his presidency by ending overflights and travel and expenditure bans for U.S. citizens. The opening of Cuban and U.S. interest sections—embassies in all but name—in 1977 followed successful negotiations on fishing rights and maritime boundaries. Smith and other State Department officials expected continuing discussions and agreements that would eventually lead to restoration of full diplomatic

relations between the two countries as part of Carter's policy of dealing with the Third World without automatically defining relations in terms of U.S.-Soviet rivalry. Soon this expectation began to be derailed by National Security Adviser Zbigniew Brzezinski, who told the press, incorrectly, that Cubans had increased troop strength in Angola and that normalization was, therefore, impossible. Smith gives numerous examples of continued failure by the Carter administration to pursue a coordinated policy toward Cuba, which included accusing Cuba of fomenting attacks on Zaire in May 1978 by exiled Katanganese from Angola when Cuba had alerted the U.S. to the invasion and offered to cooperate in stopping it. Later, the mounting of U.S.-British air and naval maneuvers and the resumption of overflights in November 1978 occurred when U.S. officials were about to go to Cuba to negotiate the release of four U.S. prisoners. Smith's account, of course, does not include any covert operations against Cuba that might have been occurring during the period, of which he may not have known, although he does discuss operations in Angola by John Stockwell.

The finale of the Carter administration's unsuccessful demarche with Cuba culminated in the Mariel boat lift. Smith has blame for both sides in these events, and by this time he was chief of the U.S. interest section. It is his belief, however, that if the United States had not encouraged marine hijackings of Cuban boats by welcoming the hijackers to U.S. shores and had dealt with Cuban complaints regarding emigration, the sea lift might never have occurred.

Any president is going to have advisers associated with the White House. Wilson had Colonel House; Roosevelt, Harry Hopkins. In foreign affairs in recent administrations, it has been the national security adviser. Under this agreement, not only is advice coming from elsewhere than the State Department, but that adviser has his own institutionalized apparatus. This apparatus has no systematic relationship with the rest of the world, however, and it has no institutional memory—both attributes of the State Department and indispensable to the formulation of an informed and effective foreign policy. Moreover, the national security adviser is biased, as the name implies, by considerations of military security, and this predisposes him—for it is never "her"—to see issues in terms of inevitable East-West conflict.

Nevertheless, the failure of the Carter presidency to realize the liberal goals for which Wayne Smith so assiduously struggled, and the ignoring of the advice of State Department professionals, who were aware of courses that could have been taken that might have led to normalization of relations, may also elicit a more worrisome conclusion. Is U.S. foreign policy still propelled by a view of U.S. interests that makes accommodation with a Latin American nation on the basis of principles applicable equally to both parties an impossibility in the 1980s as it was in 1916, when Wilson turned his back on multilateralism in his dispute with Mexico?

MARJORIE WOODFORD BRAY
California State University
Los Angeles

GILPIN, ROBERT. *The Political Economy of International Relations.* Pp. xvi, 449. Princeton, NJ: Princeton University Press, 1987. $45.00. Paperback, $9.95.

The main theme of Gilpin's book is that the world system is at a threshold of transformation. The concluding sentences are as follows:

Nevertheless, at this juncture in the transition from one economic order to another, the only certainty is that a new international political economy is emerging. It is not clear who will gain, who will lose, or what the consequences will be for global prosperity and world peace (p. 408).

Some reasons given for the world's being on the brink are the relative decline of the United States as a hegemonic leader, the ascendance of the Pacific region, and the uncertain future of Japanese-American relations.

Although the title of the book includes the term "political economy," as do the titles of three of the ten chapters, the analysis is long on economics and short on politics. One factor, for example, for the strategic importance of Japan is Soviet initiatives to contest the United States militarily in Asia rather than Europe. Navies, and now the geopolitics of inner space, are central to a new world order.

Topics covered are trade, money, finance, debt, economic inequality, multinational corporations, and ideology; noneconomic transnational movements and institutions, including religion, and the rise of world cities are not. Messages are sent to a "discourse group" of scholars but in a context general enough to inform interested readers. Heavy in description about economic relations between nations since 1945, several sections contain modern historical developments during several centuries, such as money.

Gilpin is open about his ideology: "My position is that a hegemon is necessary to the existence of a liberal international economy." He contrasts as "contending" theories liberalism, Marxism, and nationalism rather than treating them as conflicting forces of change. The relative decline of the United States is well documented, and he urges it to deal with its foreign debt, reindustrialize, and resist the New Protectionism. Speculation about the new world order focuses on the United States and Japan, whether Japan can become a financial hegemon, and whether the need for a hierarchy for world stability can come from pluralist leadership.

Too much is made of Japan as it begins to face competition, an aging population, and a new generation. Much praise is to be given for emphasizing the role of technology in growth and trade. The prediction that it is "highly doubtful that they [technologies] will cause a replication of the unprecedented postwar global rate of economic growth" can be challenged by recent developments in superconductivity, resins, synthetic materials that could end the century of steel, and the undeveloped know-how of plant production in water and air. One can argue here and there, but this is a very fair presentation of the economic, and hence political, issues confronting those who will shape the near future of a new world order.

HENRY TEUNE

University of Pennsylvania
Philadelphia

KRUZEL, JOSEPH, ed. *American Defense Annual 1987-1988*. Pp. xxvii, 387. Lexington, MA: Lexington Books; Columbus: Ohio State University, Mershon Center, 1987. Paperbound, $16.95.

As a summation of evolving American national security thinking, the yearly volumes of the *American Defense Annual* have become, in the third issuance, an indispensable guide within this complex field. Joseph Kruzel, as sole editor, proves exceptional in his choice of knowledgeable writers and in the logical progression of subject matter. The authors are lucid and fruitful in their observations, while the topics lead the reader into a satisfying, logical coverage.

A glossary and abbreviations, given at the outset, are very helpful, as is the perceptive opening chapter by the editor. Its gist is that the year 1986 was one of "transition and indirection for American defense policy." Among the debits were the Iran-contra scandal and the Reykjavik summit meeting, criticized for concealing "important politico-military initiatives from the nation's senior military officials." The presented evidence is troubling. The U.S.-Soviet rivalry, however, currently shows less range and depth.

To Samuel Huntington, the Reagan strategic innovations give more balance, with defense in nuclear exchanges and with offensive operations in conventional wars. To Richard Stubbing, while military spending has increased, it has been done on the old basis, the three major services dividing the pie with scant attention to priorities. He points out that "in 1987 there was still no comprehensive U.S. defense strategy." General Nutting echoes this in declaring "above all else, the American government and people must find a better structure for defining national interests and objectives, for articulating and executing coordinated policy." Stubbing thinks that the "verdict is still out" on the feasibility of the Strategic Defense Initiative. Drs. Davis and Steinberg, however, believe a strategic defense program of modest or broad goals "makes sense as a hedge against Soviet defenses and as a means of testing the feasibility and limits of new defensive technologies."

There are complaints. Davis and Steinberg believe that there was no willingness to face up to hard choices on strategic nuclear forces. Dr. Lambeth questions whether we could make an adequate and timely resupply of theater forces. Admiral Zumwalt cautions that the United States lacked a ready industrial base and would have to fight with equipment then available. Robert Price, Jr., assails weapons complexities and stresses the need for durable, simple weapons and systems for the average fighting man to use.

Military reform has a proponent in William Lind, who decries military exercises as "better preparation for staging an opera than for combat." Still, he thinks that Army doctrine is in good shape by favoring maneuver over its traditional firepower attrition warfare.

The overdue legislative reform of the Defense Department in 1986 is engagingly described by Vincent Davis, who had closely followed this effort. He gives a hopeful forecast of benefits from a partnership between the secretary and the chairperson of the Joint Chiefs of Staff as principal military adviser to the president, the strengthened theater commanders, and the reduction of service secretaries' powers. The new two-year budgeting system, and the unobstructed career path for joint staff trained officers, and, importantly, the new undersecretary of defense for acquisition (procurement) are deemed vital changes.

While describing the variety of views his contributors represent and while concluding that the military is well equipped, well trained, and highly motivated, Kruzel asks two pregnant questions: (1) with budget limits, can the United States "make hard choices about force strategy and force postures"? and (2) can it recognize that national security, as Lester Brown has pointed out, "requires a strong economic base on which to build military preparedness"?

ROY M. MELBOURNE
Chapel Hill
North Carolina

MccGWIRE, MICHAEL. *Military Objectives in Soviet Foreign Policy*. Pp. xiv, 530. Washington, DC: Brookings Institution, 1987. $39.95. Paperbound, $18.95.

There are a number of ways to examine Soviet foreign policy and each will provide different assessments. While many favor using the lens of ideology, others view it from the perspective of personality or institutions—party, military, bureaucracy. Mcc-Gwire, in the volume under review, suggests that an examination of military objectives provides a means by which a rigorous analysis can be made that will take into account changes in military technology, interpretations of the enemy's goals, and Marxist-Leninist thought, which, while changing, provides the basic framework for Soviet thinking.

Arguing that there is no dearth of material from Soviet sources, the problem instead lies in interpretation. Accordingly, a careful analysis of military objectives in war provides insights to peacetime diplomacy and preparedness. If one starts from the Marxist-Leninist position that the capitalist world must destroy the socialist system to survive, then the main objective of the Soviets is to win that final world war. Initially, he argues, the USSR, between 1948 and 1953, believed that the United States intended to attack it while the West had a military advantage. Thus the Soviet objective was to be strong enough to repel the attack and, in turn, go onto the offensive, defeat the North Atlantic

Treaty Organization (NATO), and deny a beachhead in Europe to the Americans. By the mid-1950s, the Soviets began to pull even with the United States in war-making potential. At the beginning of the next decade, the Kennedy administration embarked on a military buildup that alarmed the Soviets and inspired them to respond so that if war was imminent, it could launch an attack on warning and destroy its enemy. The period of arms racing began to subside after 1966, when Soviet thinking changed again, its theorists coming to believe that in an all-out war, there would be no victor, as both sides could destroy the other. Thus they began to focus upon arms reduction through negotiations so that if war came, Soviet society would not be obliterated. Throughout this period, they saw World War III as passing through two stages—the war for Western Europe and against the United States. In the first stage, the Soviets came to believe after 1966, that, using the blitzkrieg idea of the Germans in World War II and conventional weapons in the main, it could defeat NATO and not induce the United States to respond by launching its intercontinental ballistic missiles against the Russian homeland. Once victory was achieved and by developing a defensive perimeter arcing from the British Isles through North Africa and the Horn of Africa to Afghanistan, it could deprive the United States a beachhead, as it had in World War II, to launch a campaign to recover Western Europe. At that point, the Soviet thinkers believe, a long, protracted war might ensue during which neither side could totally defeat the other and some sort of peace might be effected.

The utility of this analysis is seen in the present circumstances. Beginning in the 1970s and continuing to the present, the Soviets have sought to negotiate arms reductions with the United States that might remove the U.S. ability to destroy the Soviet Union totally in an all-out war. It also sheds light on the insistence that—at this writing—current negotiations must include the nuclear missiles held by West Germany—missiles that in a war against NATO might turn it into a nuclear struggle and bring the United States in. Such reductions would both reduce tensions and weaken the West in any attempt to destroy the Soviets completely.

This volume is rich in insights to Soviet thought on weapons systems and goals and strategies to be pursued in peace and war. It responds to the uncritical arguments that the Soviet Union is an evil empire bent on world conquest, that its true objectives are fomenting world revolution, or that Afghanistan is the first stage in the USSR's plan for expansion. This volume is not a defense of the Soviet Union and it is not an apology for its behavior; instead it is a hard and realistic analysis of Soviet data and writings that gives MccGwire a sound basis for his conclusions. Finally, it is not offered as a new and only way of looking at Soviet foreign policy.

This volume should be must reading for all U.S. policymakers and negotiators and certainly will be invaluable to anyone seeking a rational analysis of Soviet thinking and analysis.

JOSEF SILVERSTEIN

Rutgers University
New Brunswick
New Jersey

SMITH, MICHAEL JOSEPH. *Realist Thought from Weber to Kissinger.* Pp. xii, 256. Baton Rouge: Louisiana State University Press, 1986. $30.00.

The strength of this book is its careful, comprehensive analysis of the ideas of a number of seminal political writers and/or statesmen during the past century who are said to share the so-called realist perception of international affairs. Smith teaches government and foreign policy at the University of Virginia, and his book appears in a series of volumes, *Political Traditions in Foreign Policy*, edited by Kenneth W. Thompson.

Smith has written a synoptic but thoroughly workmanlike summary of the political ideas of Max Weber, E. H. Carr, Reinhold Niebuhr, Hans Morgenthau, George Kennan, and Henry Kissinger. These six were chosen not because they exhaust the list of modern practitioners of realism, but because they "do fairly represent" their "range and depth."

The ideas of all six are set against a backdrop of three recurrent themes: the extent to which they attempted to develop realism as a "general theory" for all international political analysis; the manner in which realist concepts—apart from a general theory—have been applied to evaluate the particular policies of a government; and the degree to which realist approaches are used in considering the morality of foreign policy decisions. The reason why these particular themes were chosen, however, is not readily apparent, given that not all of the six principal authors discussed here made a contribution to each theme.

Two brief chapters also offer thumbnail sketches of classical progenitors of modern realism—for example, Thucydides, Machiavelli, and Hobbes—and of what Smith calls the "idealist provocateurs"—such as Alfred Zimmern and James Shotwell—during the period between the two world wars, to whom contemporary cold-war era realists reacted. A concluding chapter summarizes what Smith regards as the realists' four major assumptions—the ineluctable "evil" of human nature, the persistence of the phenomenon of the state, the "ubiquitous" dominance of the pursuit of power by both individuals and states, and, finally, the emphasis on an understanding of international politics through a rational analysis of conflicting power pursuits—and includes Smith's own critical appreciation of them. Carefully annotated and generally well balanced in the presentation of the ideas of the six major figures examined, Smith's book will long retain its value as a lucid introduction to the ideas of a group of complex foreign policy theorist-practitioners.

But is all this a "fair representation"—to paraphrase Smith—of modern realism? From beginning to end, Smith recognizes the problem of getting a firm handle on his subject. At the start, he remarks that one of the conclusions to come out of these pages is the "elusiveness" of the realist concept. Toward the end, he declares that it "may be" that realism is better viewed as a kind of personal philosophical stance, "a Weltanschauung," rather than as a "conventional theory or explanation" of international affairs and, as such, has given us simultaneously both badly simplified rationalizations and "profound insights."

Just so: Smith's attempts to show exactly what his six writers have in common, or why, for example, a Kissinger could come to a conclusion so vastly different from that of a Morgenthau or a Kennan about the significance of the Vietnam war to U.S. power interests, are noteworthy primarily for demonstrating the difficulty of the subject that Smith has chosen. What does it mean that, as Smith repeatedly emphasizes, realists in international politics invariably regard "evil" as being inherent in human nature? Is it that idealists do not? Such loose terminology invites skepticism about conceptual analysis and, in the end, it suggests that at a sufficiently high level of abstraction all writers on a given subject somehow can be classified together. And what a thicket of meandering speculation is revealed when Smith describes Kissinger as a "realist" when it comes to his ideas on power, prestige, and the role of great nations, while at the same time he is characterized as having "romantic notions" about the importance of leadership. One looks forward to a future volume by Smith that will sharpen the conceptual similarities that he suggests we should perceive in the ideas of the writers he has chosen and that he has so well presented here.

JUSTUS M. VAN DER KROEF
University of Bridgeport
Connecticut

AFRICA, ASIA, AND LATIN AMERICA

DE SILVA, K. M. *Managing Ethnic Tensions in Multi-Ethnic Societies: Sri Lanka,* *1880-1995.* Pp. xix, 429. Lanham, MD: University of America, 1986. $36.50. Paperbound, $19.75.

TAMBIAH, S. J. *Sri Lanka: Ethnic Fratricide and the Dismantling of Democracy.* Pp. xi, 198. Chicago: University of Chicago Press, 1986. $17.95.

K. M. de Silva and S. J. Tambiah are Sri Lankans, the former a Sinahlese, professor of history at the University of Peradeniya and director of the International Center for Ethnic Studies in Kandy; the latter, a Tamil, professor of anthropology at Harvard and a scholar of Thai Buddhism. Both set out to understand and explain the social history and the political sociology that underlie the current Tamil-Sinhala ethnic conflict in that erstwhile paradise called Sri Lanka.

Tambiah's book, completed in July 1984, was an immediate and impassioned response to the 1983 anti-Tamil riots in which over a thousand Tamils were killed by what is now widely accepted by most knowledgeable foreign observers as officially organized bands of thugs. An epigram to the book reads, "Who can protest and does not, is an accomplice to the act." The preface acknowledges the book as "'an engaged political tract' rather than a 'distanced academic treatise.'" Nonetheless, at no time does it lose its analytic integrity, court bridled bigotry, or stoop to political connivance. In this concise but comprehensive treatise, Tambiah traces the origins and the sustaining of Sri Lanka's interethnic violence to several related causes. A sample includes the subsumption of separate sociopolitical units by the British for administrative convenience, the colonialist disregard for indigenous cultural forms and the consequent rise of Sinhala-Buddhist nationalism turned communal chauvinism, the formation of an indigenous elite ruling class of which some consequential members unconsciously sacrificed what was just at the altar of short-term political expediency of which linguistic and religious chauvinism are the best known and the creation of a dependent economy lesser known, outright oppression of an ethnic minority by the mythicization of history and the historicization of myth by those who ought to have known better, and the rise of state terror in the name of anti-terrorism, scape-goatism, repression, and political corruption. The book ends with an optimistic but politically incorrect—vis-à-vis the Tamil separatists—proposal, conceived in the liberal democratic tradition. Missing is a strong indictment of Tamil chauvinism.

Begun in 1979, the first draft of K. M. de Silva's book was completed in 1981. He claims, "The riots of 1983 compelled me to take a more searching look at many of the chapters I had written." One is hard pressed to believe that 1983 made any difference except to update the apologetics aimed at exonerating the present Sri Lankan government.

Whereas Tambiah cautions us to his ideological commitments and convictions, de Silva claims merely to help readers "reach their own conclusions on the basis of the data provided in [his] book." Ironically, if there ever were a text that deserved to be read against itself for its rhetorical construction it is not Tambiah's but de Silva's. A few examples will demonstrate this. When Muslim politicians make a calculated move in the interest of their community, they are congratulated for competing against formidable disadvantages, pragmatically, and adaptively. The contrast is with purported Tamil belligerence. Similar adjectives, plus "accommodating," are reserved for the Sinhalese in general, but especially for the Jayewardene government. When Tamil politicians make comparable moves, they are described as manipulative, inward looking, and adventuristic. By official accounts alone—notorious for undercounting—the post-1983 death toll is placed above 6000. Most of the dead are Tamil civilians—including women and children—and almost all, killed by the armed forces occupying the Tamil areas. De Silva, who consistently calls Tamil militants "terrorists," posits himself as apologist for the occasional lapse in discipline of the "peace keeping forces" when their "patience wears thin."

Defending the government against charges of collusion in the 1983 riots, this Whig-gish historian of the Right notes that "no firm evidence has yet emerged to support that contention." This statement would be funny if it were not so perverse. In 1983 alone, by the government's own underestimated count, 400 Tamils were killed, 53 political detainees massacred while in custody, millions of dollars' worth of property destroyed; Tamils and Sinhalese citizens filed complaints with the authorities, providing witnesses and evidence. The authorities responded by ignoring them or harassing them into silence. Not one murderer has been brought to book.

Twice de Silva's passions rise to condemn atrocities. An armed attack on Sinhala villagers by Tamil militants he calls "most horrifying." No such horror is expressed over the massacre of hundreds as many Tamil civilians by the armed forces. The other instance is the burning of the famous Jaffna library, described by de Silva as a "mindless act of barbarism." Given its positioning in the text, this statement leads the unfamiliar reader to conclude that Tamils burned their own library, whereas the police were the arsonists.

In this presumably official story, atrocities become flattened down to the merely atrocious. Those very mythic histories that have legitimated so much bloodshed and for which Tambiah calls for interrogating and deconstructing, de Silva presents as "factual sources."

E. VALENTINE DANIEL
Institute for Advanced Study
Princeton
New Jersey

FINDLING, JOHN E. *Close Neighbors, Distant Friends: United States-Central American Relations.* Pp. xvi, 240. Westport, CT: Greenwood Press, 1987. $35.00.

BEST, EDWARD. *U.S. Policy and Regional Security in Central America.* Pp. 182. New York: St. Martin's Press, 1987. $32.50.

Both these well-documented and scholarly works make a strong plea for the understanding of the history of U.S.-Central American relations as an aid to the determination of a viable North American foreign policy. Edward Best, whose expertise is in the area of international relations, is affiliated with the International Institute for Strategic Studies. John E. Findling is a professor of history whose research concentrates on diplomatic sources to present a thorough picture of North American interests in Central America for the past 200 years.

U.S. Policy and Regional Security in Central America analyzes U.S. policy particularly under the Carter and Reagan administrations. Best begins with a succinct overview of U.S. policy in the early twentieth century in which he argues that North American governments relied on local elites and private U.S. interests to ensure North American national interests. When a crisis erupted, Central America was discovered anew and the United States utilized a series of traditional responses—both military and economic—which since the 1970s have not been working. As Central American wealth became concentrated in fewer hands and local elites became more entrenched, they were more resistant to U.S. pressure for change, when a sustained internal opposition to their rule was growing. Thus, for the traditional strategies to work, the costs for the United States would have to increase dramatically.

Best's book devotes considerable time to an examination of the Carter and Reagan administrations' unsuccessful and contradictory strategies in the region with specific regard to El Salvador and Nicaragua. Fragments of this misguided policy exist in other sources, but this book puts them all together: a detailed analysis of the origins of the Contadora negotiations and the bilateral U.S.-Nicaraguan talks at Manzanillo are placed in context for the reader. One can see clearly the vagaries and inconsistencies of a U.S. policy that paid lip service to negotiations in the midst of a military strategy. Best concludes with a thoughtful discussion of alternative policies that the United States might pursue.

The historical sweep of Findling's book is greater than that of Best's, and its style of analysis is quite different. Findling deals less with interpretation and scenarios and more with the historical record as compiled through diplomatic sources. He demonstrates convincingly the continuity of U.S. policy toward Central America. Findling's discussion of the American search for strategic control of the isthmus and the perceived importance of a canal dates from the nineteenth century, when British power still dominated the region. North American concern for stability in the region is longstanding: the United States tried to ensure that the Central American nations would not incur foreign debts in order to avoid any pretext for foreign intervention in a hemisphere the United States saw as its own.

Findling also brings the reader up to date with an examination of policies of the Reagan administration that sought to restore the global image of the United States as a strong foe of international communism and that designated Central America as the focal point of this shift in policy, given its strategic location. Of particular note in Findling's book is his comparison of recent events with past incidents. In 1909, U.S. Secretary of State Knox organized a surrogate army to overthrow Nicaraguan dictator José Santos Zelaya, while the Taft administration and the U.S. press reviled Zelaya as the "menace of Central America."

Both of these books are essential reading at this critical juncture in U.S.-Central American relations. Both show the continuity of U.S. perceptions toward Central America and the failures of current U.S. policy. The consistency of North American policy responses demonstrates the immense difficulty of changing course.

LAURA N. O'SHAUGHNESSY
St. Lawrence University
Canton
New York

GAUNSON, A. B. *The Anglo-French Clash in Lebanon and Syria, 1940-45*. Pp. xi, 233. New York: St. Martin's Press, 1987. $29.95.

ROBERTS, DAVID. *The Ba'th and the Creation of Modern Syria*. Pp. 182. New York: St. Martin's Press, 1987. $35.00.

In recent years, the Syrian Arab Republic has played a crucial and, often, an inscrutable role in Middle East politics. Indeed, Syrian policy in Lebanon and toward the Iran-Iraq war has baffled casual observers and even diplomatic and academic specialists.

The two major determinants shaping the foreign policy of modern Syria are its historical legacy and internal political dynamics. An important part of that historical legacy is the subject matter of A. B. Gaunson's book on the wartime Anglo-French conflict in the Levant; in contrast, David Roberts focuses on the ruling Baath party and its formative influence on Syrian domestic and foreign politics.

Gaunson presents a detailed and well-documented account of the Anglo-French confrontation that began with Churchill's decision to support the Free French forces under General Charles de Gaulle against the pro-German Vichy regime, which controlled Syria and Lebanon. Soon after the defeat of the Vichy regime, in mid-1941 by combined British and Free French forces, the divergent objectives of the two allies became manifest. De Gaulle hoped to reestablish France's imperial position in the Levant, while Churchill was intent on accommodating the rising tide of Arab nationalism by granting political independence. While some British officials considered it essential to maintain the Anglo-French alliance, the proponents of a pro-Arab policy won in the end, since forfeiting Arab goodwill would undermine Britain's interests throughout the Middle East. The result was a long series of crises that brought the two allies to the brink of armed conflict, such as the French arrest of the Lebanese ministers in November 1948, their shelling of Damascus in May 1945, and the ensuing British ultimatum leading to the

joint Anglo-French evacuation of the Levant in August 1946.

De Gaulle never forgave Churchill for having insulted France and forcing it to leave the Levant; as president of the Fifth Republic, he vetoed Britain's second application in 1967 to join the European Economic Community. Nor was Britain destined to retain Arab friendship after its policy failures in Palestine and Egypt. Meanwhile, Syria and Lebanon had become independent republics, although successive Syrian governments refused to recognize a separate Lebanese entity.

David Roberts observed Syrian politics firsthand as a British diplomat in Damascus and subsequently as ambassador to Syria, from 1973 to 1976, and to Lebanon, from 1981 to 1983. His book represents a *historie événementielle* of the Baath, combining personal observations, analysis of political events, and documentary evidence from primary and secondary sources. Throughout the book, the insights of the diplomat-practitioner are interwoven with scholarly scrutiny to produce a highly readable, if not well organized, study of the Baath. Special attention is given to the party's official ideology, its Hegelian ancestry and evolution, and its permeation throughout Syrian society. Successive chapters cover the politically dominant Alawite sect, the coup d'etat politics of the 1950s, the union with Nasserist Egypt, the Baath takeover of March 1963, the ascendance of the Neo-Baathists, and the rise of General Hafez al-Assad as president in 1970.

While much of the coverage parallels that found in other books, some of Roberts's conclusions are worth noting. Roberts pays tribute to Assad's leadership abilities and the performance of the Syrian army against Israel in the 1973 war. He makes a strong case for Assad's cold pragmatism, which placed Baathist ideology into the deep freeze. Instead, Roberts argues, Assad is guided by the Syria-first doctrine, which is rooted in the greater-Syria ideology of the Partie populaire syrien. The other important factor, to

Roberts, is sectarianism—the tenuous status of the Alawite sect in the eyes of the Muslim Brotherhood that claims the support of Syria's Sunni majority. The willingness of Iranian clergy to recognize the Alawites as a branch of Islam has accorded much needed legitimacy to Assad's regime vis-à-vis his domestic and external Sunni opponents. Hence the close ties between Islamic Iran and secular Syria against the Sunni Baath of Iraq—a relationship that has been tested recently by the growing challenge of pro-Iranian Shiite groups in Lebanon. The book concludes with a good discussion of the problems facing the Baath and Syria in the post-Assad era.

Both studies are valuable contributions to the scholarship on the Levant. Together they contain a great deal of solid information and insightful analysis that should prove useful both to area specialists and to general readers.

RICHARD DEKMAJIAN
University of Southern California
Los Angeles

RUBENBERG, CHERYL A. *Israel and the American National Interest: A Critical Examination.* Pp. xvi, 446. Champaign: University of Illinois Press, 1986. $24.95.

This volume is a challenge to U.S. policy toward the Arab-Israeli conflict over the last 40 years. Rubenberg willingly states that her book is not "value-free and scientifically neutral." This work is, in fact, overtly in favor of the Palestinian Liberation Organization (PLO) and criticizes all other actors in the Middle Eastern drama: Israel, the United States, the Arab governments, and the radical Palestinian organizations, among others.

The book deserves praise as a bold statement of an unpopular thesis on U.S. policy in the Middle East. Rubenberg does not shy away from positions that most analysts in this country, and certainly public opinion, reject as invalid. Her commitment to a just

solution to the Arab-Israeli conflict is commendable.

Yet, in an effort to promote her perspective, Rubenberg makes numerous inaccurate claims; furthermore, her position is altogether extreme and one-sided. Thus she accuses Israel for being responsible for practically every regional war in the Middle East over the last four decades. The Israelis, she maintains, rejected all the efforts of the Arabs to establish peace. The United States is perceived as Israel's loyal ally, encouraging and facilitating Israeli aggression. Even the 1967 war is described as a conflict prompted by America's desire to depose Nasser, although no evidence is given in this, as in many other, cases.

One of the most obvious problems with the book is that while Rubenberg performs heroics in a determined effort to understand the Arabs, she refuses to give the Israelis similar treatment. Thus, while she highlights the "transformation of the PLO" from a radical to a compromising organization, she describes Israel's position as invariably aggressive. The reader is left with a heavy feeling that a double standard is at work resulting from Rubenberg's ideological commitments.

Rubenberg fails to recognize some of the most important aspects of Israel's political system and society. She minimizes the differences between the political blocs in Israel, a critical task for the understanding of Israel's foreign policy since 1948. Rubenberg mistakenly sees Begin's rise to power as merely the emergence of "a new style." Similarly, she describes the Israeli emphasis on the Holocaust as merely instrumental, a means to gain world sympathy. She fails to recognize the authentic force of the Holocaust experience. For her the tragedy is "a useful pathology for rallying mass support."

Structurally, the book is organized around six major events between the 1947 partition of Palestine and the 1982 war. These historical chapters are sandwiched between a general introductory chapter, tackling the "fallacies" of "the elite consensus" on the Middle East, and a summary, which discusses the pro-Israel lobby in Washington. The historical chapters are comprehensive and well written, but inaccuracies and mis-interpretations are not uncommon.

In the final analysis, although the volume makes a strong case for the Palestinians, especially as their case is represented by the PLO, it is less successful in demonstrating that Israel does not serve the U.S. national interest in the Middle East, as this interest is defined by most Americans. Toward the end of the book, Rubenberg says that "Israel exists at the expense of the Palestinians." The meaning of her message is simple: Israel ought to disappear.

ILAN PELEG

Lafayette College
Easton
Pennsylvania

RUSTOW, DANKWART A. *Turkey: America's Forgotten Ally.* Pp. xv, 154. New York: Council on Foreign Relations, 1987. $14.95.

Forgotten? If not, then underrated or disparaged in the face of special pleading by vocal partisans such as philhellenes and Armenian Turkophobes.

Professor Rustow presents a brief but sound, well-rounded view of the easternmost member of the North Atlantic Treat Organization, without stooping to hackneyed bangs-per-buck parsimony—so many *Mehmetçiks* for the cost of one GI grunt. With appreciation for the Turks' character and society, assets and diminishing disadvantages, attitudes and aspirations, this little book persuasively seeks better attention by Americans and their policymakers and lawmakers to Turkey's geopolitical hazards and challenges and how the republic is meeting them.

As a people, the Turks are worthy allies. Their economy has been so much improved since decrepit empire mutated into youthful democracy that, were it unencumbered by strategic predicaments, foreign aid would not be an issue. The aberrations of excessive pluralism that disrupted multiparty behavior after 1961, mostly the failure of the two major, centrist parties to undertake any coalition together, resulting in unworkable *mariages de convenance*, seem now replaced by more pragmatic competition, promising vital stability. Hardly even vestigially Third World, Turkey is increasingly worthy of American cooperation.

Rustow correctly stresses Turkey's immunity to Khomeinism, and the minor impact of quasi-Islamist parties on the political scene. Rustow may, however, understate the potential for future disarray inherent in the prime ministry's Department of Religious Affairs, and the precarious concessions of some major party leaders to religious fundamentalists.

The half chapter on the Cyprus question would make a good journal article, deserving wide attention to countervail the influence on the White House and Congress of ex parte pleaders. Without relating how much Ankara and Athens have exploited intercommunal friction on the island to distract attention from domestic discord, Rustow delineates the background and treaty justification for Turkish intervention begun in 1974.

While "Turkey and Israel are America's closest partners in the Middle East," the former's strength and location are more pertinent to the North Atlantic Treaty Organization's program. Meanwhile, Turkey's now-warm-now-cool relations with the Zionist state exemplify its independent pursuit of its own "peace at home, peace in the world" master principle. Now, "Turkish and American interests in the Middle East converge and coincide more closely than ever. Turkey remains a crucial barrier to Soviet expansion. Historically and strategically, culturally and commercially, Turkey is the West's bridge to a more peaceful Middle East," concludes Rustow. I conclude: this book is a standard, up-to-date, must work in its field.

DONALD E. WEBSTER

Claremont
California

SCHAHGALDIAN, NIKOLA B. *The Iranian Military under the Islamic Republic.* Pp. xiii, 163. Santa Monica, CA: Rand, 1987. No price.

LIMBERT, JOHN W. *Iran: At War with History.* Pp. xviii, 186. Boulder, CO: Westview Press, 1987. $28.00.

Nikola Schahgaldian's study of the Iranian military was sponsored by the U.S. under secretary of defense for policy and conducted by the Rand Corporation. Its findings are based primarily on interviews with about 110 Iranian former military personnel now living in exile in Western countries. Although Schahgaldian concedes that his sample is biased, he argues that it was the only available source for such a study and could yield useful information when balanced with the existing academic and journalistic information on contemporary Iran. Given these considerations, this book is certainly of interest to Middle East specialists and policy analysts. It provides an account of the transformation of the old regime's professional armed forces into a relatively loyal and disciplined organ of the Islamic Republic, a guided transformation achieved through purges, restructuring, and reduction in size to half of the armed forces' former 500,000-man strength. More important, the new professional armed forces are now counterbalanced by the 350,000-man Islamic Revolutionary Guard Corps, which grew out of the politically heterogeneous self-styled revolutionary militias into the primary armed organ of the clerical faction that emerged dominant at the head of the Islamic Republic. According to Schahgaldian, within both of these armed organizations, the dominant individuals have close family ties to powerful Persian clerical families, but this claim, although plausible, is not substantiated. The major thesis of the book, however, is that in the post-Khomeini period, threats of military intervention in political conflict are more likely to arise from the Islamic Revolutionary Guard Corps than from the professional military. This, too, seems a reasonable projection, given the present predominance of the Guards over the regular armed forces. Even if one agrees with Schahgaldian's assessment that any successful alternative will emerge from within the present power structure, however, it is not clear why Schahgaldian assumes that all contenders for power—including factions of the Guards—must inevitably support clerical candidates, because it is conceivable to have an Islamic Republic without clerical domination, especially if the new rulers come to power through a military struggle.

John Limbert's *Iran: At War with History* is one of the series *Profiles: Nations of the Middle East.* A former hostage in Iran, Limbert is with the U.S. Foreign Service and displays considerable knowledge and intimate familiarity with Iranian culture and history. The book, however, is based almost entirely on secondary sources and is thus intended not for the specialists but for the educated layperson, to whom Limbert wants to explain that "Iran did not come into existence in 1979 with the inauguration of ABC's 'America Held Hostage.'" To this end, Limbert pays a learned homage to the richness and diversity of Iranian history, and thus his account is a welcome antidote to the polluted atmosphere of hostility and ignorance that permeates the perceptions the United States and Iran have of each other. But as the book's title suggests, Limbert takes the present rulers of Iran to task for their imposition of an obscurantist reign of terror upon an essentially tolerant and creative background of Iranian history. This point of view is certainly appealing to Iranian dissidents and their sympathizers, but as Limbert's own account clearly indicates, the present regime is also a product of Iranian history and not something imposed from outside. There are a few factual errors—for example, the assertion that the Feda'i guerrillas originated in the Tudeh party—and a tendency on Limbert's part to deemphasize events such as British involvement in the early rise of Riza Khan or the U.S. role in the 1953 overthrow of Premier Mossadegh, which were important in undermining the legitimacy of the Pahlavi dynasty and in causing among Iranians much resentment of and paranoia toward foreigners.

AFSHIN MATIN
University of California
Los Angeles

YANIV, AVNER. *Dilemmas of Security: Politics, Strategy, and the Israeli Experience in Lebanon.* Pp. xii, 355. New York: Oxford University Press, 1987. $24.95.

Avner Yaniv has written an interpretation of Israel's foreign policy conduct in Lebanon from 1982 to 1985 based on a model of the security dilemma. Additionally, he briefly applies this model to all Israel's foreign policies since the inception of the state—and before, during the period of the Yishuv—and in conclusion predicts future conduct based on the model. Yaniv presents his security dilemma as a universal situation faced by all states in the international system resulting from the anarchic nature of the system. Yaniv considers the human condition—and the nature of states—to be essentially insecure and thus prone to aggressive action out of fear. Yaniv claims repeatedly that Israel's behavior is no different from that of most states throughout world history, which he argues derives from an iron law that pushes states, "logically, into a game of preemption against not only their adversaries but also their allies."

Because the book focuses on Israel's campaign against the Palestinians in Lebanon, Yaniv is most explicit about Israel's security dilemma vis-à-vis Palestinians. He argues that this dilemma involves the necessity for Israel to oppose the establishment of an independent Palestinian state in any part of Palestine because such a state would be a mortal threat to Israel's security. Yaniv never explains why a Palestinian state would be a mortal danger to Israel. He argues, however, that this aspect of the security dilemma has remained unchanged since the pre-state period, which at that time impelled

Ben-Gurion to seek an arrangement with Emir Abdullah of Transjordan to prevent the actualization of the Palestinian state stipulated in U.N. Resolution 181, through the present. It mandated the 1982 war in Lebanon not because Israel faced a military threat from the Palestinian Liberation Organization (PLO)—Yaniv candidly, and correctly, admits that it did not—but because the PLO's political accommodation since 1977, when it formally agreed to a two-state solution and declared its willingness to participate in a peace process; its increasing international recognition and legitimacy by 1980-81; and its increasing emphasis on diplomacy coupled with a declining inclination to resort to force even when intensely provoked by Israel made the threat to Israel even greater than a military threat. With these changes regarding the PLO, the international community, particularly the United States, might expect Israel to negotiate with the PLO and achieve a compromise with the Palestinians based on the two-state formula. "To escape this trap without running the risk that a political settlement with the PLO would entail, Israel could do only one thing—go to war."

The bulk of the book—chapters 2 through 5—discusses in detail Israel's invasion, occupation, and slow withdrawal from Lebanon beginning in the summer of 1982 through the summer of 1985. Yaniv provides no new information; all of the details have been previously discussed in a variety of other solid works. But Yaniv is an Israeli who is highly supportive of his government's policies, and his analysis of Israel's behavior as consistently offensive, preemptive, and aggressive provides a useful source for those critical of Israel's policies, faced with unremitting Israeli government declarations—as well as much purportedly scholarly literature—about the defensive nature of Israel's conduct. Indeed, Yaniv's candor is quite revealing. For instance, in discussing Israel's policies during its occupation of south Lebanon, particularly its difficulties in controlling the predominantly Shiite population, Yaniv writes:

The implicit unspoken assumption of the former West Bank/Gaza administrators who were put in charge of south Lebanon was, to put it bluntly, that all Arabs are the same—more dangerous verbally than in practical terms, cowardly, submissive, greedy, untrustworthy, emotional, bribable, and easily intimidated into collaboration with any authority, Arab or not. Such an assumption was not born of racism but of a long experience with Israel's own (mainly Sunni) Arab minority of half a million and their compatriots in the mainly Sunni West Bank and Gaza (p. 232).

. . . the closely knit social structure of the Shi'ite community in south Lebanon together with the intensely religious aura of resistance to occupation made the intelligence-gathering task of the various security services exceedingly difficult. In the West Bank and Gaza almost any type of simple intimidation and bribery could easily lead the population to divulge valuable information. Indeed, owing to this intrinsically collaborative predisposition of the Palestinians, the Israelis were very seldom required to resort to physical torture in order to obtain information. In south Lebanon, none of these techniques were effective (p. 236).

Israel's inability to control the Lebanese Shiites led to the Iron Fist policy, initiated in February 1985:

The raids were conducted methodically. A large force in armored cars would suddenly surround a village chosen for a raid. Israeli soldiers would take the hills around it, and block all entrances to the village with physical barriers. The troops would enter the village shooting at anything that moved while commanding the residents through loudspeakers to stay at home. They would search every home thoroughly, and round up all the men aged sixteen to sixty and assemble them in the village square. Then, assisted by hooded informers, the Israelis would begin to identify suspected al Amal supporters and take them for further interrogation. Houses owned by suspected supporters of al Amal would be blown up. Any attempt to resist arrest would lead to shooting. Fifteen Shi'ites were killed this way within the first ten days of the new policy (p. 281).

This, according to Yaniv, constituted a natural response to a security dilemma.

The individual who wishes to read something that genuinely attempts to understand Israel's invasion of Lebanon would be better served by Zeev Schiff and Ehud Yaari's

Israel's Lebanon War (New York: Simon & Schuster, 1984). Though it, too, tends to reductionism in laying most of the responsibility for the war at the feet of Defense Minister Ariel Sharon, it nevertheless makes a serious effort to evaluate and analyze Israel's policies and behavior. Schiff and Yaari are considered quite respectable mainstream Israelis. The readers of this volume, at the very least, should balance their reading with Yehoshafat Harkabi's *Fateful Choices before Israel* (Claremont, CA: College Press, 1987). Harkabi, a former chief of Israeli Military Intelligence and former head of Strategic Research for the Ministry of Defense, argues that Israel's security would be best served by the establishment of an independent Palestinian state alongside Israel.

Too often theories are taken as objectively existing truth; the fact that they are the product of subjective human thought, developed to explain and typically to justify the behavior of existing institutions—in the case of realpolitik, the nature of interstate behavior in the international system—is frequently lost in their presentation as historical, universal, scholarly, and objective. Few books illustrate so clearly the bankruptcy of realpolitik theory as does Yaniv's *Dilemmas of Security*. The fallacies are too numerous to outline in a short review, but I shall suggest the most important. First, there is no quantitative data to prove that the normal behavior of states throughout history has been to choose aggressive over accommodative behavior. This is purely an assumption, though Yaniv—and realist writers in general—present it as a priori truth. Second, the entire body of thought and practice in international law and world order beginning with Hugo Grotius through the creation of the League of Nations and the United Nations, culminating in the world-order studies project presently headed by Richard Falk, Saul Mendlovitz, Samuel Kim, Robert Johansen, and others suggests the felt need to strive for an international system based on law and order—even in the absence of an all-powerful international authority capable of enforcement—as the best means of maximizing security for all the peoples of the globe. It also suggests the dual and plastic nature of human beings—their capacity for aggressive behavior and for just, lawful, and orderly behavior, both refuting the determinist and negative nature-of-man assumptions implicit in the realpolitik school. Third, that theory too often serves to justify, legitimize, and excuse behavior—the state's or human beings'—rather than affording real explanations for it has never been more starkly apparent than in Yaniv's book. His theory absolves all Israeli decision makers of any moral responsibility for any action they have undertaken because all actions are considered rational responses to security threats. The amoral presumable logic of political realism carried to its ultimate conclusion, as Yaniv comes close to doing, could as well rationalize Stalin's gulag and Hitler's ovens. Finally, the history of Israel is by no means typical of states in the international system. In forty years of existence, it has fought seven major wars and has been engaged in constant military aggression of various other sorts. The explanation for such behavior resides in something quite different from Yaniv's reductionist security dilemma. The attempt to fit reality to theory results in a lessening of our understanding rather than a broadening.

CHERYL A. RUBENBERG
Florida International University
North Miami

EUROPE

CHASE, WILLIAM J. *Workers, Society, and the Soviet State: Labor and Life in Moscow, 1918-1929.* Pp. xviii, 344. Champaign: University of Illinois Press, 1987. $29.95.

The social history of Soviet Russia in the 1920s and 1930s has long been neglected due to a traditional scholarly emphasis on the role of the state and leadership in Soviet historical development. This traditional emphasis has recently been challenged by revisionist scholars who have sought to explore the complex interrelationships between Soviet state and society through studies of workers, peasants, officials, and members of the professions. The emerging view from below is gradually altering the traditional image of Soviet Russia as the gray, totalitarian monolith of cold-war fantasy. Among the pioneers in this new direction is William J. Chase, who, in *Workers, Society, and the Soviet State*, has written the first American scholarly monograph of labor in the USSR since the 1950s.

Chase traces the development of Moscow's working class from its disintegration during the Russian civil war through its gradual reformation in the 1920s. Chase's view of the Soviet working class is one of a class divided internally—according to such factors as skill level, age, degree of urbanization, and so on—but united in the face of outside pressures threatening, in workers' eyes, to resurrect the prerevolutionary factory regimen and class relationships. According to Chase, class consciousness gradually reemerged among Moscow's workers in the course of the 1920s as a host of social and economic problems intrinsic to the New Economic Policy helped to radicalize important sectors of Soviet labor. By the end of the 1920s, Communist Party radicals formed a kind of alliance with disgruntled workers to push through the maximalist policies of Stalin's First Five-Year Plan revolution. Chase concludes, therefore, that Stalin's revolution was based on a complex web of political voluntarism and social pressures. The revolution known traditionally as a revolution from above becomes, in Chase's interpretation, a "revolution from above *and* below." Chase's analysis is a major revision of traditional thinking regarding the relationship of state and society in the years leading up to the First Five-Year Plan revolution. Chase has successfully challenged long-entrenched cold-war views that considered the Communist Party, and, in other cases, Stalin alone, to be the locomotive force of Soviet historical development.

In addition to the general historio-graphical contribution of his work, Chase offers the reader one of the very few regional studies of Soviet history in the early years. In so doing and in choosing Moscow as his base, Chase has joined with an important group of historians who have studied Moscow before or during 1917 to add further to our general picture of this important region's development.

Chase's source base is sound and his writing style smooth. This book will soon become standard fare in university courses and seminars on Soviet social history. Chase's book will be read to advantage by both specialists in Soviet history and labor historians of other national areas. My only criticism is the high price of this book; a plea for an early paperback edition is in order.

LYNNE VIOLA
State University of New York
Binghamton

CLAYTON, ANTHONY. *The British Empire as a Superpower, 1919-39.* Pp. xiv, 545. Athens: University of Georgia Press, 1986. $30.00.

JACKSON, WILLIAM. *Withdrawal from Empire: A Military View.* Pp. xvii, 285. New York: St. Martin's Press, 1987. $29.95.

These two books, taken together, make an admirably intelligible whole, marred, unfortunately, by the fact that the authors are the product of the world they are trying to describe. Jackson is a former assistant chief of the General Staff of the British army. Anthony Clayton is the son of a former officer of the Royal Artillery and is presently senior lecturer in history at Sandhurst. Their books reflect these factors.

The title of Clayton's book is unfortunate, as it gives the impression that it is some sort of comparative study, informed by the concepts of policy studies, rather than the simple historical narrative it is. As a historical narrative, it is the product of a great deal of study and, were it not for certain basic flaws,

would be a dry but quite readable account of a significant period of history. If anything, it might be thought a bit too conscientious with regard to detail. Few readers will find interest in the move of the Second Suffolks, in December 1926, from Gibraltar to Hong Kong.

The period between the wars represented the high tide of British imperial expansion. The treaties signed at the end of the war gave Britain substantial territorial gain. Its colonies and client states were more numerous and included Palestine, Iraq, and Trans-jordan as well as a substantial part of East Africa. Britain was the leading naval power in Europe, and British financial strength a major factor in world politics. This was, however, counterbalanced by budget stringency and the antiwar sentiments of a large part of the British public. Continual costs for policing the empire were not popular, and, by 1939, Britain's armed forces were either small or poorly equipped or both.

Clayton does discuss the changes in military strategy brought about by the introduction of tanks and aircraft, but sparsely. A thoroughgoing discussion of the debates around the value of strategic bombardment, the use of armor in large formations, and the debate between the Royal Navy and the Royal Air Force over control of the Fleet Air Arm would have added greatly to the book's merit.

Jackson's book is in a much lighter vein, and it is difficult to understand why St. Martin's Press classifies it as scholarly. It is a simple account of the military operations and strategic considerations that governed Britain's withdrawal from its empire and covers the years 1945-72.

The withdrawal is covered fairly meticulously, from the standpoint of a staff officer, to whom it looks, at least in retrospect, like a series of rational responses to a changing balance of forces. The withdrawal, naturally, was conducted with great politesse, and anybody, we are led to believe, other than British nationals, who were killed in the process, only got what they deserved. Trifling details such as how the British determined if someone killed in a free-fire zone was a civilian or a terrorist are omitted, leaving the reader with the impression that all dead people are, by definition, terrorists. The only exception I can find to this rule is in Jackson's reference—for reasons known only, I suspect, to senior British officers—to "Egyptian Fedayeen Commando" raids on Israeli settlements. Merely on grounds of consistency it is not possible to maintain this view and then refer to the Malayan Peoples Anti-British Army as terrorist.

Consistency is not Jackson's strong point. His use of the word "race," for instance, would make most anthropologists wince. Sometimes he uses it to refer to linguistic nationality, at other times to citizenship in a state, at still other times in so confused and ethereal a sense as to drive the conscientious reader up a wall.

Neither writer has seen the matter at hand from any viewpoint other than that of Whitehall or the War Office. Neither the views of the peoples fighting for national self-determination nor that of the ordinary British serviceman is presented. Has it ever struck either of these writers that, say, some poor sod of a lance corporal in the Second Howards, stringing wire in some godforsaken bit of Malayan jungle may have thought his commanding officers a bit potty and the whole game not worth the candle, or that some poor Iraqi villager whose family had just been killed in a Royal Air Force bombing raid might think that this, somehow, is not part of the onward march of progress?

I suspect not.

MURRAY SMITH

Notre-Dame de Grâce
Quebec
Canada

GOTTFRIED, ROBERT S. *Doctors and Medicine: In Medieval England 1340-1530.* Pp. xvi, 359. Princeton, NJ: Princeton University Press, 1986. $45.00.

Between the Black Death in 1348 and the founding of the Royal College of Physicians (RCP) of London in 1518 there occurred fundamental changes in English medicine that have been ignored by historians. Robert S. Gottfried shows that clinical medicine was improved by surgeons, and he ascribes this change to the death of influential physicians, medical teachers, and authors during the plague and their replacement by surgeons who had gained firsthand experience on the battlefields. Improving their techniques through experimentation, the surgeons developed more effective methods than the physicians did to treat disease. Upon returning home after war, those surgeons who distinguished themselves were awarded royal patronage and were given other opportunities to practice due to a shortage of physicians brought about by the Black Death, and, therefore, were in a position to apply the techniques they learned during the war. Further opportunities for surgeons to learn on the battlefield diminished after 1450, when fewer and less bloody wars were waged. At the same time, new discoveries linking medicine and surgery were brought from Italy, so that in 1518, when Henry VIII wished to reform medical practice, he chose physicians to create the RCP, from which he excluded surgeons. Gottfried argues that the RCP did not add a new dimension to medicine but, in fact, brought an end to innovative changes in clinical practice introduced by military surgeons.

This provocative study has drawn upon biographical information and the history of ideas, institutions, and diseases, as well as the social and cultural experiences of medical practitioners. A vast quantity of data on the lives of 2282 practitioners—mostly men, with only 1 percent who were women—who lived between 1340 and 1530 provide crucial information to place this study of the history of medieval medicine within the "mainstream of social and cultural history." The data on each individual encompass one or more of the following items: dates and types of practice, residence, royal service, legal and social standing, education, family information, occupations of other family members, manuscripts or books owned or written, property owned, where educated, other occupations such as cleric, gender, and religion. The data reveal some generally unknown information such as that surgeons were very successful according to the criterion by which all medical practitioners measured their achievements, selection for royal service. To add to their professional esteem, surgeons demonstrated an unusual sense of public service. Of those surgeons in royal service, 40 percent donated money and services to the poor, whereas most physicians gave very little to the poor. Other surprising and informative interpretations of the data provide rich understanding of this hitherto neglected period in medical history. This is Gottfried's major contribution.

Gottfried's reassessment of this period in English medicine begins with a study of a missing link in the historical framework of the period: the corporate structure of medieval English medicine. In challenging the view that the RCP advanced English medicine, he concludes that the college permitted physicians to function without rivals, did not inspire them to new insights and techniques, and gave them no basis for making changes in their techniques. As a medical corporation, the RCP preserved wealth, privilege, and dignity for physicians. By protecting the status of English-trained physicians and ignoring the surgeons, who had proven their ability to advance clinical medicine, the college helped to destroy the source of innovation and the most dynamic branch of medicine during the later Middle Ages. When English medicine was poised to undergo dramatic change through the methods and discoveries of surgery and anatomy, the institutional priority given to physicians through the RCP stopped further progress. Thus the gain of one and a half centuries was squandered in a generation, and it would take another two centuries before English medicine would be transformed into a viable clinical enterprise.

If anyone wishes to challenge Gottfried's exciting thesis, he or she must mine all the data Gottfried used and discover a good deal more. Given the model presented by Gottfried, it is evident that this will take intensive study, but, in the meantime, the history of medieval medicine has been given its due and has been incorporated into the history of the period, at least as general historians view it. For this Gottfried is to be congratulated. To understand English medieval medicine, this is the book to read.

AUDREY DAVIS

Smithsonian Institution
Washington, D.C.

NISSMAN, DAVID B. *The Soviet Union and Iranian Azerbaijan: The Use of Nationalism for Political Penetration.* Pp. viii, 123. Boulder, CO: Westview Press, 1987. Paperbound, $18.95.

MOTYL, ALEXANDER J. *Will the Non-Russians Rebel? State, Ethnicity, and Stability in the USSR.* Pp. xii, 188. Ithaca, NY: Cornell University Press, 1987. $24.95.

It is very encouraging to see an increase in scholarly attention focused on the non-Russian populations of the Soviet Union. The Soviet Union's problems with the perennial nationality question and how it deals with them are at least as important in understanding the USSR as its economic problems or its dealings with its Eastern European satellites. The addition of these two volumes to the available literature is most welcome, although they are by no means of equal quality.

David Nissman's book is a brief but thorough and competent examination of the relationship between the Azerbaijani communities on either side of the Soviet-Iranian border. In particular, it studies Soviet policy toward each community and how it attempts to use Iranian Azerbaijan's nationalist sentiment to its own advantage.

Nissman is well aware of the complexity of his subject matter. He correctly points out that, in the Azeri case, nationalist sentiment that would have been censured in a strictly Soviet context is allowed public exposure. This is because, he claims, "of the three countries on the Soviet border which are not now under Soviet influence—Iran, Turkey and the Peoples Republic of China—Iran is easily the most susceptible to Soviet penetration." Nissman documents this thesis with a clear and precise history of Azerbaijan since Persia gave roughly half of it to Russia in 1828.

The most enlightening section of Nissman's study deals with the USSR's successes and failure in its policy toward Iranian Azerbaijan since 1979. Briefly, Nissman documents an initial period of success as the new Iranian regime sought to break with the Pahlavi precedent. The shah had banned expression of Azeri nationalism, fearing another Soviet occupation in the event of destabilization of the region. Khomeini pledged freedom for all and loosened anti-Azeri controls. The Soviets immediately responded, drawing upon the knowledge of Azeri nationalism gained during their occupation in the 1940s, with a barrage of broadcasts of nationalist poetry and increased contacts between various Azeri cultural groups. But this revived Iranian suspicion of Soviet motives, and, by 1982, Tehran again had taken steps to thwart the perceived advance of Soviet hegemony. The Soviets responded accordingly, shifting to a more active cultivation of nationalist longing for "one Azerbaijan."

Nissman deserves special credit for clearly distinguishing the significance of apparent Soviet flexibility in dealing with Azerbaijan. "The ambiguity in the Soviet approach lies in the fact that neither the meaning nor the consequences of a people sharing a common ethos have been resolved in modern Soviet political literature." In addition to being well organized, carefully documented—primarily with Soviet sources—and highly readable, then, this book has interest well beyond its specific subject of Azerbaijan.

This is not the case with Motyl's *Will the Non-Russians Rebel? State, Ethnicity, and Stability in the USSR*. Despite its ambitious title and the claim on its dust jacket that it "is an integrated conceptual study of the nationality question in the Soviet Union," this work in fact deals only with the Ukraine. Motyl defines stability as "a state's effective pursuit of survival" and state survival as "the survival of political, class, and ethnic authority patterns." He concludes that, barring nuclear war, "insurrection will be well-nigh impossible." The final sentence of his book sums up his position: "Because they *cannot* rebel, non-Russians *will not* rebel."

Motyl's point is that the Soviet Union is a Russian state, the Russians have key positions sewn up, they disallow any public attempts to mobilize anti-Russian activity and carefully control expression of antistate sentiment through the KGB. Therefore, the type of activity necessary to bring about rebellion cannot take place and the Soviet Union will remain stable for the foreseeable future. But his work suffers from serious flaws. Its style is needlessly pedantic, as in the following: "In view of the epistemological arrogance involved in claiming perfect knowledge about any social phenomenon, it is not unreasonable to acknowledge the sociopolitical importance of both ethnicity and class." Many of its conclusions are tautological: "In other words, the greater the accumulation of antistate challenges, the greater the cumulative challenge." More important, however, the work is based on an unsubstantiated premise. Motyl claims in his introduction that the only real challenge to the Soviet state's stability "comes from the regional hegemonies of the non-Russians in general and the Ukrainians in particular.... If the Ukrainians will not or cannot undermine the USSR's ethnic stability, then neither can any other non-Russian nation." Dismissing the serious nationality problems existing in Soviet Central Asia, Motyl simply states that "the Ukraine is still the key to the Soviet Russian state's ethnic stability." Readers interested in the nationality problem beyond the Ukraine are, therefore, advised to consult such scholars as Alexandre Benigsen, Marie Broxup, S. Enders Wimbush, and Chantal Lemercier-Quelquejay, whose work presents compelling evidence undermining Motyl's hypothesis.

TAMARA SONN
St. John Fisher College
Rochester
New York

TAYLOR, SIMON. *Prelude to Genocide: Nazi Ideology and the Struggle for Power.* Pp. xii, 228. New York: St. Martin's Press, 1985. $27.50.

SORGE, MARTIN K. *The Other Price of Hitler's War: German Military and Civilian Losses Resulting from World War II.* Pp. xx, 175. Westport, CT: Greenwood Press, 1986. $32.95.

Little in the history of civilization compares with the horrors of Nazi genocide. Armenian massacres were dominantly nationalistic; Stalin's liquidation of the kulaks was essentially economic; Mao's slaughter of intellectuals was his contribution to Chinese culture.

Hitler's plan to exterminate the entire religion of Judaism—in his ignorance calling it a race—was primarily a biological phenomenon without precedent. It was a stupid effort by a nearly insane person.

The origins, development, and results of the Holocaust have stimulated a cascade of studies. Many advocate the never-forgive, never-forget syndrome. There are even books claiming that the Holocaust never took place.

Simon Taylor's *Prelude to Genocide* was supported partly by the presumably democratic republic of East Germany. Taylor claims that though the Final Solution may, indeed, have been ordered in 1941, "there can be no doubt that the intention to annihilate the Jews physically was publicly stated well before the seizure of power by the NSDAP."

Describing the evolution of Nazi ideology, Taylor also presents a selection of Nazi propaganda posters and election leaflets. He shows how the German middle classes *(Mit-*

telstand) were strongly attracted to Nazi ideology and how they became victims of the Nazi *Weltanschauung,* or worldview.

This book demonstrates again how scholars can draw differing conclusions from the same set of facts. Taylor calls it a "tragic irony" that much of the postwar literature on German fascism identifies Hitler as the initiator, mentor, and dynamic force of national socialism. Great-man theory of history? This, he says, "reinforces the image created by the German propaganda machine." He criticizes Golo Mann, Ernst Deuerlein, Ernst Nolte, and John Toland for defending ideology as an exclusive product of the führer. Hitler, he writes, did not represent the nation but was rather the champion of a politics reflecting particular class interests.

Taylor also rejects Wilhelm Reich and Erich Fromm and their psychoanalytical category of the irrationality of Nazi ideology. He describes their views as "vague and undefined," as "little more than speculative," and as "lacking any form of comparative verification."

Taylor holds that powerful German industrial interests were not only instrumental in founding and financing the early Nazi party but that they also manipulated public opinion "to offload" the consequences of all social ills on the Jews. Yale expert Henry Ashby Turner, Jr., in his *German Big Business and the Rise of Hitler* (1985), however, asserts that industrialists did not, on balance, support Hitler in his program, that their financial contributions were negligible, and that Nazism was essentially self-supporting thanks to self-organized funding devices.

The Other Price of Hitler's War, number 55 in Greenwood Press's excellent series *Contributions in Military Studies,* concerns German military and civilian losses in World War II. German-born author Martin K. Sorge came to the United States in 1955 and served in the U.S. Air Force for twenty years.

Drawing upon official archival documents, Sorge chronicles losses by regular German ground, air, and naval forces, the Afrika Korps, and Hitler Youth and losses inflicted by enemy partisans. He gives special attention to civilian casualties.

Sorge does commendable work in one of the most difficult areas of war research—obtaining accurate figures. His tone throughout is sympathetic for a people trapped in the Nazi national prison. He claims "negative stereotyping" by the English-speaking media "as perpetuating themes of German guilt and brutality."

As long as he remains in the statistical field, Sorge's work is valuable and impressive. But he is less effective when he ventures into the debatable ground of historical judgment. For example, he underestimates the impact of genocide when he quotes "Jewish research" as giving a total of 125,000 Jewish victims of the Holocaust, plus 65,000 more in Austria. What happened to Raul Hilberg's estimate of 5.1 million Jewish dead? Sorge judges the terrible bombing and fire storms at Hamburg, Dresden, and Berlin as unnecessary vengeance: "It is to the credit of civilized man that during the reign of death unleashed against Germany, a few voices were heard on the Allied side questioning this genocidal warfare." Genocidal? Other opinions merely point to the earlier Nazi terror bombing of Rotterdam, Coventry, London, and other cities. General Sherman's dictum remains: "War is hell!" Finally, Sorge's opinions on the Malmédy incident and the judgment at Nuremberg are open to question.

Nevertheless, Sorge's study is a welcome compendium of German losses in Hitler's war. One can well imagine the consequences of a Hitler victory!

LOUIS L. SNYDER

City University
New York

YELLING, J. A. *Slums and Slum Clearance in Victorian London.* Pp. x, 160. Winchester, MA: Allen & Unwin, 1986. $34.95.

Yelling's book, despite its title, deals primarily with the late Victorian period, beginning with the Artisans' Dwelling Act

passed by Disraeli's ministry. He focuses on the various clearance plans from then into the early twentieth century, using a wealth of charts and diagrams. He examines the preconceptions of various groups charged with implementing policy as to what constituted a slum. He moves on to discuss the work of the authorities mostly involved in that implementation, at first the Board of Works and then the London City Council. He shows the difficulties inherent in awarding fair compensation to those people—whether landlords or renters—whose properties would be cleared. Fair market value seemed to emerge as the primary consideration, however, in evaluating properties. He shows that slum clearance usually did not and could not provide, in the new buildings that arose, housing for the former tenants, who tended nonetheless to take up quarters near the new construction. He examines the concept of the suburb as alternate housing. He even attempts in a statistical way to show that people who lived in the slum to be cleared did not differ greatly in the way they planned their finances and tried to live their lives from others more fortunate. He describes in considerable detail a sort of model program, the Boundary Street project. He analyzes thoroughly each of the particular topics he has chosen to examine.

Yelling does not put his story in the context of national political development. Rather, he focuses on local influences, the London County Council records constituting his most important source. His book is not for the general reader. He assumes his audience to be familiar with a host of writers on the topic of Victorian housing, some of whom he introduces into the text by their last name. More important, although one can glean by dint of application a general idea of the content of various legislative enactments, the book cries out for at least one appendix. Yelling starts with the Artisans' Dwelling Act. Thereafter he refers repeatedly to Torrens' Act—Torrens is never identified—which preceded it, and then says that an 1890 measure incorporated both of them. As he points out that the assumptions behind the

Torrens and Artisan acts were mutually incompatible, a succinct summary of the 1890 measure in an appendix would help the reader.

FRANKLIN B. WICKWIRE
University of Massachusetts
Amherst

UNITED STATES

ARON, CINDY SONDIK. *Ladies and Gentlemen of the Civil Service: Middle-Class Workers in Victorian America.* Pp. viii, 234. New York: Oxford University Press, 1987. $29.95.

The thousands of men and women who went to work as clerks in the federal government between 1860 and 1900 helped create "the first large, sexually integrated, white-collar bureaucracy in America." They thus became the somewhat unlikely vanguard of a new middle class. Drawing on a variety of primary sources—application files in the Treasury and Interior departments, manuscript census schedules, congressional and executive reports—Cindy Sondik Aron paints a detailed portrait of these "reluctant pioneers." She describes their backgrounds, motivations, working conditions, problems, and progress, and at the same time she explores the reciprocal relationship between class and occupation.

Although the pay and hours were relatively good, many of those who were compelled by economic necessity to seek federal clerkships felt uneasy about their new work. The men, overwhelmingly white and U.S.-born, with better than average education, feared a loss of autonomy and independence. The women, also U.S.-born whites and often from professional families, knew they were violating the norms of submissiveness and domesticity. Determined to maintain their status as gentlemen and ladies, these new clerks tried "to shape white-collar labor according to their own middle-class image." As a result, rationalization came slowly to the federal workplace. Variety and flexibility

characterized many jobs until the first decades of the twentieth century. Thus it is a mistake, Aron contends, "to see the history of clerical work in the nineteenth century as one of unremitting decline."

Ladies and gentlemen though they remained, federal clerks did face novel conditions. Sexual integration imposed new standards. Men had to give up smoking, drinking, and cursing in the office, and women had to become more aggressive and competitive. This melding of the male and female spheres did not always proceed smoothly, however. The average pay for women was significantly lower than that for men, and even after the Pendleton Act introduced merit examinations, women failed to win their fair share of government jobs. Aron suspects that sexual harassment was also a problem, but direct evidence on that issue is understandably thin. She can document more cases of political infighting than of "overt gender conflict."

Aron's study ends at the turn of the century, with the work force she has portrayed with such care on the brink of further rapid and dramatic change. There is much still to learn about the evolution of the modern white-collar middle class; *Ladies and Gentlemen of the Civil Service* offers a clear and persuasive account of its formative years.

CAM WALKER
College of William and Mary
Williamsburg
Virginia

BLACK, EARL and MERLE BLACK. *Politics and Society in the South.* Pp. ix, 363. Cambridge, MA: Harvard University Press, 1987. $25.00.

Nearly forty years ago, V. O. Key, Jr., wrote his path-breaking *Southern Politics in State and Nation.* Key's book is now badly dated, but well into the civil rights era anyone who wanted to understand Southern politics had to come to grips with its arguments. Veteran political scientists Earl and Merle Black have now masterfully updated *Southern Politics in State and Nation* with their new book, *Politics and Society in the South.*

When Key wrote in 1949, Southern politics was dominated by the agrarian conservatives of the black belt, the plantation region whose economy was driven by cheap black labor and whose politics were animated by the most extreme forms of Southern racism. Key placed his hopes for liberating the white South from the burden of racism not on a moral critique of black subordination but on the secular processes of urbanization and industrialization, which would undermine the power of the black-belt plantation owners. The Blacks' study is devoted to examining how the economic and demographic transitions of the postwar era that created a large white middle class have, as Key expected, transformed the once solidly Democratic South into an increasingly two-party region. Writing in a crisp, jargon-free prose, the Blacks move systematically through the effects of the growth of cities and industry in the South, the out-migration of blacks and the in-migration of whites, to show how Southern politics have become far more like that of the rest of the nation.

The economic modernization of the South has, as the Blacks show, done far more to emancipate the white from the Negro than the reverse. For all the progress they have made, black Southerners are still politically dominated, albeit in far more subtle ways, by a white population largely united across class lines. In a region that has only recently tasted the fruits of economic growth, leadership has passed from the black-belt traditionalists to the entrepreneurially oriented, and often Republican, businessmen of the cities. Entrepreneurial upper-middle-class whites and working-class whites, the Blacks show, share a political culture that is intensely individualist and suspicious of socially interventionist government. "Ask God for help in your work," goes a Protestant prayer, "but do not ask him to do it for you." By contrast, black Southerners are strongly

supportive of government guarantees for both jobs and the overall level of social welfare. "Almost half of black Southerners advocated *total* governmental responsibility in providing a job and a good standard of living," compared to 11 percent of white Southerners. The net effect of these differences is to produce a region that, despite residual Democratic strength on the local and state level, will continue to be a bastion of Republicanism on the presidential level.

There are two minor problems with the book. One is a paltry index that hardly does justice to the richness of the material. The other is the absence of any discussion of the polarizing mésalliance between Republican and black leaders aimed at redrawing political boundaries at the expense of white Democrats. These matters aside, anyone who wants to consider the questions raised by V. O. Key will now have to read the Blacks' book as well.

FRED SIEGEL

Cooper Union
New York City

EDEL, WILBUR. *Defenders of the Faith: Religion and Politics from the Pilgrim Fathers to Ronald Reagan.* Pp. x, 261. New York: Praeger, 1987. $38.95.

FRANKL, RAZELLE. *Televangelism: The Marketing of Popular Religion.* Pp. xviii, 204. Carbondale: Southern Illinois University Press, 1986. $19.95.

These two quite different books contribute something to the literature on religion in the United States, but both would have benefited from closer editorial supervision.

Edel's general problem appears in his first chapter, a sweeping survey of religious and political development through the Reformation, which, though informative, provides no central question, general thesis, or other organizational device to keep his narrative on track. Lacking such a framework, his book begins as a scholarly history of religion and politics in the United States but ends with a lengthy diatribe against Ronald Reagan and his foreign policy. Edel's historical scholarship suffers with this unhappy transition.

Edel's best chapters thus come early in the book and concern the uneven development of religious tolerance in the American colonies, divided church loyalties during the Revolutionary War, and the prevalent view of established religion at the Constitutional Convention. His account of slavery and civil war nicely sets out sectarian differences but oddly neglects the abolitionist movement, with all its religious fervor. Edel's discussion of First Amendment protections absorbed by the Fourteenth Amendment is very substantive but seems a bit rich given that so many topics of obvious relevance are slighted or ignored altogether. For example, there is one passing reference to superpatriot preacher Billy Sunday and none whatever to Father Coughlin. Edel takes no notice of the crucial role of black and white clergy in the civil rights movement of the 1960s or of the importance of black churches in Jesse Jackson's 1984 presidential campaign. Black Muslims, Moonies, and other elements on the fringe of American religion and politics are similarly overlooked.

Edel unfortunately devotes his last chapters to a largely ad hominem and not wholly consistent attack on Reagan. In chapter 9, he suggests that Reagan's moral pronouncements are little more than empty posturing because the president's formative years appear to have been uncomplicated by deep religious convictions. But in chapter 12, Edel portrays Reagan as a true believer embarked on a dangerous "crusade" against godless communism.

He also scores Jerry Falwell, Pat Robertson, and the New Christian Right in an account wholly innocent of the substantial social science literature on who supports the religious Right. Edel's brief account of the nuclear freeze and refugee sanctuary movements is more approving but scarcely more substantive. Finally, his extended discussion of religious passion in the Third World is solid enough but should have been supplemented by, or sacrificed to, topics obviously central to the history of religion and politics in the United States.

A better editorial job on Frankl's manuscript would have pruned this doctoral dissertation of its more ponderous jargon and needless genuflections to revealed sociological authority. Frankl should also have been encouraged to review her use of such terms as "charismatic leadership" and "urban revivalism."

Frankl's basic thesis is that the "electric church" is best understood as a complex social organization with clear antecedents in earlier forms of "urban revivalism." This highly plausible notion is needlessly complicated by an unconvincing argument that television evangelism is uniquely different from earlier forms of revivalism. What Frankl does convincingly demonstrate is a fairly clear evolution from early camp-style revivalism to contemporary televangelism. In my opinion, Frankl makes too much of television's programming and marketing formats and pays too little attention to the continuity of revivalist themes. Even though Charles Finney, Dwight Moody, and Billy Sunday predated television, virtually all of their major themes evidently are repeated by contemporary media revivalists. Moreover, as Frankl reveals in her chapters on these earlier preachers, they, too, stood apart from mainstream Protestant denominations and were preoccupied with fund-raising and productivity. Although Frankl studied the content of different religious broadcasts, her book does not systematically examine the possible continuity of evangelist messages in this and earlier periods.

Frankl's analysis also is not well served by characterization of late nineteenth- and twentieth-century revivalism as distinctly urban. This label rests chiefly on a sweeping assertion that America was abruptly transformed from a gemeinschaft to a gesellschaft society after the Civil War. Frankl never provides an operational definition of urban and never acknowledges the rural and small-town setting of so much American revivalism in this and the previous century. Nor does she examine the possibility that the audience for contemporary televangelism is disproportionately drawn from country folk, small-town residents, and migrants from these areas to larger cities.

EMMETT H. BUELL, Jr.

Denison University
Granville
Ohio

GARROW, DAVID J. *Bearing the Cross: Martin Luther King, Jr., and the Southern Christian Leadership Conference.* Pp. 800. New York: William Morrow, 1986. $19.95.

In an interview, Ella Baker, former associate director of the Southern Christian Leadership Conference (SCLC), said, "The movement made Martin rather than Martin making the movement." This sentence captures the thrust of David Garrow's biography: that Martin Luther King, Jr., was a reluctant leader who stepped forward in Montgomery—and later—because it seemed to be his duty to do so. Garrow's King is thus a quite human figure rather than a charismatic demigod.

This narrative history weaves together the life of Dr. King and the story of the SCLC in the years from Montgomery to Memphis. The book is a well-written, exhaustive—almost exhausting—thoroughly documented chronicle of the events of King's career in the civil rights movement. Although Garrow centers on King's involvement with the SCLC, he is able to place these events in the overall struggle for civil rights in the years from 1955 to 1968. Part of this success is Garrow's making and part is due to the central role of Martin Luther King, Jr., in the movement.

Ella Baker's comment is a particularly apt appraisal of the relationship of Dr. King and the civil rights movement. It is easy to see the movement as one that started with his role in the Montgomery bus boycott and that came to an end with his death in Memphis. Such is not the case. The National Association for the Advancement of Colored People and leaders such as A. Philip Randolph had long worked to combat racial inequality in the United States, and the struggle still continues today. This is not to deny Martin Luther King an important role in the movement but to indicate that circumstances were right in 1955 for a moderate leader to step forward.

J. Edgar Hoover's vicious attacks notwithstanding, King remained the voice of moderation throughout his career. His calls for reform were more forthright and his tactics less polite than those of the NAACP, which had come to be a middle-class movement by the mid-1950s. On the other hand, some students were critical from an early date of his moderation and advocacy of nonviolence.

King's humanity was both a strength and a weakness of the movement. He remained a humble, unassuming leader who had time for everyone, which was certainly a strength but which also created scheduling nightmares. At times his self-doubt, reinforced by his awareness of spying by the Federal Bureau of Investigation on his private life, threatened to become overwhelming. On occasion his morbidity became damaging, but only a fool would have been unaware of the physical danger that often confronted civil rights leaders in the 1960s. King's, and other leaders', attitudes toward women in the movement were costly in the long run as accomplished women, such as Ella Baker, sought other avenues after one put-down too many.

All of these facts are unsurprising to scholars of the period. It is here that Garrow's admirable book is disappointing. Narrative history certainly plays an important role in our understanding of the past, a point underscored by Lawrence Stone in his essay "The Revival of Narrative." Yet, after finishing *Bearing the Cross*, some readers may still have questions concerning the evolution of King's views on nonviolence and socialism or even his leadership abilities. From Garrow's account, it can be inferred that King was not a strong organizer nor that he was good at consolidating his gains, feeling a need to go on to other projects, but he does not address these or other questions explicitly. It is in answering these questions that analysis plays an important part in gaining understanding.

In sum, *Bearing the Cross* is a superb book for the general reader. The narrative format is likely to attract readers, and the length is not insurmountable. The only criticism concerning this audience is that a list of acronyms might be helpful. Students can profitably consult *Bearing the Cross*, although its length may preclude its assignment in some courses. Scholars might wish for more than narrative. Garrow displays such a command of the sources that some measure of analysis should have been possible.

Even though David Garrow could have done more with his material, he has produced a book that will continue to be referred to for factual insights. That is no mean feat.

JOHN THEILMANN
Converse College
Spartanburg
South Carolina

HUNT, MICHAEL E. *Ideology and U.S. Foreign Policy*. Pp. xiv, 237. New Haven, CT: Yale University Press, 1987. $22.50.

Michael E. Hunt has written an interesting and provocative book. He believes that "ideology remains the obvious starting point for explaining both the American outlook and American behavior in world affairs." Starting with Thomas Paine, he traces in a mere 200 pages the rise of what he perceives as "the core ideas in the ideology of U.S. foreign policy": an active quest for national greatness closely coupled to the promotion of liberty; a concept of racial hierarchy through which the white elite that dominated U.S. policy has viewed other nations and cultures; and an opposition to all revolutions that did not conform to the moderate upheaval that brought the United States into being. The "deep and pervasive impact" of this ideology, he believes, and the activism that it has inspired have yielded unfortunate

results both at home, in strengthening executive authority and weakening liberty, and abroad, where it led to imperial expansion in the name of liberty and involved the United States in costly overseas ventures. The Vietnam experience, understandably, is the climax of his argument.

The bald summary hardly does justice to Hunt's thesis, which is presented cogently and persuasively in smooth flowing prose that is buttressed and enlivened by myriad quotations from the extensive literature on U.S. foreign policy that he has so clearly mastered. He includes an interesting "Essay on Historical Literature." His chapters on the development of ideology from the eighteenth century are followed by a chapter on the role of ideology in the twentieth century and a concluding one in which he looks ahead and advances some suggestions. His book should contribute to the continuing debate on new directions for U.S. foreign policy. He is careful to note at several points—on page 191, for example—the importance of comparing the U.S. experience and that of other powers. But, as a non-American reviewer may presume to suggest, he has not entirely escaped from the tendency to criticize U.S. attitudes and policies in isolation from the shortcomings of others. He calls for the acceptance of "the limits of our ability to transform a world prone to violence, chaos, exploitation, brutality, and oppression," for an "instinctive wariness towards political entanglements." He insists that this is not a plea for a new isolationism but rather a call for a more restrained, self-limiting policy in which the despised doctrines of spheres of influence and balance of power might figure. It makes sense to argue, as others have done in the past and are doing in the present, for a recognition of the limits of U.S. power and for a discriminating look at its real interests. But the problem is that the United States is not a power like others, it has willy-nilly inherited a special role, and it is difficult to see how, in a troubled world, the antidote of international education and the inspiration of a new republicanism could reverse the impact of the history of two centuries. As Hunt notes toward the end, "Fashioning a new policy will prove a formidable task."

ROBERT SPENCER

University of Toronto
Ontario
Canada

LINK, ARTHUR S. et al., eds. *The Papers of Woodrow Wilson.* Vol. 56. Pp. xix, 646. Princeton, NJ: Princeton University Press, 1987. $52.50.

"While these men talk the world is falling apart," Ray Stannard Baker of Woodrow Wilson's entourage confided in his diary. He was passing on the policy debates between the Allied victors in Paris. It took no great perspicuity to observe the dilemmas the war's end laid before them. Hunger was all but universal in Europe. Defeated Germany seethed with unrest and might even, given hope, resume fighting. The Bolshevik government had not collapsed and was even being given new possibilities by the Béla Kun Communist revolution in Hungary. With France's Clemenceau interested only in binding down Germany forever, and Lloyd George and Woodrow Wilson curbed in their decisions by parliamentary and Senate threats, statesmanship was not readily available to concerned leaders.

This latest volume in the continuing *Papers of Woodrow Wilson* is invaluable in modifying and even changing apparently long-established judgments of the Peace Talks. Only the notorious reparations problem remains as grimly questionable as it was seen in earlier accounts, and even here apportioning blame remains difficult. Wilson's idealism stands at its best. He urged Lloyd George to defy Parliament and if necessary go down honorably to defeat. Lloyd George was never inclined to accept splendid cashiering, but the issue does point to public pressure as the real impediment to a sane settlement. Wilson had said in his famous war declaration that his government was not fighting the German people, only their masters. But he could not control the French and English masses in their lust for vengeance.

The protracted debates and negotiations merit close reading. Wilson's faith in democratic speech and belief that food would settle most discontent in mid-European countries proved ill-founded. Herbert Hoover's heroic efforts to satisfy basic needs in Russia, Rumania, and elsewhere could not by themselves further peace or democracy. War between Ukrainian patriots and the Polish raised the specter of Bolshevik expansion to the west. Yet old legends of Allied reactionary measures do not hold up in these detailed accounts. The Allied leaders discussed newborn Czechoslovakia in terms of the rights of its mixed population. Lloyd George talked of returning Germany to the family of nations, if only to fend off Communist threats in the west. Even Colonel House expressed willingness to recognize the Bolsheviks as a de facto government with which they could deal.

Meanwhile Wilson, heavily pressured by his European colleagues and his foes at home, labored for his League of Nations, separate from his peace proposals yet part of the mechanism he dreamed would control the narrow demands of his associates, at home and abroad. He was less rigid and authoritarian than tradition has pictured him. Socialists and liberals at home pleaded that he free Eugene V. Debs from prison, where he had been placed for defying wartime regulations against speech calculated to harm the war effort. Wilson is willing to satisfy such valuable coadjutors as Charles Edward Russell, Upton Sinclair, and Charlotte Perkins Gilmore, among others. But he felt that he could not hobble Attorney General A. Mitchell Palmer in maintaining the law. It was Palmer, not Wilson, who insisted on Debs's remaining confined. The conclusion must be that Wilson must be judged, not only in terms of his will and judgment, but also by the forces that shared power with him.

LOUIS FILLER

The Belfry
Ovid
Michigan

MILLER, WARREN E. and M. KENT JEN-NINGS. *Parties in Transition: A Longitudinal Study of Party Elites and Party Supporters*. Pp. xxv, 284. New York: Russell Sage Foundation, 1986. $22.95.

This volume, based on mail questionnaires and personal interviews with delegates to the 1972, 1976, and 1980 Republican and Democratic national conventions, covers a period of turbulence for both parties. While "the transition of leadership within the Republican Party has been fueled by an ideological drive that has become politically viable through the failures of Republican liberals and centrists," the changes within the Democratic Party stemmed from "a series of reforms intended to restore legitimacy to its leaders by changing the process of their selection." Rather than legitimating the established leadership, however, those reforms allowed two outsiders, George McGovern and Jimmy Carter, to gain the Democratic presidential nomination.

During this period, the parties were moving in opposite directions at one level, but in a similar direction at another. The Republicans moved toward an ideologically based politics, while the Democrats were moving away from ideology: "Carter did not represent a 'movement' or a cause—only an alternative to apparent losers." These contradictory trends, however, led to a "drift to the right" on the part of both parties. Within the Republican Party, "conversion" has occurred, with long-time activists becoming more conservative as Reagan gained the nomination and then the presidency; the increasing Democratic conservatism was due to "circulation," with conservative delegates replacing liberals who became inactive. Other differences, also related to the varying importance of ideology, are discussed: Republican activists became less attached to party and less concerned about the personal advantages they would gain from participation in the election process while Democrats became more concerned with these incentives for participation.

While there are some interesting findings contained in this book, it is not a work written for a general audience interested in the political process or the dynamics of social change. The book has an extremely narrow focus. It is almost totally ahistorical, detaching the conventions of 1972-80 from the ongoing stream of political life that preceded and followed them. It deals only with delegates to party conventions and makes the questionable assumptions that these delegates are representative of party activists in general and that they provide a crucial link in the election process between formal campaigns and the public. While this is a work that students of political parties no doubt will find useful, its limitations outweigh its value for the nonspecialist.

STEVEN D. EALY

Armstrong State College
Savannah
Georgia

SIEGEL, FREDERICK F. *The Roots of Southern Distinctiveness: Tobacco and Society in Danville, Virginia, 1780-1865*. Pp. xiii, 205. Chapel Hill: University of North Carolina Press, 1987. $22.00.

Histories of the pre-Civil War South have focused on the question of whether the institution of slavery ensured Southern distinctiveness and was the key factor affecting the South's relative economic backwardness and failure to develop a more diversified agricultural and industrial economy. Some historians have argued that slavery retarded Southern economic development while others have claimed that the creation of a plantation system based on slavery gave rise to a feudalistic antimarket ideology and thus the South's distinctive political economy.

In his tightly researched monograph examining the economic development of Danville, Virginia, and the surrounding county of Pittsylvania, Frederick Siegel challenges these two competing interpretations. Recounting the history of Danville's and Pittsylvania's economic development from 1780 through 1865, with the rural sector's dependence on tobacco production and Danville's belated development in the decades after 1820 as a commercial and manufacturing center based on tobacco, Siegel documents that Pittsylvania's failure to diversify and Danville's emergence as a manufacturing town was the consequence of the cultivation of tobacco. The dependence on tobacco production, he concedes, created a distinctive tobacco culture that both benefited and limited the region's economic development. Siegel nonetheless concludes that the failure to diversify was not the product of the constraints imposed by the emergence of a plantation system based on slavery so much as the limitations imposed by soil and climate. Because of these natural limitations, Pittsylvanian agriculturists could not profitably shift to other commercial crops. Concurrently, the particular labor needs of tobacco manufacturing allowed Danville's merchant investors to rely on hired slaves and to prosper—in contrast, such a labor force could not meet the needs of other forms of manufacturing, notably textiles.

Siegel's monograph adds another dimension to our understanding of the South's different economic and political development and thus the factors bringing about the crisis of secession and Civil War. Yet Siegel makes no attempt to correlate his particular findings with those of other historians who have researched other Southern geographic regions having either similar or dissimilar soil and climate. As such, his research leaves unanswered the question of Southern distinctiveness. Representative of the shift in recent historiography toward local quantitative history, with the attendant ability to test the validity of generalizations that were often based on a limited data base or that failed to recognize distinctiveness, Siegel's study is a useful beginning and offers the prospect for resolving the question of the inevitability of the Civil War.

ATHAN THEOHARIS

Marquette University
Milwaukee
Wisconsin

SPITZER, MATTHEW L. *Seven Dirty Words and Six Other Stories: Controlling the*
Content of Print and Broadcast. Pp. xii, 163. New Haven, CT: Yale University Press, 1987. $15.00.

This brief book is itself a brief. Matthew L. Spitzer, a professor of law at the University of Southern California, sees little justification for "differential regulation" between print and broadcast media. An articulate advocate of First Amendment equality, Spitzer makes a persuasive case that the stricter controls placed on radio and television are no longer pertinent to our communications environment.

A principal virtue of *Seven Dirty Words and Six Other Stories* is its methodical questioning of the reasoning behind the different treatments of print media—newspapers, magazines, and books—as opposed to broadcast media. For example, the rationale that scarcity of the airwaves demands greater control and regulation might have had merit in the early days of radio and television. Today, however, as technology mushrooms and becomes more sophisticated, possibilities for broadcasting widen and allow greater diversity of programming. Given the wealth of choice, especially with cable and satellite transmissions, the original argument about limited sources becomes as obsolete as an elder American's crystal set radio receiver.

After dispensing with the shibboleth of scarcity, Spitzer investigates the effects of specific print and broadcast messages on the public. Through close analysis of social and behavioral research, he finds that sexually explicit and violent printed matter has pernicious effects similar to the effects of the same kinds of material that arrive on the airwaves. It is possible—indeed, civilly responsible— to question the ethical propriety of such messages; however, Spitzer's concern centers on the unequal regulatory treatment of print and broadcast media. If the impact of material is actually quite comparable, why does the government exercise greater control over broadcast media than print forms? What justifies this double standard?

Although Spitzer demonstrates that differential regulation rests on a weak foundation, he is by no means absolutist in favoring the removal of barriers between the various kinds of media. He acknowledges that broadcast media are more easily accessible to young children than print media, making the delivery of potentially harmful messages a legitimate reason for special measures. Spitzer advocates the zoning of explicit sex and violence by limiting such material to adult channels delivered through special receivers and at late night hours. Specifically designed television locks would also help parents shield children from certain programming.

Spitzer makes extensive use of social science research in building his argument for more equitable treatment of print and broadcast media. He emphasizes, however, that much of such research possesses inherent shortcomings that make relevance to policy guidance dubious. As he notes at one point:

One cannot be certain that the behavioral tendencies observed in the laboratory will also manifest themselves in natural settings. Several considerations counsel caution: subjects watch the screen more in the laboratory than in natural settings; experimental films are quite short, and are shown without commercials; subjects are usually given an immediate opportunity to aggress in the laboratory; and . . . subjects are not punished for acts of aggression in the laboratory, while they often are in natural surroundings (pp. 115-16).

In addition, there is considerable ambiguity among studies, with conclusions being contradictory and befuddling.

On 4 August 1987, the Federal Communications Commission voted to abolish the Fairness Doctrine, an anachronism—in Spitzer's opinion—deserving such a fate. In future years, *Seven Dirty Words and Six Other Stories* will continue to offer the necessary direction to the fulfillment of the broadcast media's First Amendment freedom.

ROBERT SCHMUHL
University of Notre Dame
Indiana

WASTE, ROBERT J. *Power and Pluralism in American Cities: Researching the Urban Laboratory.* Pp. xvi, 176. Westport, CT: Greenwood Press, 1987. $32.95.

Power and Pluralism in American Cities assesses Robert A. Dahl's concept of polyarchy—political regimes in which nonleaders exercise relatively high degrees of control over their leaders. In this study, Robert J. Waste, associate professor of urban studies at San Diego State University, raises compelling questions. How democratic are American cities? How do we measure degrees of democracy? What can be done to enhance citizen participation?

At various times, Dahl has been portrayed as a committed democratic theorist, an apologist for the status quo, a neo-elitist, and a value-free behavioral scientist who overlooked key issues. While bringing disciples and dissenters into the forum, Waste never misleads us. Dahl is his mentor and friend. The critics' positions are succinctly stated, but Waste ultimately dismisses them as straw men whose arguments are "incorrect," "not helpful," "methodologically deficient," or "wide of the mark."

Waste rejects the notion that Dahl is an apologist for the status quo or an elitist masquerading as a democrat. He contends that Dahl is evenhanded in exposing undemocratic practices in giant corporations, trade unions, totalitarian governments, and boss-ridden municipalities. He concurs with Dahl's premise that inequalities in wealth and status undermine democracy. Winners and losers in urban contests are unduly determined by the political skills, incentives, and resources of the combatants.

Still, this is not a paean to pessimism. Even in *Who Governs?*—the classic account of polyarchy in New Haven—Dahl found a republic of unequal citizens, but a republic nonetheless. Waste supports Dahl's emphasis on three policy issues—urban redevelopment, public education, and party nominations—as salient indices that affect vast numbers of people and cut across a variety of interests. In short, they meet the tests of "centrality, financial magnitude, scope and breadth."

Going beyond New Haven's borders, Waste proffers an empirical model for determining the presence of polyarchy in other cities. He identifies eight institutional conditions: freedom of association, free speech, the right to vote, citizen eligibility for office, alternative sources of information, fair elections, leadership competition for support, and linkages between public preferences and official policies.

Waste applies this model to Foster and Providence, Rhode Island. Foster, a suburban community of 3400 inhabitants, is small enough to retain town meetings and linkages between those who govern and are governed. The political system, substantially Republican, is a social network of neighbors, friends, and relatives. Providence, with a population of 157,000, has shifted from its patrician past to the politics of immigration controlled by a Democratic machine attempting to cope with urban unrest and economic decline. On the basis of size and homogeneity, Foster appears to be more polyarchical. Empirical testing, however, reveals that the two municipalities generate surprisingly close scores. Even the expectation that Providence's political machine might alienate the populace is tempered by the fact that many residents accept politics as a participant sport in which entire families can engage.

The defense of Dahl consumes most of the book. Researching the urban laboratory is limited to the final chapter, which ends rather abruptly. Apart from his excellent notes, Waste overlooks community empowerment projects in most parts of the country. He does acknowledge that his two-city sampling is too small to determine the universality of his empirical model. With these caveats in mind, the reader will appreciate this useful synthesis of the theory of polyarchy, and the suggestions for further exploration.

LEONARD P. STAVISKY
Columbia University
New York

SOCIOLOGY

BOSKIN, JOSEPH. *Sambo: The Rise and Demise of an American Jester.* Pp. ix, 252. New York: Oxford University Press, 1986. $20.95.

SOUTHERN, DAVID S. *Gunnar Myrdal and Black-White Relations: The Use and Abuse of an American Dilemma, 1944-1969.* Pp. xviii, 341. Baton Rouge: Louisiana State University Press, 1987. No price.

Two recent books of note revive the issue of the black image in the white mind. Joseph Boskin traces the comic black stereotype back to the early renaming of Africans with humorous tags, a white ritual of control. By 1830, Sambo and his antics had evolved into a white American convention, as the Southern slave darkie and the Northern burnt-cork minstrel man. His dancing, his bug-eyed mugging, and his social pretensions confined the black male to a performance role in white culture. Sambo became the theatrical fool but without the traditional sly wisdom.

For Boskin this is a dual-edged American tradition that was borne from the complex interplay between white and black peoples. At his richest, "Sambo was the first truly indigenous American humor character throughout the culture" but also an unthreatening guise that whites liked and needed to believe. Nonetheless, this began as a white creation, which could assuage guilt, rationalize slavery, redirect black energies, and even help to pretend interracial harmony.

More than a static racist image, Sambo was an evolving character that came increasingly under the control of more sensitive white practitioners and, ultimately, of blacks themselves. Customarily scorned types, especially Uncle Remus, Amos and Andy, and Eddie "Rochester" Anderson, were really central to the broadening of the image. Boskin rightly concludes that Sambo finally became a self-reflexive stereotype, even a tool for liberation. "Mocking features of black behavior effectively undercut whatever notion remained of blacks as fools."

In order to show the pervasiveness of the image in American culture, Boskin's use of evidence can seem excessive and heavy-handed. Nonetheless, Boskin's study is laudable, as both American popular culture and Afro-American history. He makes good use of a general approach; main points of Afro-American history and scholarship are reiterated in succinct, unobtrusive fashion. *Sambo* certainly deserves a reading outside of the historical guild.

David Southern's study of *An American Dilemma* is far removed from the realm of popular culture, as it chronicles the approach of intellectuals, predominantly white, to the problem of racial segregation and social equality. Gunnar Myrdal, a Swedish economist and political activist, told Americans in 1944 that their sincerely held democratic ideals were at odds with the nation's continuing disregard and mistreatment of blacks. Despite the indictment, however, Myrdal's thesis rested on idealistic ground. Human goodness, American values, and, of course, the toolbox of social engineering promised a brighter day. As Southern argues, the Myrdal thesis had a pervasive effect on American attitudes toward race among policymakers, educators, and participants in the civil rights movement itself.

Southern is sensitive to the ideological and social worlds of ideas, and the strongest chapters weave both into first-rate narrative history. The academic infighting, tales of Myrdalian charisma and cheek, and the wartime state of social theory are not only important but compelling. He guides us ably through the intellectual nuances of modern social theory, where Myrdal stood within it, and how subsequent shifts in the intellectual wind have challenged the dilemma explanation of inequality.

As Southern understands, intellectual influence is a tough rap to make stick. So, in addition to the clear citations of Myrdal by the likes of the Truman Committee, Dr. King, and the *Brown* case, he unearths conservative, Southern, Marxist, activist, and academic responses to the milestone study. Unfortunately, Myrdal's influence up-

on black movers and shakers—after all, the heart of the civil rights movement—seems more tenuous, and Southern never really confronts the key issue that is raised here, the intellectual relationship between white liberals and the movement's germination. Within its narrower scope, however, Southern's study is an able analysis of liberalism's evolving attitudes toward race.

STEVEN SMITH

Brown University
Providence
Rhode Island

BURGHARDT, STEVE and MICHAEL FABRICANT. *Working under the Safety Net: Policy and Practice with the New American Poor.* Pp. 180. Newbury Park, CA: Sage, 1987. Paperbound, $9.95.

KATZMANN, ROBERT A. *Institutional Disability: The Saga of Transportation Policy for the Disabled.* Pp. ix, 211. Washington, DC: Brookings Institution, 1986. $28.95. Paperbound, $10.95.

Burghardt and Fabricant are social service activists who set out to portray human distress in the United States among varied groups—older Americans, blacks, single-parent family heads, the disabled, the hungry, and especially the new unemployed. The latter refers to persons caught up by current political and economic conditions, such as the decline in industries that once offered numerous well-paying jobs and the explosion in the number of low-paying high-technology and service jobs. Burghardt and Fabricant also comment upon the evils that accompany unemployment, such as increased alcoholism, substance abuse, domestic violence, alienation, and despair. They do not discuss the plight of one group, which suffers from the acquired immune deficiency syndrome. Of course, this infection was recognized only in 1981, and a blood test has familiarized millions of Americans to it.

The previous half century had witnessed a vast expansion of social entitlements, such as unemployment insurance, disability benefits, aid for dependent children, and the like. The safety net is now, however, less capable of meeting the new unemployeds' basic needs, operating as it does against a backdrop of cuts in government allowances and the gradual withdrawal of discrete federal services for vulnerable groups by government agencies and private institutions.

In July 1987, a White House aide filled a gap in a speech being prepared for President Ronald Reagan; the president delivered the message without seeing the passage in advance.

This incident should not surprise readers of *Institutional Disability*. It deals with a narrower area than *Working under the Safety Net*; however, until Katzmann wrote it, relatively few policymakers in this domain could view it comprehensively. The federal government had declared that the elderly and disabled could claim the same rights as others to the use of public transit. Millions of disabled, however, could use it only with difficulty; others, not at all. This was largely due to the failure of the national government to formulate effective policies to guide the carriers, state and local governments, and the disabled community.

The reasons were varied and complex. First, Congress is divided into authorization and appropriation committees, plus some with crosscutting jurisdiction. Again, scores of officeholders related to Congress, whom Katzmann names, have dabbled in this area without close scrutiny by Congress. Congressional "entrepreneurs," for example, could tack amendments to bills only distantly related to transit. Finally, administrators often—mistakenly—assumed committee reports represented congressional consensus. In short, Congress seemed to behave irresponsibly when staff members, like the president's aide, acted "unseen by the whole house." The cumulative effect of these actions has been to create a "grab bag of programs that ill served the target population."

Administrators have added to the confusion: three cabinet-level departments that dealt in this area generated the principle of "personal accountability," mentioned earlier, as well as the principle of "effective mobility," which emphasized the transit aspect. Unfortunately, agencies like the Department of Transportation frequently oscillated between these two approaches. Finally, Katzmann finds no evidence that an "imperial" judiciary sought to impose monolithic preferences. In fact, 740 overworked district and appellate judges responded only to suits initiated by scattered plaintiffs.

In the absence of coherent and consistent federal efforts, the disabled concentrated on state and local institutions. There the thrust has always arisen not only out of state law but also out of the political strength of interested groups.

Both books serve important purposes, to show (1) how increasing numbers of Americans are affected by new and intensive forces of poverty and difficulties for the disabled in public transportation; (2) how the services recently organized to meet their needs are inadequate; and (3) how improvements may be undertaken realistically and efficiently. Buttressed by extensive notes and bibliographies, both recommend remedies for the flaws they uncover that merit careful consideration by statesmen and political scientists.

FREDERICK SHAW
City University of New York

COLQUHOUN, ROBERT. *Raymond Aron.* Vol. 1, *The Philosopher in History, 1905-1955.* Pp. xi, 540. Newbury Park, CA: Sage, 1986. $40.00.

COLQUHOUN, ROBERT. *Raymond Aron.* Vol. 2, *The Sociologist in Society, 1955-1983.* Pp. xv, 680. Newbury Park, CA: Sage, 1986. $48.00.

If one were to think of the most famous French intellectual of the past fifty years, probably the names of Sartre or Camus would come to mind. Raymond Aron, philosopher, journalist, and sociologist, was a classmate of Sartre at the École normale supérieure and graduated first in his class. Sartre, by contrast, was failed by the faculty because he presented his new views. Sartre passed the next year first in the class, with Simone de Beauvoir in second place. Sartre and de Beauvoir went on to become internationally known for their new contributions to literature and philosophy, while Aron went on to become well known for his brilliant reinterpretation of other people's work and a dedication to pragmatism in a culture that loved metaphysics. Unfortunately, Aron ended up being publicly and privately alienated from not only Sartre and de Beauvoir but Albert Camus as well.

Robert Colquhoun's intellectual history of Aron is chronological. First we read of Aron's school days, and we end with his last written work. In all there are 45 chapters. Each chapter is largely self-contained and is organized about events or lectures in the author's life. Probably no human will ever be able to read or digest all Aron's writings. A man who wrote a daily newspaper column for most of his life leaves behind too much to digest. Colquhoun does not list the daily writings in the bibliography. Even then the bibliography contains for some years over 20 books and articles, not counting the translations from the French original.

Aron's work, being massive, is hard to categorize. Combining metaphysics with pragmatism, Aron attracted great praise for his life-long summary and reinterpretation of the place in history of Marx, Pareto, and Weber. Thinkers such as Toynbee applauded the effort, while others, especially in England, criticized any effort to disagree with Aron as "like trying to argue with a frog," a very nasty interpretation indeed. Although Parsons in the United States also based theory on the work of Marx, Pareto, and Weber, Aron criticized Parsons's efforts, too. Aron himself, however, was popular at Harvard even if he is not well-known to the majority of sociologists in the United States who seem to follow Parsons's lead today. If Aron were France's sociological equivalent of Talcott Parsons, Colquhoun would imply that Aron was much more brilliant. Aron's

efforts at understanding the causes of war and peace were extensive, but in the end he only counseled both the United States and the Soviet Union to be "prudent" when dealing with each other. Aron's followers will find much to enjoy in these books; his critics are not likely to have their minds changed.

Colquhoun is to be complimented for his clear writing style. The chapters are short, and each is a nicely presented summary of one or more pieces of Aron's work. Graduate students will especially enjoy volume 2, because it contains an excellent review of most of the major classical thinkers in sociology. Unfortunately, the chronological approach means that many issues are covered in more than one place. I tried to trace convergence theory in the book, to find it mentioned only in the index of volume 2, even though two of the references were to volume 1. Aron rejected convergence theory himself. Why he did so is not explained by Colquhoun, who is much better at explaining final conclusions than Aron's thought process. We are not given too much information on the alternatives Aron considered in reaching his conclusions.

These books are essential for any college library, graduate or undergraduate. For classroom use, especially at the graduate level, professors should consider volume 2. Perhaps the publisher should bring out a one-volume edition suitable for use as a textbook.

GEORGE H. CONKLIN
North Carolina State University
Durham

GOGGIN, MALCOLM L. *Policy Design and the Politics of Implementation: The Case of Child Health Care in the American States.* Pp. xv, 296. Knoxville: University of Tennessee Press, 1987. $29.95.

TAYLOR, D. GARTH. *Public Opinion & Collective Action: The Boston School Desegregation Conflict.* Pp. xiii, 241. Chicago: University of Chicago Press, 1986. $29.00.

208 OF THE AMERICAN ACADEMY

Policy Design and the Politics of Implementation, by Malcolm L. Goggin, and *Public Opinion & Collective Action*, written by D. Garth Taylor, each involve the dynamics of policy implementation. Goggin's effort, which, on the whole, is superb, involves state implementation of child health diagnosis services. In contrast, Taylor's work, which I found somewhat disappointing, concerns the response of the public and the politics of the racial integration of Boston's public schools.

Goggin, at the outset of his volume, describes the essence of the Early and Periodic Screening, Diagnosis, and Treatment (EPSDT) Act passed by the Congress in 1967, signed by President Johnson in 1968, and initially scheduled to commence on 1 July 1969. Basically, EPSDT is a federal-state program designed to screen children for dental, physical, and mental health problems and provide for appropriate treatment. Following his general discussion of EPSDT, Goggin elaborates upon various theories of policy implementation that conceivably have some bearing on the success of state efforts to implement EPSDT.

Goggin's research focus inordinately involved the experience of California, although, to provide his work with a comparative dimension, Goggin includes the experience of Arkansas, Louisiana, New Mexico, Oklahoma, and Texas. Its core concern was to seek to determine which factors and variables accounted for the relative success or nonsuccess in implementing the programs and goals of EPSDT. Goggin concludes that the economic, political, and implementation setting capacity models of policy implementation are each insufficient in bearing upon the implementation success of EPSDT; he finds more appropriate his suggested differential theory of policy implementation.

Goggin is not to be praised so much for his findings, which are hardly novel, but for the rigor, longitudinal analysis, and the quasi-comparative focus of his research effort.

Taylor commences his volume with a nice general discussion of the politics of racial school integration, and this is followed by a review of the events leading up to Judge Arthur Garrity's order in the mid-1970s to the Boston School Committee to utilize busing to achieve some measure of racial integration in the public schools. Taylor provides the reader with a good understanding of the way in which local politicians, the Church, and the mass public reacted to the busing order. He notes the mass communication, organizational, and attention-calling resources, in addition to the long political hostility between Boston and the state government, which were available to and utilized by the anti-busing forces. He advances the base argument that the vast majority of Boston's white citizens opposed busing for racial integration not because they were racists but because they viewed busing as a perceived injustice and as constituting social harm; further, busing was viewed as undermining the concept of voluntary compliance.

This book contains a wealth of empirical data pertaining to the mass public's attitude about the employment of busing as a vehicle to promote racial integration in the Boston public schools; unfortunately, Taylor does not relate this data to the various socioeconomic groups that populate the city. We never learn, for instance, whether the Irish of Southie—South Boston—were more opposed to busing than their more prosperous kin who reside in Jamaica Plan.

I did not learn a great deal from this work because I have already done a fair amount of reading on the politics of school integration. For the uninitiated, this is a worthwhile empirical study of the politics surrounding mandated school busing in one Northern city.

NELSON WIKSTROM
Virginia Commonwealth University
Richmond

JONES, DAVID A. *History of Criminology: A Philosophical Perspective*. Pp. xii, 243. Westport, CT: Greenwood Press, 1986. $35.00.

There exists no universally accepted definition of what criminology is. The terse dictionary description of it as the study of crimes and criminals can be interpreted in various ways, but all agree that it deals with actions and actors defined by law. Actually "criminology" is an umbrella term covering studies mainly done by persons trained in various branches of the social and psychological sciences and searching for the causes of crime in the makeup and personality of the criminal or in the criminal's social environment and for means and methods of reducing and preventing criminal conduct. Therefore, it is surprising to find that David Jones, who regards criminology as a scientific discipline, claims that Cesare Beccaria is the founder of modern criminology. Beccaria, who published a remarkable tract in 1764 titled "Of Crimes and of Punishments," was a great penal law reformer, whose ideas have had a powerful influence on American penal legislation in recent decades. Outside the United States, at least, criminology is but one component of what the French call the *sciences criminelles*, the others being penology or criminal policy, and penal law. Recently, even the basic structure of criminology has been challenged. At an international conference sponsored by the Council of Europe a few years ago, a Dutch professor proposed that criminology be replaced by "deviology," that is, the study of deviancy and deviants, including crimes and criminals as well as violations and violators defined by normative social groups other than legislative bodies. Consequently, anyone who plans to write a history of criminology faces a dilemma. What is criminology?

Jones has solid credentials as legal scholar, writer, and practitioner and is professor of interdisciplinary studies in law and justice and of sociology at the University of Pittsburgh. His history is notable. It shows that he is well acquainted with the philosophy of law and much of the literature, past and present, dealing with the subject matter of his book. His style of writing is graceful. Furthermore, his history is the first of its kind written by an American, but the reader should not share his confident belief that, having perused it, the reader will know what criminology really is.

The plan of the book is original. An introductory chapter, giving a conspectus of the content of the work, is followed by seven chapters, each of which is designed to show the influence of successive schools of philosophy on the pursuit of knowledge about criminality and the penal system, beginning with "classical realism," followed by "classical idealism," utilitarianism, positivism, naturalism, pragmatism, and "analytical criminology." A final chapter on existentialism is an essay that is interesting but seems to lack any substantial relationship to the subject matter of the book. The early chapters deal mostly with penal law, criminal procedure, prison management, and police agencies. The fifth and the following three chapters examine the theories and research produced by physical anthropologists, psychiatrists, psychologists, and sociologists during the last hundred years, and some of them are analyzed at length. Most attention is paid to the criminological theories and studies of Americans—all but two of whom are males—since the first world war. No mention is made of many top-ranking European criminologists of this century, nor is the rest of the world given any attention, which is understandable given that nobody has an encyclopedic knowledge of the subjects covered by Jones's history.

THORSTEN SELLIN

Gilmanton
New Hampshire

MORONE, JOSEPH G. and EDWARD J. WOODHOUSE. *Averting Catastrophe: Strategies for Regulating Risky Technologies.* Pp. x, 215. Berkeley: University of California Press, 1986. $17.95.

In their book, *Averting Catastrophe: Strategies for Regulating Risky Technologies,* Morone and Woodhouse attack an "intriguing puzzle." Why, despite close calls, have risky civilian technologies produced no catastrophes in America? Is it the result of luck or is it the result of a somewhat deliberate and successful regulatory planning process? While they claim that it is too premature to answer the question, due to the unseen impact of late somatic effects of some of these risky systems, they nevertheless conclude that the United States has "done better at avoiding catastrophe than most people realize." This, obviously, is a controversial issue, and their answer is bound to continue the heated debate concerning a risky technology's threat to the ecosystem and to society.

Morone and Woodhouse view five types of technological risk: toxic chemicals, civilian nuclear power, recombinant DNA research, threat to the ozone layer, and the greenhouse danger. They analyze these activities in order to understand how—or whether—the system has learned to deal with the potential for catastrophe. In this analysis, which leads to the development of a system of risk reduction, Morone and Woodhouse enter a few caveats: theirs is not a comprehensive study; there is no examination of the "politics" of each controversy. The book is limited to civilian technologies and does not discuss risky, top-secret military technologies, such as the atomic testing program at the Nevada Test Site, radiation experiments, Star Wars, space shuttle technology, and so forth. The book focuses only on severe threats, that is, catastrophes. Finally, Morone and Woodhouse strive to be "as unpoliticized as possible." Some of these caveats are very critical limitations that will be commented on in the concluding paragraphs of this review.

Morone and Woodhouse, in a sparse, descriptive manner, examine (1) the inherent dangers of each "technology"; (2) how industry and regulatory agencies—without the authors' writing about the politics of each controversial and risky technology—have interacted mostly, with the exception of nuclear power, in trial-and-error-fashion, to develop controls on the technology; and (3) how successful these interactions have

been—as far as can be determined at this point.

After reviewing these five risky technologies, Morone and Woodhouse generalize from these examples and discuss the possibility of creating a systematic strategy for averting catastrophe. The integrated system they discuss consists of five strategies identified in earlier chapters: protect against hazards, proceed cautiously, test risks, learn from experience, and set new priorities based on testing and experience. The risk-avoidance system they envision (1) protects against hazards, (2) reduces the level of uncertainty in risky technologies, and, as the first two goals are met, leads to the closing of a circle with (3) the revision of original precautions. In this regard, they emphasize the importance of strategic planning and decision making, given the complexity of the technological problems and the uncertainty of the data, over analytic decision making—that is, cost-benefit analysis—as administrators and scientists choose among risky options, monitor feedback, and adjust their earlier choices.

A final chapter, "Can We Do Better?" raises some natural value questions of fundamental importance: if a system of risk avoidance protects against hazards, which ones are the "egregious" hazards? What is an "acceptable" level of risk? How safe is safe enough? How does a regulator, public or private, measure risk in these risky systems? These questions pose basic obstacles to the questioner because they reflect value and factual uncertainty. But they have to be addressed in order to develop a viable catastrophe-aversion system. Morone and Woodhouse argue that to have a workable system of risk management, it must be compatible with society's values about that particular system, its perceived dangers to the society, and so forth.

I do have some concerns about the character of the book and the message it conveys. First, technology itself is not defined in an appropriate fashion. In addition, I am concerned about the omission of any discussion of new military technologies—Star Wars, shuttle technology, continued nuclear testing of weapons systems at the Nevada Test Site—that probably pose a greater risk of catastrophe than do a number of the technologies discussed in the book. If the truth, that is, the dangers to the public and to the ecosystem, were known, the essential governmental program might have to be curtailed or, worse, shut down. (For example, for the U.S. atomic testing program's scientific and moral dilemmas, see Howard Ball, *Justice Downwind: America's Atomic Testing Program in the 1950s* [New York: Oxford University Press, 1986]).

As to the question of the rareness of catastrophes, while Morone and Woodhouse talk of the development of a good monitoring system by federal agencies, Perrow is probably closer to the reality of the issue when he states that catastrophes are rare

not only because risky systems are safety-conscious but because it takes a combination of infrequently occurring conditions to produce a catastrophe. It is not so much that we have been lucky not to have had more disasters, which is the usual observation, but that it is *difficult* to have them (Perrow, "Habit of Courting Disaster," p. 347).

My last concern about *Averting Catastrophe* involves one of Morone and Woodhouse's caveats, namely, that they did not examine the politics of these technological controversies. This lack points to a fundamental weakness of the book. Without more fully examining the politics of the regulatory process, that is, the impact of the executive branch's ideology on regulatory politics (see, for example, Howard Ball, *Controlling Regulatory Sprawl: Presidential Strategies from Nixon to Reagan* [Westport, CT: Greenwood Press, 1984]), the reader is left, as in this case, with a largely descriptive account of five civilian technologies.

While the subject matter of this book is timely and important, and while the reader does receive a sense of the complexity of trying to manage and prioritize the problems associated with risky systems in order to avoid catastrophes, there are, as I have suggested here, some basic weaknesses in the

book that detract from its value for political science and public policy students.

HOWARD BALL

University of Utah
Salt Lake City

STEARNS, CAROL and PETER STEARNS. *Anger: The Struggle for Emotional Control in America's History.* Pp. vii, 295. Chicago: University of Chicago Press, 1986. $24.95.

This work is the result of a successful collaboration between a wife, who is a psychiatrist, and a husband, who is a historian. Practitioners of the new social and cultural history, a field that in the last two decades has brought a whole new range of human experience under examination, the Stearnses provide us with a first guide to the history of anger in the United States.

Methodologically sophisticated, the Stearnses avoid trying to define anger as a single thing and they do not join as partisans those polemics that turn on the either-or questions essentially asking whether anger is either necessary and purifying or unwanted and disposable. They realize that anger has multiple definitions, takes a variety of forms, and has numerous interconnections with other feelings and forms of actions.

Not unfamiliar to many of those who have written histories of love and intimacy, the Stearnses' interest is to write a history of changing American prescriptions about anger at home and in public. That is, in yet more abstract terms, they seek to locate the main historical contours of the evolving ethical and scientific emotionology offered by the representatives of the controlling upper-class Protestant culture. Their assumption is that this culture has supplied the dominant voice in the American conscience regarding anger. They do acknowledge that their "study deals with the emotionology produced by the Protestant middle class," and that this emotionology, while having been widely preached, has not been "necessarily so widely adopted."

For the Stearnses, four stages characterize the history of American anger. First, in colonial America, as in Western Europe in that era, there were few signs of concern about anger. Second, in the first half of the nineteenth century, Americans began to preach as desirable an anger-free home, which served as a refuge from the world in which anger was inevitable. Third, roughly from the second half of the century until World War I, Americans continued to focus on familial control of anger, especially in their notions of socializing children, while ambivalently believing that anger might serve a necessary public function—the righteous need their wrath. Fourth, in the last period, which begins in the 1920s and has continued in one form or another to the present, Americans have undertaken that often confusing and contradictory effort to treat anger at home and at work therapeutically. Increasingly, in the workplace, anger has been treated by management as unacceptable, as personnel relations have become the key to jobs; and anger at home, especially in the middle class, has been surrounded by varying strategies to control and manage it.

Believing that contemporary Americans continue to live within the ambivalences, confusions, and contradictions of this therapeutic understanding of anger, the Stearnses use history as the therapy of therapies. History provides, for them, a vital self-knowledge. While recognizing how many real and valid reasons there are for anger in contemporary mass and bureaucratic society, and yet what a hideous and threatening role violence plays in twentieth-century public and international life, the Stearnses conclude that our only hope is knowing where we come from emotionally. By recognizing the assumptions, aspirations, and contradictions of our emotionologies, we may at least liberate ourselves from past compulsions of behavior and feeling and be able to make new choices.

The Stearnses have provided us with a useful primer of the history of American anger. They have written an important history of a subject that has not received nearly as much attention as have love and intimacy. To complete their work, they wisely set aside questions that other historians are now invited to investigate. They did not undertake a comparative history of anger in America and Europe; nor did they explore the different forms and prescriptions of anger in varying classes, cultures, and ethnic groups; nor, finally did they seek to establish a causality that would determine whether and to what degree American prescriptions about anger commanded conscience or followed the movement, transformation, and practices of American institutions.

Rather, in accord with their intentions, Carol and Peter Stearns have offered us an important guide to a subject that, even though its heterogeneity and ambiguity may ultimately exceed our historical powers of conceptualization, we dare not ignore. After all, we know that anger destroys individuals, families, and whole nations, and we dare not forget what the Greek playwright taught: "Whom the gods would destroy, they first make mad."

JOSEPH AMATO
Southwest State University
Marshall
Minnesota

WILKINS, LEE. *Shared Vulnerability: The Media and American Perceptions of the Bhopal Disaster*. Pp. xiii, 168. Westport, CT: Greenwood Press, 1987. $29.95.

The media play a critical role in the public's understanding of significant events such as the Bhopal disaster. They can be an effective means of public education about the technological hazards that we all face in today's world. In reality, however, the media not only fall short in this role but often distort the message because of an emphasis on short-run, event-oriented reporting that emphasizes stereotypes. The differences in the reporting of the December 1984 gas leak at Union Carbide's plant in Bhopal by the American media and that by the Indian media bear out this generalization because the two viewed the disaster from ethnocentric points of view and thus formed in the two countries different perceptions about the disaster. A comparative analysis of the reporting by the media of both countries would be a useful contribution to the study of the role of the mass media and their shortcoming.

Lee Wilkins, an assistant professor of journalism and mass communication, has done one part of the comparative analysis by investigating media coverage in the United States and the public perceptions formed as a result of this coverage. The first of his book's eight chapters describe the year after the accident in Bhopal, from December 1984 to December 1985. The second provides a justification of the scholarly framework that flows out of critical events theory. Chapters 3 and 4 analyze the media coverage using content analysis of the print and visual—or televised—media; chapter 5 describes the patterns of power implicit in the coverage. Chapter 6 reports on the public's perception. The seventh chapter sets forth the ethical implications of the reporting. The last chapter gives the conclusions and Wilkins's recommendations.

Content analysis is used for a two-month period immediately following the disaster for the three commercial networks, three wire services—the Associated Press, United Press International, and Reuters—the *New York Times* and the *Washington Post*, and three newsmagazines—*U.S. News & World Report*, *Time*, and *Newsweek*. The print media concentrated on the short-term stories with an emphasis on the event rather than on long-term issues and background information. Despite the worldwide ramifications of the disaster in a variety of fields—technology, safety, law, environment, relations of developing countries with multinationals—television in the United States portrayed Bhopal primarily as an Indian tragedy and its effects as largely limited to Union Carbide. It also tended to portray corporate and government institutions as being powerful and knowledgeable and indi-

viduals as helpless. Wilkins asserts that the media created a new myth—that Bhopal was an accident in which institutions played a part but individuals were basically impotent.

The material on the public reaction is based on two 400-person telephone surveys conducted seven months after the gas leak, one in an area similar to Bhopal—Charleston, West Virginia—and the other in a control area—Eugene, Oregon. Respondents from both groups had similar recall as to their sources of information with television as the primary source of information (54.5 percent), followed by newspapers (26.4 percent), radio (7.3 percent), magazines (3.2 percent), and talking with others (3.2 percent). The Charleston residents were more likely to have a command of the facts on Bhopal, reflecting the influence of their higher-risk environment as compared to Eugene.

Wilkins suggests a four-point program for the media in reporting disasters related to man-made technology: provide the context of the event; provide a discussion of the science of the event; broaden and significantly alter existing sourcing patterns; and shift the tone of news reports to include discussion of long-term issues. These recommendations are important, but they are limited in that they do not address the ethical and stereotyping issues raised in the book. This is surprising in view of the books's title and its intent to prove the "shared vulnerability" in today's technology-dominated world. It is, however, a useful book in the analysis of the lessons to be learned from Bhopal and its aftermath, using a tested but limited methodology.

ASHOK BHARGAVA
University of Wisconsin
Whitewater

ECONOMICS

BERGER, PETER L. *The Capitalist Revolution: Fifty Propositions about Prosperity, Equality, and Liberty*. Pp. v, 262. New York: Basic Books, 1986. $17.95.

TULLOCK, GORDON. *The Economics of Wealth and Poverty.* Pp. 210. New York: New York University Press, 1986. $40.00.

Berger has developed a masterful theory of social change to challenge the Marxian theory. He has integrated the traditional theories of capitalist development from Weber, Rostow, von Hayek, Schumpeter, and Kuznets to explain the social, political, and cultural consequences of capitalism. He does a particularly good job of showing the revolutionary aspect of capitalism in terms of productive capacity, class mobility, income distribution, and the expansion of political and individual freedom. He is careful to separate capitalism and modernization and to show the distinction between political and economic freedom. He also addresses the authoritarian-totalitarian distinction of Jeane Kirkpatrick in terms of the political and social consequences.

The fifty propositions developed are stated in such a manner that they could be empirically tested. Although it is doubtful that some of the propositions could be verified, the general conclusions of these propositions are basically nondogmatic and insightful. The examples used, the sociological definitions, and the positive methodology often close the propositions and bias the conclusions; however, this is the most balanced argument for the market over the state both as a vehicle for economic development and as a social system.

The emphasis on the individualism of Western culture as a cause as well as an effect of capitalism is stressed, but the successful development of Japan and the Four Little Dragons—South Korea, Taiwan, Hong Kong, and Singapore—shows the success of state intervention in the economy via the democratic elite as a development rather than a regulatory power. This conclusion appears to be inconsistent with his condemnation of democratic socialism and the evils of bureaucracy and "hereditization."

The attack on the imperialistic theory of dependency as a theory of exploitation of Third World countries is succinct. The success in overcoming the physiological standards of material life via capitalism rather than socialist development is persuasive, but the briefness of this topic is a weakness in the presentation.

The last chapter is an explanation of the impotency of the myths that support capitalism. The intellectuals or knowledge class and the underclass seek redistribution from a symbiotic political force that is antagonistic to capitalism. If advocates of the market and unfettered capitalism spent more time explaining the success of capitalism and less on the dogma, the myths would be more acceptable to Third World countries and its own citizens.

Tullock's book is a collection of previously published articles on social choice and the economics of transfers and redistribution with four unpublished chapters on how to redistribute income. Tullock is a most articluate spokesperson for the market as the most efficient allocator of resources.

Several recurrent themes flow through the book. The first is that transfers most often do not go to the poor but are a form of rent-seeking via the political distortion of market decisions. The second theme is that poverty in the United States is relative affluence by world standards and that the welfare state and equalitarians treat their own citizens very differently from foreigners in this respect. The third theme is that behavior is more accurate than noble professions with respect to equality and income distribution. The fourth theme is that transfers are not costless activities. The fifth theme is an attack on the Rawlsian concept of justice and equality. The sixth theme is that any attempt to increase equality must not alter the efficiency of the economy. The last theme is that the activities of both government transfer policies and charitable institutions are guided by good intentions but hampered by muddled thought and inefficient institutions.

The book is readable by the noneconomist, although several of the republished articles have basic welfare economic graphs but no significant mathematical barriers. Game theory payoffs are used to justify inheritance and to deny the public defender system of providing free legal services. The reasoning is, as always with Tullock, exceptional and the expansion of economic thinking to political issues is rewarding and insightful. To use his market analysis to justify such an expenditure for republished articles, however, would not be in my preference schedule.

W. E. SPELLMAN

Coe College
Cedar Rapids
Iowa

BIRD, GRAHAM. *International Financial Policy and Economic Development: A Disaggregated Approach.* Pp. xvi, 348. New York: St. Martin's Press, 1987. $37.50.

One of the problems with writing a scholarly treatment of a subject like the international financial problems of developing countries is that the subject is likely to change before one's eyes. By the time almost any book in this area actually reaches print, there are apt to be dramatic new developments that affect much of the tone—and frequently the substance—of the presentation that is being made.

Having voiced that preliminary qualm, there is much that is positive to say about Graham Bird's work in this new book. Although Bird could not, of course, have been aware of the unilateral debt payment delays initiated by several countries in Latin America or the dramatic decision by a number of U.S. banks to write off significant portions of their Third World loans, he is quite persuasive in his analysis of the differences between the financial situation of midrange developing countries, such as those in Latin America and the Far East, and those countries at the lowest economic level, those in Africa and on the Subcontinent. Indeed, one of the key themes of Bird's book is that these material differences in economic circumstances justify not only differences in developmental policy within these countries but differences in treatment by international

financial institutions as well, on both a multilateral and a bilateral basis.

One of the most pointed suggestions made by Bird in furtherance of his differentiation approach to respective groups of developing countries is that the International Monetary Fund should take greater account of such differences in structuring the nature and scope of the conditionality it will apply to borrowing countries in connection with International Monetary Fund loans. For Bird, the damages caused by strict conditionality standards in the least developed countries produce not only political and social unrest but poorer economic performance as well.

Given the other strengths of Bird's work in this volume, it is unfortunate that he did not cover the more intriguing of the developmental tools now being used in the Third World: privatization, debt-for-equity swaps, and country funds. Also, it would have been interesting to have included in this treatise a discussion of the impact of the work of the International Finance Corporation, particularly in the area of international capital markets.

JAMES R. SILKENAT

New York Bar
New York City

CASSON, MARK. *The Firm and the Market.* Pp. xii, 283. Cambridge, MA: MIT Press, 1987. $27.50.

Mark Casson's objective here is to provide the foundation for a general theory of the firm across spatial markets. This work has largely developed within the somewhat narrower context of the multinational enterprise (MNE), which provides most of the illustrative material found in the book. Casson pursues his analysis within the Coasian vision of the firm as a nexus of various contractual arrangements that reduce or eliminate transaction costs and internalize external economies of information and knowledge, leading, under various institutional structures, to horizontal and vertical spatial integration.

The first two chapters contain a useful review of recent MNE literature, drawing a good deal of it together with the common thread of the internalization hypothesis. Casson critically evaluates the demonstrated strengths and weaknesses of this analysis, and then contrasts it to other perspectives—for example, that of the neoclassical school.

The middle three chapters then extend the basic model in three directions, examining international oligopolistic rivalry, vertical integration and its import for quality control, and alternative spatial contractual relationships within diverse institutional contexts. The first discussion is particularly interesting because it argues that to sustain a credible threat against rivals, MNEs must penetrate their rivals' principal spatial markets. This is consistent with observed multilateral investment patterns by MNEs among developed economies. The analysis further suggests that MNEs will eschew price warfare in individual markets, anticipating credible retaliation elsewhere. Confronted with the prospects of universal warfare or universal cooperation, the latter is preferred and enforced by MNEs in this iterative prisoner's dilemma.

The last theoretical chapter explores the different institutional characteristics of firms, industries, and national markets that would favor alternative contractual forms of technological transfer, ranging over the spectrum of control from direct greenfield investment through merger, joint venture, collaboration, subcontracting, and franchising to licensing agreements. Extracting the optimal contractual form requires somewhat arbitrary weighting of the several institutional factors, and is illustrated for four diverse firm/industry groups.

Casson completes his analysis with three extended case studies of the construction, shipping, and automotive industries. The first two provide additional insight especially into the questions of vertical integration. The third case, the divestment of Chrysler's European operations to Peugeot, reflects a rather tenuous relationship to the preceding

theoretical discussions. Indeed, this illustrates one of the difficulties of the overall presentation. All but two of these chapters have appeared independently elsewhere, and while all address a common theme, there is inevitably some unevenness and lack of unity. For example, some theoretical propositions are not well illustrated empirically while some empirical material does not appear to address supporting theoretical arguments. Moreover, certain thorny questions such as MNE political power or the feasibility and desirability of public policy for MNEs go largely undeveloped in theory or example. Thus, while Casson probably falls short of developing his comprehensive theory, he does provide a thoughtful exploration of several central topics. To be fair, this is implicitly recognized by Casson, who is generous throughout with perceptive suggestions for further research. The text is complemented by an extensive bibliography and an adequate index.

ALEXANDER M. THOMPSON III
Vassar College
Poughkeepsie
New York

HARVEY, CURTIS E. *Coal in Appalachia: An Economic Analysis.* Pp. viii, 219. Lexington: University Press of Kentucky, 1986. $21.00.

In this examination of the Appalachian coal industry, Curtis Harvey, a professor of economics at the University of Kentucky, reviews the industry's structure, economics, and problems within the traditional framework of supply and demand analysis.

Appalachia and coal are virtually synonymous in the public mind because the region contains some of the world's richest coal reserves in sufficient quantities to supply the nation's energy needs for centuries. For that reason, demand is the most critical side of Harvey's analysis. After World War II, the markets for coal contracted with the declining significance of the railroads, the abandonment of coal for residential heating, and the more recent demise of the American steel industry. Now two-thirds of Appalachian coal production is consumed by electric utility plants, and much of the remainder is exported for similar uses abroad. The health of the coal industry, therefore, is chronically dependent upon the vitality of the Western industrial economies. When the economy catches a cold, it is said, Appalachia comes down with pneumonia.

The dependency of the coal industry on forces beyond its own control is amply illustrated by the fact that the market for coal is actually determined by the price of oil rather than by competing alternate sources of coal. As the price of oil rises, coal becomes more attractive as a substitute fuel and its price also climbs. Conversely, when the price of oil declines, that for coal falls as well. Legislation to protect the environment also affects demand for Appalachian coal by aggravating the price spread between coal and its competitors. Considering the recent trend among oil corporations to acquire coal subsidiaries, we might expect greater concentration and a moderation in the dependency status of coal. Harvey demonstrates that this has not occurred and that coal remains one of the least concentrated of American industries. Indeed, the lack of concentration probably has hindered the industry in dealing with the myriad difficulties it confronts.

In Harvey's view, the future of Appalachian coal remains bleak. The price of oil is expected to remain comparatively low, thereby depressing the markets for coal. Also, environmental problems, such as acid rain, will continue to dampen demand until technological advances permit coal to be burned in ways consistent with public welfare. Only when some of these technological obstacles are overcome, and there is a resurgence in worldwide economic activity, Harvey concludes, will the "sick industry" begin to recover.

RONALD L. LEWIS
West Virginia University
Morgantown

STOLZ, BARBARA ANN. *Still Struggling: America's Low Income Working Women Confronting the 1980s*. Pp. xviii, 205. Lexington, MA: Lexington Books, 1985. $20.00.

ZABALZA, A. and Z. TZANNATOS. *Women and Equal Pay: The Effects of Legislation on Female Employment and Wages in Britain*. Pp. vi, 140. New York: Cambridge University Press, 1985. No price.

These two slender volumes form a complementary pair of studies about the progress of women toward equality in the areas of work and wages. One author, reporting on her subject's personal experiences, is basically pessimistic about women's prospects. The other authors, offering statistical analyses of wages in Britain, present an optimistic view of legislative reform and implementation.

In *Still Struggling*, Barbara Ann Stolz interviews 105 low-income women. Her subjects worked full-time but earned less than "poverty line" wages—$10,000 in 1981-82, when these interviews were conducted—in a variety of jobs in various regions of the country. In her sampling, if not in her analysis, Stolz makes a heroic effort to disentangle the effects of race, class, and ethnicity by interviewing urban white women, rural and urban blacks and Hispanics, and Native American women in the Southwest. Some of the respondents worked in traditional women's jobs—as quilters, secretaries, beauticians, clerical workers. Others had made their way into jobs, such as truck driving and mining, previously monopolized by men.

Yet, despite the differences in their regional and ethnic origins and in their jobs, these women's stories are remarkably similar. Many of them hold a set of beliefs and attitudes that Stolz calls "the captive mentality." This mind-set is composed primarily of very low self-esteem and little sense of personal effectiveness. It is augmented by a reluctance to take risks, a perception that women have no rights and that, therefore, any attempt on their part to pursue a career can only be made by slighting family obligations and victimizing children, and, finally, a fear of bosses and strangers that makes a retreat into the family all the more plausible. Stolz also posits a "master mentality" in which women feel a sense of efficacy and entitlement to participate fully and equally in the world of work. She then makes two further observations. First, although these views are logical opposites, many women, in fact, endorse elements of both. But, second, while they sometimes are able to articulate elements of the master mentality, they act, more often, on the basis of the captive mentality.

Is this account of working women yet another analysis that blames the victim? Stolz says no. In part 3 of her book, she tries to show the interplay between individual beliefs and social forces that make the captive mentality at least a partially realistic response to adverse circumstances. She shows how a broad cultural consensus, the logistics of child care and transportation, the widespread failure of the schools to serve poor children, and the aversive character of jobs for the unskilled all conspire to keep poor women in their place. Against this array of forces, the elements that sustain women's moves toward a master mentality seem slight indeed. Some women discover strength in adversity, becoming aware of their own talents when a crisis—such as death, illness, or desertion of a spouse—forces them into an aggressive search for better jobs. Others have been immeasurably helped by a single individual—a nun, social worker, or job-training counselor—whose faith in them becomes a self-fulfilling prophecy. But, as the foregoing summary shows, this analysis leaves Stolz in the position of implying that the forces that promote equality are much weaker than those that support the status quo.

In sharp contrast is the monograph of Zabalza and Tzannatos, which reports on the British experience of legislating wage equity between the sexes. According to the authors' statistical analyses of public data on earnings, this legislation has been singularly effective both in increasing women's earnings and in closing the gender gap in wages. Moreover, these positive effects are real and have been secured directly within all occupations and industries. They are not the by-product of other changes, such as women's increasing inclination to move into previously male-dominated occupations or to switch from part-time to full-time work. Zabalza and Tzannatos conclude that the effectiveness of reform legislation depends upon its implementation. In the British case, a majority of workers are covered by a few, centrally administered wage agreements. For example, a mere four contracts cover 3 million workers. According to Zabalza and Tzannatos, this centralization has made it possible to defeat evasions and to achieve sweeping changes in the span of a few years. Thus *Women and Equal Pay* is the bearer of good news. It also contributes an interesting case study to the ongoing American debate about the relative merits of centralized—that is, federally mandated—and decentralized, state-level, social reform.

EVE SPANGLER

Boston College
Chestnut Hill
Massachusetts

OTHER BOOKS

ADAMS, JAMES LUTHER. *Voluntary Associations: Socio-Cultural Analyses and Theological Interpretation.* Pp. 404. Chicago: Exploration Press, 1986. $26.95. Paperbound, $14.95.

ARLACCHI, PINO. *Mafia Business: The Mafia & the Spirit of Capitalism.* Pp. 239. London: Verso, 1986. $17.95.

ATE, BASSEY E. *Decolonization and Dependence: The Development of Nigerian-U.S. Relations, 1960-1984.* Pp. 282. Boulder, CO: Westview Press, 1987. $26.50.

BALL, DESMOND and JEFFREY RICHELSON. *Strategic Nuclear Targeting.* Pp. 385. Ithaca, NY: Cornell University, 1986. $29.95.

BATES, ROBERT H. *Essays on the Political Economy of Rural Africa.* Pp. 178. Berkeley: University of California Press, 1987. Paperbound, $9.95.

BILLMAN, CAROL. *The Secret of the Stratemeyer Syndicate: Nancy Drew and the Hardy Boys and the Million Dollar Fiction Factory.* Pp. 187. New York: Crossroads, Unger Continuum, 1986. $14.95.

BOUCHER, JERRY et al., eds. *Ethnic Conflict: International Perspectives.* Pp. 331. Newbury Park, CA: Sage, 1987. Paperbound, no price.

BROWN, EUGENE. *J. William Fulbright: Advice and Dissent.* Pp. 171. Iowa City: University of Iowa Press, 1985. No price.

BUDGE, IAN et al., eds. *Ideology, Strategy and Party Change: Spatial Analysis of Post-War Election Programmes in 19 Democracies.* Pp. xvii, 494. New York: Cambridge University Press, 1987. No price.

BURSTEIN, LEIGH, HOWARD E. FREEMAN, and PETER H. ROSSI. *Collecting Evaluation Data: Problems and Solutions.* Pp. 318. Newbury Park, CA: Sage, 1985. No price.

CAMILLERI, J. A. *The State and Nuclear Power: Conflict and Control in the Western World.* Pp. 347. Seattle: University of Washington Press, 1984. $25.00.

CARTWRIGHT, JOHN et al. *The State of the Alliance 1986-1987: North Atlantic Assembly Reports.* Pp. 376. Boulder, CO: Westview Press, 1987. Paperbound, $33.50.

CHARLTON, MICHAEL. *The Eagle and the Small Birds: Crisis in the Soviet Empire: From Yalta to Solidarity.* Pp. 192. Chicago: University of Chicago Press, 1984. Paperbound, no price.

CHAY, JOHN and THOMAS E. ROSS. *Buffer States in World Politics.* Pp. 245. Boulder, CO: Westview Press, 1986. Paperbound, $23.50.

CHEN, YUNG-PING and GEORGE F. ROHRLICH, eds. *Checks and Balances in Social Security.* Pp. 357. Lanham, MD: University Press of America, 1986. $32.25. Paperbound, $17.50.

CUDDIHY, JOHN MURRAY. *The Ordeal of Civility: Freud, Marx, Levi-Strauss, and the Jewish Struggle with Modernity.* Pp. 272. Boston: Beacon Press, 1987. Paperbound, $9.95.

DANZIG, RICHARD and PETER SZANTON. *National Service: What Would It Mean.* Pp. 306. Lexington, MA: Lexington Books, 1986. $30.00.

DANZIGER, SHELDON H. and DANIEL H. WEINBERG, eds. *Fighting Poverty: What Works and What Doesn't.* Pp. 418. Cambridge, MA: Harvard University Press, 1986. $27.50. Paperbound, $10.95.

DEFLEUR, MELVIN L. and OTTO N. LARSEN. *The Flow of Information: An Experiment in Mass Communication.* Pp. 302. New Brunswick, NJ: Transaction Books, 1987. Paperbound, $16.95.

DEUTSCH, MORTON. *Distributive Justice: A Social-Psychological Perspective.* Pp. 313. New Haven, CT: Yale University Press, 1985. $27.50.

EISENSTADT, S. N., ed. *Patterns of Modernity.* Vol. 1. Pp. ix, 185. New York: New York University Press, 1987. $30.00.

EISENSTADT, S. N., ed. *Patterns of Modernity.* Vol. 2. Pp. vii, 223. New York:

New York University Press, 1987. $30.00.

ELDER, NEIL et al. *The Consensual Democracies: The Government and Politics of the Scandinavian States.* Pp. 244. New York: Basil Blackwell, 1985. $49.95. Paperbound, $11.95.

FAY, BRIAN. *Critical Social Science.* Pp. 242. Ithaca, NY: Cornell University Press, 1987. $35.00. Paperbound, $12.95.

FEATHERSTONE, KEVIN and DIMITRIOS K. KATSOUDAS, eds. *Political Change in Greece: Before and after the Colonels.* Pp. viii, 301. New York: St. Martin's Press, 1987. $37.50.

FISHER, JOHN E. *The John F. Slater Fund: A Nineteenth Century Affirmative Action for Negro Education.* Pp. 166. Lanham, MD: University Press of America, 1987. $19.75.

FRASER, ARVONE S. *The U.N. Decade for Women: Documents and Dialogue.* Pp. 235. Boulder, CO: Westview Press, 1987. $18.85.

GABRIEL, RALPH HENRY. *The Course of American Democratic Thought.* Pp. 568. Westport, CT: Greenwood Press, 1986. $45.00.

GELBER, MARILYN G. *Gender and Society in the New Guinea Highlands: An Anthropological Perspective on Antagonism toward Women.* Pp. 180. Boulder, CO: Westview Press, 1986. No price.

GIBBONS, WILLIAM CONRAD. *The U.S. Government and the Vietnam War: Executive and Legislative Roles and Relationships.* Pt. 1. Pp. 364. Princeton, NJ: Princeton University Press, 1986. Paperbound, $8.95.

GIBBONS, WILLIAM CONRAD. *The U.S. Government and the Vietnam War: Executive and Legislative Roles and Relationships.* Pt. 2. Pp. 422. Princeton, NJ: Princeton University Press, 1986. Paperbound, $9.95.

GOTTFREDSON, STEPHEN D. and SEAN McCONVILLE, eds. *America's Correctional Crisis: Prison Populations and Public Policy.* Pp. 260. Westport, CT: Greenwood Press, 1987. $37.95.

GREELEY, MARTIN. *Postharvest Losses, Technology, and Employment: The Case of Rice in Bangladesh.* Pp. xvii, 345. Boulder, CO: Westview Press, 1987. Paperbound, $35.00.

HAMMER, DARRELL P. *The USSR: The Politics of Oligarchy.* Pp. 260. Boulder, CO: Westview Press, 1986. $35.00. Paperbound, $14.95.

HARRIS, GEORGE S. *Turkey: Coping with Crisis.* Pp. 240. Boulder, CO: Westview Press, 1985. $28.00.

HAYWARD, FRED M. *Elections in Independent Africa.* Pp. 318. Boulder, CO: Westview Press, 1987. Paperbound, $23.95.

HELLEINER, GERALD K., ed. *Africa and the International Monetary Fund.* Pp. 277. Washington, DC: International Monetary Fund, 1985. Paperbound, $10.00.

HELLER, THOMAS C. et al., eds. *Reconstructing Individualism: Autonomy, Individuality, and the Self in Western Thought.* Pp. 365. Stanford, CA: Stanford University Press, 1986. $39.50. Paperbound, $11.95.

HIMMELFARB, GERTRUDE. *The New History and the Old.* Pp. 209. Cambridge, MA: Harvard University Press, 1987. $20.00.

HIRSCHMAN, ALBERT O. *Rival Views of Market Society and Other Recent Essays.* Pp. 197. New York: Viking Penguin, 1986. $18.95.

HOPE, KEMPE RONALD. *Economic Development in the Caribbean.* Pp. 215. New York: Praeger, 1986. $39.95.

HUGHES, DEAN W. et al. *Financing the Agricultural Sector: Future Challenges and Policy Alternatives.* Pp. 254. Boulder, CO: Westview Press, 1986. No price.

JAIN, B. M. *India and the United States, 1961-1963.* New York: Advent Books, 1987. $25.00.

JASANI, BHUPENDRA, ed. *Space Weapons and International Security.* Pp. 366. New York: Oxford University Press, 1987. $59.00.

JASANI, BHUPENDRA and TOSHIBOMI SAKATA, eds. *Satellites for Arms Control and Crisis Monitoring.* Pp. xv, 176.

New York: Oxford University Press, 1987. $37.00.

JOHNSTON, BRUCE F. et al., eds. *U.S.-Mexico Relations: Agriculture and Rural Development*. Pp. 401. Stanford, CA: Stanford University Press, 1987. $42.50.

KATZ, JACOB. *Toward Modernity: The European Jewish Model*. Pp. 279. New Brunswick, NJ: Transaction Books, 1987. $24.95.

KATZENSTEIN, PETER J. *Small States in World Markets: Industrial Policy in Europe*. Pp. 268. Ithaca, NY: Cornell University, 1986. $39.50. Paperbound, $11.95.

KELLEY, MICHAEL P. *A State in Disarray: Conditions of Chad's Survival*. Pp. 222. Boulder, CO: Westview Press, 1986. Paperbound, $28.50.

KINDLEBERGE, CHARLES P. *International Capital Movements*. Pp. vi, 99. New York: Cambridge University Press, 1987. No price.

KINSBRUNER, JAY. *Petty Capitalism in Spanish America: The Pulperos of Pueblo, Mexico City, Caracas, and Buenos Aires*. Pp. 159. Boulder, CO: Westview Press, 1987. Paperbound, $19.50.

KRUGMAN, PAUL R., ed. *Strategic Trade Policy and the New International Economics*. Pp. 313. Cambridge, MA: MIT Press, 1986. Paperbound, $12.50.

KYOGOKU, JUN-LCHI. *The Political Dynamics of Japan*. Pp. ix, 239. Tokyo: University of Tokyo Press, 1987. Distributed by Columbia University Press, New York. $24.50.

LAIRD, ROBBIN F., ed. *French Security Policy: From Independence to Interdependence*. Pp. 180. Boulder, CO: Westview Press, 1986. Paperbound, $18.50.

LOONEY, ROBERT E. *The Jamaican Economy in the 1980's: Economic Decline and Structural Adjustment*. Pp. 257. Boulder, CO: Westview Press, 1987. Paperbound, $22.50.

LOONEY, ROBERT E. *The Political Economy of Latin American Defense Expenditures: Case Studies of Venezuela and Argentina*. Pp. 325. Lexington, MA: Lexington Books, 1986. $39.00.

MacINTYRE, STUART. *The Oxford History of Australia*. Vol. 4, *1901-1942*. Pp. xx, 399. New York: Oxford University Press, 1987. $36.00.

MACKINTOSH, IAN. *Sunrise Europe: The Dynamics of Information Technology*. Pp. 288. New York: Basil Blackwell, 1986. No price.

MADISON, G. B. *The Logic of Liberty*. Pp. 293. Westport, CT: Greenwood Press, 1986. $37.95.

McCAULEY, MARTIN, ed. *The Soviet Union under Gorbachev*. Pp. 247. New York: St. Martin's Press, 1987. $39.95. Paperbound, $14.95.

McGHEE, GEORGE C., ed. *Diplomacy for the Future*. Pp. viii, 108. Lanham, MD: University Press of America, 1987. Paperbound, $7.50.

MILLER, ROBERT T. and RONALD B. FLOWERS, ed. *Toward Benevolent Neutrality: Church, State, and the Supreme Court*. Pp. 612. Waco, TX: Baylor University Press, 1987. $36.00.

MILLER, STEVEN E. and STEPHEN VAN EVERA, eds. *The Star Wars Controversy*. Pp. 327. Princeton, NJ: Princeton University Press, 1986. Paperbound, $9.95.

MOHAN, BRIJ. *Denial of Existence: Essays on the Human Condition*. Pp. xiii, 111. Springfield IL: Charles C Thomas, 1987. No price.

NEVITTE, NEIL and CHARLES H. KENNEDY, eds. *Ethnic Preference and Public Policy in Developing States*. Pp. 203. Boulder, CO: Lynne Rienner, 1986. $25.00.

NIEHANS, JURG. *International Monetary Economics*. Pp. 340. Baltimore, MD: Johns Hopkins University Press, 1986. $37.50. Paperbound, $12.95.

OBASANJO, OLUSEGUN. *Africa in Perspective: Myths and Realities*. Pp. 51. New York: Council on Foreign Relations, 1987. $10.00.

O'MALLEY, ILENE V. *The Myth of the Revolution: Hero Cults and the Institutionalization of the Mexican State, 1920-1940*. Pp. 199. Westport, CT: Greenwood Press, 1986. $29.95.

PAREKH, BHIKHU and THOMAS PAN-THAM, eds. *Political Discourse: Explorations in Indian and Western Political Thought.* Pp. 314. Newbury Park, CA: Sage, 1987. $27.50.

PARK, JAE KYU et al., eds. *The Foreign Relations of North Korea: New Perspectives.* Pp. xiii, 491. Boulder, CO: Westview Press, 1987. $39.50.

PASTOR, ROBERT A., ed. *Latin America's Debt Crisis: Adjusting to the Past or Planning for the Future?* Pp. xiii, 176. Boulder, CO: Lynne Rienner, 1987. $20.00.

PATRICK, HUGH. *Japan's High Technology Industries: Lessons and Limitations of Industrial Policy.* Pp. 277. Seattle: University of Washington Press, 1987. $40.00.

PATTERSON, JAMES T. *America's Struggle against Poverty 1900-1980.* Pp. 268. Cambridge, MA: Harvard University Press, 1981. $17.50. Paperbound, $9.95.

PENNOCK, J. ROLAND and JOHN W. CHAPMAN, eds. *Authority Revisited: Nomos XXIX.* Pp. 344. New York: New York University Press, 1987. $42.50.

PIERRE, ANDREW J., ed. *A High Technology Gap? Europe, America and Japan.* Pp. xii, 114. New York: New York University Press, 1987. $20.50.

PORTER, FRANK W., III. *Strategies for Survival: American Indians in the Eastern United States.* Pp. 232. Westport, CT: Greenwood Press, 1986. $35.00.

PRADOS, JOHN. *Pentagon Games: Wargames and the American Military.* Pp. 81. New York: Harper & Row, 1987. Paperbound, $9.95.

PRADOS, JOHN. *The Soviet Estimate: U.S. Intelligence Analysis and Soviet Strategic Forces.* Pp. 391. Princeton, NJ: Princeton University Press, 1986. Paperbound, no price.

REIN, MARTIN. *Stagnation and Renewal: The Rise and Fall of Social Policy Regimes.* Pp. 190. Armonk, NY: M. E. Sharpe, 1987. $35.00.

RIDGE, MARTIN. *Frederick Jackson Turner: Wisconsin's Historian of the Fron-tier.* Pp. 71. Madison, WI: State Historical Society, 1986. Paperbound, $6.95.

RINGER, BENJAMIN B. *"We the People" and Others: Duality and America's Treatment of Its Racial Minorities.* Pp. 1165. New York: Methuen, 1985. $75.00. Paperbound, $25.00.

ROFES, ERIC E., ed. *Gay Life: Leisure, Love, and Living for the Contemporary Gay Male.* Pp. 305. Garden City, NY: Doubleday, 1986. Paperbound, $12.95.

ROSNER, LYDIA S. *The Soviet Way of Crime: Beating the System in the Soviet Union and the U.S.A.* Pp. 140. South Hadley, MA: Bergin & Garvey, 1986. No price.

ROTHSCHILD, BRIAN J. *Dynamics of Marine Fish Populations.* Pp. 277. Cambridge, MA: Harvard University Press, 1986. No price.

ROY, RAMASHRAY. *Self and Society: A Study in Gandhian Thought.* Pp. 205. Newbury Park, CA: Sage, 1985. No price.

SCHOLZMAN, KAY LEHMAN and JOHN T. TIERNEY. *Organized Interests and American Democracy.* Pp. 448. New York: Harper & Row, 1986. Paperbound, no price.

SCHNEIDER, LOUIS, ed. *Paradox & Society: The Work of Bernard Mandeville.* Pp. 248. New Brunswick, NJ: Transaction Books, 1987. $39.95.

SEALE, PATRICK. *The Struggle for Syria.* Pp. xxii, 352. New Haven, CT: Yale University Press, 1987. Paperbound, $15.95.

SEMLER, ERIC, JAMES BENJAMIN, and ADAM GROSS. *The Language of Nuclear War: An Intelligent Citizen's Dictionary.* Pp. 318. New York: Harper & Row, 1987. Paperbound, $9.95.

SHORT, JAMES F. *The Social Fabric: Dimensions and Issues.* Pp. 366. Newbury Park, CA: Sage, 1986. Paperbound, $29.95.

TAYLOR, DONALD M. and FATHALI M. MOGHADDAM. *Theories of Intergroup Relations: International Social Psychological Perspectives.* Pp. viii, 223. Westport, CT: Praeger, 1987. No price.

TECKENBERG, WOLFGANG, ed. *Comparative Studies of Social Structure*. Pp. viii, 214. Armonk, NY: M. E. Sharpe, 1987. $35.00.

TERRY, MAURY. *The Ultimate Evil: An Investigation of America's Most Dangerous Satanic Cult*. Pp. 512. Garden City, NY: Dolphin Books, 1987. No price.

THORP, ROSEMARY and LAURENCE WHITEHEAD, eds. *Latin American Debt and the Adjustment Crisis*. Pp. xv, 359. Pittsburgh, PA: University of Pittsburgh Press, 1987. $42.95.

ULAM, ADAM B. *Stalin: The Man and His Era*. Pp. 760. Boston: Beacon Press, 1987. Paperbound, $15.95.

UTTON, M. A. *The Economics of the Regulating Industry*. Pp. 243. New York: Basil Blackwell, 1986. No price.

WARD, ALAN J., ed. *Northern Ireland: Living with the Crisis*. Pp. xvii, 248. Westport, CT: Praeger, 1987. $37.95.

ZALD, MAYER N. and JOHN D. McCARTHY. *Social Movements in an Organizational Society*. Pp. x, 435. New Brunswick, NJ: Transaction Books, 1987. No price.

NEW from Sage

CRISES IN THE CARIBBEAN BASIN

edited by RICHARD TARDANICO, *Tulane University*

**Published in cooperation with the
Political Economy of the World-System Section of
the American Sociological Association**

The term "Caribbean Basin" has gained favor among scholars and policymakers in their efforts to understand contemporary crises in U.S. relations with Central America, the Caribbean islands, Mexico, and the northern coast of South America. The term implies that the region's societies have been transformed into an "American Mediterranean" since the late-nineteenth-century ascendance of the U.S. as an industrial and military power. It also implies that today's conflicts in such countries as Nicaragua, El Salvador, and Haiti represent challenges not only to the wealth and power of local oligarchies but to the global hegemony of the U.S. and the foundations of capitalism as a world system. What are the national and international causes, dimensions, and consequences of such challenges? This volume sheds light on this question by focusing on the past and present interplay of economic transformations, social struggles, and political conflicts in the Caribbean Basin with the world-scale dynamics of capitalism. The contributors emphasize the initiative of the peoples of the Caribbean Basin in grappling with the region's past and present forms of domination and underdevelopment. Their analyses invite comparison with the changing forms of domination, underdevelopment, and struggle in such other Third World regions as the Middle East, Southern Africa, and Southern Asia. And they raise fundamental questions about the interrelationship of crises in the Caribbean Basin with transformations of U.S. society and the world capitalist system.

CONTENTS: Preface / Introduction: Issues in the Study of Caribbean Crises R. TARDANICO // **I. Labor, Economy, and Crisis** // 1. White Days, Black Days: The Working Day and the Crisis of Slavery in the French Caribbean D.W. TOMICH / 2. Labor and Ethnicity: The Caribbean Conjuncture S.W. MINTZ / 3.Economic Development and Dependency in Nineteenth-Century Guatemala R.L. WOODWARD, Jr. / 4. Employment Crises and Economic Development in the Caribbean: Jamaica and the Dominican Republic D. BRAY / 5. The Informal Sector Revisited: The Case of the Talleres Rurales Mini-Maquilas in Colombia C. TRUELOVE // **II. State, Economy, and Crisis** // 6. State Responses to the Great Depression, 1929-1934: "Revolutionary" Mexico and "Nonrevolutionary" Colombia R. TARDANICO / 7. Coffee and Politics in Central America J.M. PAIGE / 8. Sandinista Relations with the West: The Limits of Nonalignment R.P. MATTHEWS / 9. Restratification After Revolution: The Cuban Experience S. ECKSTEIN / 10. The International Monetary Fund and Crisis in the Dominican Republic M.F. MURPHY

**Political Economy of the World-System Annuals, Vol. 9
1987 (Summer) / 320 pages (tent.) / $29.95 (c)**

SAGE PUBLICATIONS, INC.
2111 West Hillcrest Drive,
Newbury Park, California 91320

SAGE PUBLICATIONS, INC.
275 South Beverly Drive,
Beverly Hills, California 90212

SAGE PUBLICATIONS LTD
28 Banner Street,
London EC1Y 8QE, England

SAGE PUBLICATIONS INDIA PVT LTD
M-32 Market, Greater Kailash I,
New Delhi 110 048 India

NEW from Sage

CONFLICT IN SPAIN, 1931-1939
Democracy and Its Enemies
edited by MARTIN BLINKHORN, *University of Lancaster*

Few events in the twentieth century have aroused as much passion, or resulted in as much violence, as the Spanish Civil War. Even though fifty years have elapsed since the final shots were fired, the political fallout continues to haunt the social fabric of modern Spain. **Spain in Conflict** not only explores the causes of this tragic episode, but also reflects on the profound ramifications of its aftermath.

Beginning with the socio-political polarization under the Spanish Republic, **Spain in Conflict** investigates the gradual fragmentation of Republicanism and the Left, the coalescence of conservative and right-wing interests, and the impact of foreign involvement in the war. In addition, the contributors provide new evidence about Spanish political development from 1931-1939, as well as a distinctive re-evaluation of this dramatic event.

CONTENTS: Introduction // **I. The Republicans and the Left** 'Responsibilities' and the Second Republic, 1931-1936 C. BOYD   The Struggle Against Facism in Spain: Leviatan and the Contradictions of the Socialist Left, 1934-1936 P. PRESTON   Anarchism in Aragon During the Second Republic: The Emergence of a Mass Movement G. KELSEY / The Socialist Youth in the JSU: The Experience of Organizational Unity, 1936-1938 H. GRAHAM // **II. Conservatives and the Right**   / The Forerunners of Spanish Fascism: Union Patriotica and the Union Monarquica S. BEN-AMI / 'Moderate' Conservatism and the Second Republic: The Case of Valencia S. LYNAM & M. BLINKHORN / Alfonsist Monarchism and the Coming of the Spanish Civil War P. PRESTON / Right-Wing Utopianism and the Harsh Reality: Carlism, the Republic and the 'Crusade' M. BLINKHORN / Falange Espanola, 1933-1939: From Fascism to Francoism S. ELLWOOD // **III. Foreign Involvement in the Civil War**   Gold, the Soviet Union, and the Spanish Civil War A. VINAS / How Franco Financed His War R. WHEALEY

1986 (December) / 304 pages / $40.00 (c)

SAGE PUBLICATIONS, INC.
2111 West Hillcrest Drive
Newbury Park, California 91320

SAGE PUBLICATIONS, INC.
275 South Beverly Drive
Beverly Hills, California 90212

SAGE PUBLICATIONS LTD
28 Banner Street
London EC1Y 8QE, England

SAGE PUBLICATIONS INDIA PVT LTD
M-32 Market, Greater Kailash I
New Delhi 110 048 India